INTERNATIONAL
CONFLICT
and
SOCIAL
POLICY

PRENTICE-HALL SERIES IN SOCIAL POLICY

Howard E. Freeman, Editor

Marc Pilisuk

with the assistance of
Mehrene Larudee

INTERNATIONAL CONFLICT and SOCIAL POLICY

prentice-hall, inc.,
englewood cliffs, new jersey

©1972 by Prentice-Hall, Inc.
Englewood Cliffs, N.J.

C–0–13–472431–3
P–0–13–472423–2

JUL 6 '72

Library of Congress Catalog Card No.: 78–160541

10 9 8 7 6 5 4 3 2 1

Printed in the United States of America

Prentice-Hall International, Inc., London
Prentice-Hall of Australia, Pty. Ltd., Sydney
Prentice-Hall of Canada, Ltd., Toronto
Prentice-Hall of India Private Limited, New Delhi
Prentice-Hall of Japan, Inc., Tokyo

To My Parents, Louis and Charlotte,
Who First Taught Me About
The Ultimate Brotherhood of Mankind,
And to My Students, Who Work to Make
That Brotherhood a Reality.

PREFACE

I want to acknowledge several debts. Bill Gamson first suggested my name for the assignment. Anatol Rapoport, with whom I once worked, has greatly influenced my thinking about military strategy; I have drawn heavily from his writings in my chapter on "Real Politik and the Strategists." Tom Hayden worked with me on an article about the military–industrial complex, for which we shared a prize from the Society for the Psychological Study of Social Issues for research approaches to potential threats to peace. That article has been revised to form the chapter, "Is There a Military–Industrial Complex?" Michael Locker first taught me the methods for investigating power in the United States. He now works for the North American Committee on Latin America, a group that has done excellent work in an area of inquiry which, while shunned by the universities, should be familiar to every educated person. His contribution to the chapter on the Dominican Republic was great. To the editors of the former *Viet-Reports,* particularly to Carol Brightman and John McDermott, I am indebted for some of the best analyses of American policy that I have yet seen. I. F. Stone remains my hero among journalists. What passes as news among the major wire services has largely degenerated into self-serving statements by officials, and *I. F. Stone's Weekly* continually filters the facts and exposes the lie in what we have often come to believe is true. Without the actual facts, the scholar who tries to theorize is impotent. I am indebted as well to the students at Berkeley. Although my analyses of contemporary events have sometimes been a source of their despair, their efforts to change the world have provided me with a source of hope.

During the three years I worked on this book, many friends, students, and research assistants helped me. I am particularly indebted to Mehrene Larudee, who brought great dedication and ability to the organization and extensive documentation of the entire work, and to Ann DeRosa, who typed and corrected the chapters through countless revisions. Finally, I am grateful to my wife, Phyllis, who understood what I was trying to do.

MARC PILISUK
University of California,
Berkeley

CONTENTS

INTERNATIONAL
CONFLICT
and
SOCIAL
POLICY

INTRODUCTION

The man on the street believes that nations are real things which willfully act on one another, conquering, trading, threatening, and aiding. He imagines that the geographical boundaries of nations are entirely orderly and are somehow made real by formal procedures of national recognition. He tends to believe that a nation can be readily categorized by its form of government, that the government controls the nation (rather than vice versa), and that the government makes foreign policy in what it seems to be its own best interests. The layman assumes that the national interest is increasing the security and power of his country and protecting its citizens. The layman's most primitive view of the nation is that its purpose is to maintain internal order, to defend itself, and to expand its influence. That so many people appear to hold such views makes them neither right nor wrong. However, since so many people, government officials as well as ordinary citizens, believe unquestioningly that nations are the actors in the drama of world conflict, then in fact the world probably does tend to conform to the image. What is at issue here is not the objective truth or validity of the image, but merely the observation that, true or false, it is but a theory of the state of the world; there are other theories that merit attention.

Like all theories, the one we described selects certain elements and ignores others. In this case nations are emphasized as the prime movers in international conflict. Unfortunately this is a poor abstraction, for it misses completely the entire network of internal forces such as military service, secret intelligence organizations, international corporations, and federal agencies that underlies the actions of nations. This book will emphasize the internal structures that create and enact the events which, taken together, come to be considered public policy. The guiding premise is that while policies must indeed be rationalized for explanation to the public or the Congress, the policy process is not basically a rational one. Instead, policies are the political end products of the pressures exerted by certain interests on their own behalf. In matters of international conflict the most enduring and powerful forces of policy are often concealed from public view and immune to public accountability. This book will try to reveal the persistent forces of foreign policy.

It is not an accident that the general public selects a theory of international conflict which permits the powerful interests of policy to remain out of view. The public view is itself a product of the media institutions which translate world events into "news." Chapter 3, which describes management of public opinion, concludes that public opinion generally adds little to the formation of policy.

Expert knowledge has added little of fundamental significance to the average citizen's understanding of the theory of international conflict. One reason for this is that the system of policy formation in the United States presents only a facade of responsiveness to the needs of the populace. This facade hides those more durable loci of power in society which respond mainly to their own interests. A look at these latent political forces makes it possible to explain the harsh facts of international conflict as predictable products, rather than as accidents, of the system that produces them. Yet the most potent underlying forces of our society have so far escaped the full spotlight of social science inquiry.

The contribution of social science has also been limited by the sheer enormity of the task of bringing order to the morass of international events. For example, we illustrate the difficulties in the task of trying to identify the characteristics of the international system which are correlated with the outbreak of war. Before setting up and carrying out such a study, the scientist must first define what the international system is. This was actually done, in this case, in terms of economic and military treaties between nation-states during particular historical periods. The researcher soon found that the historical record is not always adequate for his classification scheme, nor are the sources of information even consistent with one another. He must decide whether a nation which divides is to be considered two nations or whether a territory in revolt is to be considered a new nation. He must further consider whether a non-aggression treaty is to be placed in the same category as a mutual assistance treaty or a trade agreement. When he wishes to relate the number and kind of such agreements in the world system to the outbreak or severity of wars, he is faced with an additional dilemma: what is war? Is it one plane shot down, one territory occupied—for two weeks or for years—with five or five thousand battle deaths? Or must war be formally declared, which would exclude certain major armed conflicts like Vietnam?

Given the magnitude of the task, it is remarkable that the relatively inexperienced interdisciplinary scholars of conflict have taught us anything —but they have. We do know, for example, a good deal about the conditions which have been associated with the outbreak of violent international conflict. Polarization of nations into armed alliances; the increased rate of information transmission during a crisis, exceeding the ability of officials to handle it; and the escalation of hostile imagery in the press are all now understood to be associated with the onset of armed conflict. We also know something, both from historical data and from laboratory and computer simulations, of how the belligerent or conciliatory moves of one nation are likely to be countered by similar moves of its adversaries. Recently, we have learned much about the forces involved in European unifications and about the conditions under which the institution of war may pass away among these same European nations with their intensely violent histories of recurrent warfare.

I think it is fair to include in our dividends from social science the serious scholarly attention given to the problems of a future without violent war. How will international disputes be settled without war? Will there be an international tribunal and police agency? What sanctions will be exercised against violators of agreements? Who will control existing armaments during a period of disarmament? Will revolutions be permissible in a peaceful world? What will happen to American productive capacity, to its aeroframe industry, its military employees, and its giant Southern California defense corporations, in the event of disarmament? Questions such as these have surrendered, in theory, to ingenious schemes of law and policy which might replace the prevailing rule of force and power.

But the difficulties of scholarly research are great. The findings are tentative and always subject to further confirmation, to repudiation, or to refinement. Moreover, the task has hardly begun. For those who possess a naive faith that science will discover and thereby eliminate the causes of war, the first lesson from our early attempts is that the problem is significantly more complex than we ever anticipated.

I say these things by way of apology for what is being left out. This book does not attempt to survey the diligent efforts of the newly developing scientists of international conflict. Some research studies will be described where they are relevant, but by and large research attempts are bypassed—not because they have failed to find the scientifically correct answers, but because they have failed to ask some very critical questions. No rules of scientific inquiry guide the choice of questions to study. That task is left to the values of the investigator. My own approach derives from my background as an interdisciplinary behavioral scientist (a relatively new breed) and as a liberal humanist (very possibly a dying breed).

My own values suggest that open inquiry into concealed data is more vital than systematic ordering of easily available data. This book concludes with two case histories dealing with American actions in the Dominican Republic and in Greece. The cases provide a chronicle of brutal and manipulative events which abuse the dignity of the human being. Many of the facts in these cases have been concealed or distorted by official sources; however, any sound comprehension of international conflict will have to include these factual details of human exploitation and degradation.

Again, my values draw my attention to the question of how wealth is accumulated and perpetuated in certain hands while half the world's population lives in the shadow zone between bare subsistence, malnutrition, and starvation. How are policies made which permit this inequity and maintain it, even by force? Why is it that so vast an intellectual army can be harnessed to the task of national security in a nation which already has the power to destroy the population of the entire world many times over, yet so little effort is spent to determine why a complete dismantling of the machinery of force is never even an item for discussion on the official policy agenda? What kind of social order can establish costly overseas military bases in more than forty nations while permitting people in those nations to die from hunger or at the hands of police trained and paid by the United States to suppress revolutionary movements?

Thousands of people and thousands of procedures form the policies which assign to the national bankroll a fixed set of priorities, condemning some to poverty and others to positions in the expanding machinery for the application of science to the manipulation of people. Surely there is some reason why only the details of the allocation procedure are contested, while the basic allocations and actions go on as if by some hidden hand of injustice.

This book will attempt to uncover that hidden hand as it operates in the international arena. The first and second chapters delineate the context of international conflict. The first deals with the change in the American role in world affairs over the past two decades, from that of competitor in a technological arms race with the Soviet Union to that of policeman over the underdeveloped world. Chapter 2 examines the problem of development and revolution from the perspective of the people of the poorer countries.

Chapter 3 examines several possible sources of armed conflict—the emotions and the ideas of people, both public and ruling elite. Chapter 4 continues the inquiry into the domestic sources of policy by focusing on the workings of two federal agencies, the Department of State and the Central Intelligence Agency. The two chapters together suggest that neither the opinions of the public, nor those of officials elected or assigned responsibility for international policy, are important in generating policy. The CIA, which has no such charge, on the other hand creates immediate policy by its daily monitoring and manipulating of events in other countries—and at home.

Chapter 5 deals with ideology. It examines a way of thinking about international conflict which makes reasonable—even necessary—the most extensive arsenal of arms imaginable. The importance of the ideology is that it is almost universally accepted among the decision managers and scholars in key policy positions, and it justifies the major diplomatic and military directions of social policy without mentioning the particular interests which stand to benefit from these directions. The ideology also helps to create a sense of national purpose which is, in fact, destructive to the purposes this nation professes.

Chapter 6 asks whether there is, in fact, a military–industrial complex. The chapter raises the major theoretical issues of this book. What are the most central institutions in the process of creating foreign policy? How powerful are they, how widespread through society, and how do they relate to one another? The chapter suggests that those policies that emerge are in accord with the interests of the institutions which generate them, but are not consistent with the prerequisites for a peaceful world. That conclusion is illustrated by the details of two case studies in the final chapters. Each illustrates the operation of the various forces already described: the media, the strategic ideology, the State Department and the CIA, military and corporate interests, the privileged ruling elites of the two countries, and the radical reform movements.

The tragedy in Greece and the Dominican Republic is repeated in Thailand, Indonesia, Brazil, Nigeria, and most destructively in Vietnam. It is by and large an American tragedy. The greatest dedication to American society may be found in efforts to modify the institutions that generate such policies. If there is a way for ordinary people to stand up against adverse institutions, it may be found through an appreciation of the operating system that dominates international conflict and reaches far into the domestic order as well.

Chapter 1

EVOLUTION OF THE CURRENT AMERICAN MILITARY OUTLOOK

The Cold War Stalemate

Whatever the origins of the cold war, its evolution during the 1950s produced a relatively stable balance of terror between the Soviet and American camps. The threat of massive retaliation with nuclear weapons provided a protective perimeter within which each of the antagonists could dominate its respective alliances, make the most of its markets, and, where necessary, crush disturbing opposition. The last was illustrated on the Soviet side by the direct military suppression of the 1956 Hungarian uprisings and on the American side by the covert coup arranged by the Central Intelligence Agency to bring a pro-American military junta to power in Guatemala in 1954. Hostilities during the fifties, apart from the Korean War, were largely verbal. Of course there were crises, as in West Berlin, where the boundaries between the armed camps were precariously drawn. When the Chinese began shelling the offshore islands of Quemoy and Matsu, which could hardly be considered to lie within the defensible limits of the American fortress, another crisis ensued. But on the whole, crisis eruptions such as those in the Congo or the Suez were ameliorated by an awed mutual respect for Soviet and American nuclear arsenals and an awareness that the populations of the United States and the USSR were in reality hostages against a larger war.

Most of the American political and diplomatic effort during John Foster Dulles's term as secretary of state was to draw lines and cement ties which could separate the "free world" from the "communist world." Starting with NATO and extending to SEATO and into Eurasia, the United States forged a series of military alliances, frequently using the promise of economic or military assistance to persuade other governments to take sides.

It was Dulles's belief that communism was both evil and foredoomed to die of its own inadequacies. A content analysis of Dulles's speeches shows that he had a closed belief system with regard to the USSR. No conciliatory action by the USSR could be attributed to conciliatory intensions by Soviet leaders. No sign of economic or social advancement in the USSR could be taken to indicate a strong point of the Soviet system (Holsti 1962). When human beings have strong fears or hatreds, their psychic apparatus provides them with great flexibility in interpreting information to support their deeper reactions.

So sure was Dulles of the inevitable decline of communism and of its inability to spread except by directly military conquest that he was content to make and to strengthen major military alliances as the free world's bulwark against communism. If the defense perimeter could be secured against Soviet attack, especially by the threat of massive retaliation, then all that remained to be done in the cold war was to wait for the internal collapse of international communism. This black–white image of international affairs fit well with the domestic efforts of Senator Joseph McCarthy, the Senate's Internal Security Subcommittee, and the House Committee on Un-American Activities to purge the "good side" from contamination by leftists or by those whose desire for international conciliation might undermine American attempts to isolate communist states militarily and economically. The target of American opposition was clearly defined as the ruling dictatorship of a monolithic Soviet society. All other communist states were viewed as puppets, and the view tended to persist even against the evidence of strong anti-Soviet forces in Yugoslavia and China. The administration showed little concern for small countries in Asia, Africa, and Latin America. It assumed that colonial status would continue at least on a de facto basis even after the colonies gained formal independence. The United States encouraged the French to retain colonial control in Southeast Asia and was critical of the sudden Belgian military withdrawal from the Congo, even though the withdrawal was only partial and retained the major wealth of the Congo under Western domination.

Meanwhile, the Soviet Union and China, protected by the their own massive retaliation umbrella, were surrounded by American bases in Greece, Turkey, Germany, Norway, Formosa, Taiwan, Japan, and the Philippines. The same game of threatening massive retaliation and cementing alliances was played within the Communist camp. However, there were no friendly colonial powers to include in such alliances, and at least some factions within Soviet and Chinese society saw advantages in association with the nationalist aspirations of emerging nations.

However hostile its tone, the Dulles policy built on massive retaliation was static in its objectives. It had no sustained policy for dealing effectively with the emerging nations, many of whom found military alliances against communist nations to be, at best, irrelevant to the overwhelming problems of food production and nation building. The Dulles foreign policy held no place for dealings with revolutionary movements. Its tacit assumption was that revolts in the "free world" countries were originated and executed in accord with orders from a central communist oligarchy. Revolts within the Communist camp, however, were a response to oppression and a result of the fallacies of communism. Such uprisings could be cautiously encouraged within the Communist camp, but must be immediately subdued in the Western camp. It was the large and apparently growing neutralist area which hamstrung the policy of massive retaliation. Anti-American (at least not anti-Communist) reactions in underdeveloped countries were becoming visible to an American population whose perpetual grooming for war readiness had led them to expect that the American fortress was too strong for setbacks. The Eisenhower administration of the fifties extended the American mandate somewhat with its call for stopping indirect aggression. But this same administration did not see American power or prestige tied to the fates of thrown-off colonies and economically impoverished areas of the world. The Kennedy administration, however, saw in these struggling areas the new frontier.

It is possible to place too much emphasis on the personalities and world views of particular leaders. To a large extent, political leadership emerges to meet and give voice to economic and social forces already present. The cold war had boosted certain larger industries, but a substantial recession followed the post–Korean War cutbacks and a massive deterrent force, invulnerable to enemy surprise attack, could be maintained without new increases in defense contracting. The research and development specialists among the corporations were already pioneering new weaponry and with it a new way of playing the strategic game of the cold war. Defense contracts meant the promise of jobs and votes in communities hard hit by recession. It was President Kennedy who gave voice to a more active, more broadly based, more internationalistic, and more expansionistic foreign policy.

"Limited Wars"

In his first major address on defense policy in 1961, Kennedy stated:

The Free World's security can be endangered not only by a nuclear attack but also by being slowly nibbled away at the periphery, regardless of our strategic power, by forces of subversion, infiltration, intimidation, indirect or non-overt aggression, internal revolution . . . or a series of limited wars. (Quoted in Brightman, June/July 1966, p. 11)

Kennedy's view of democracies, expressed in his early book *Why England Slept*, was that they were intrinsically isolationist and complacent. They needed external shocks and threats if they were to remain alert to danger; they needed outside challenges if they were to unleash their own productive and ideological resources. The Kennedy administration saw a specific rather than a general military function for the threat of nuclear annihilation: to preserve a power balance which would prevent the onset of global war while smaller conflicts could be pursued with every means possible.

Every means possible was indeed a popular strategy. Those who saw grave risks and dangerous instabilities evolving as the balance of terror moved into the no-warning ballistic missile era could find common cause with the Kennedy administration's efforts to seek an end to nuclear testing, a method of arms control, and more flexible relations with communist states, for these measures held the promise of lessening the chances of unwanted nuclear war. Those who saw need for concern with the impoverished majority of the world's population could applaud the ideals of the Alliance for Progress and the Peace Corps.

The change toward a more encompassing, active, and fluid foreign policy was not the work of President Kennedy alone. In the 1950s the testing of high-megaton hydrogen bombs provoked the question of whether military preparedness had come to its logical end; whether the entire idea of a war involving the great powers had become technologically obsolete. But economic and psychological involvement in war preparedness on the part of the most powerful segments of American society was not to be diminished merely by a fear of annihilation. For this reason a number of special government and extragovernment committees met to deal with the question of the proper function of military preparedness in the nuclear age. The select committees which came together to plan and recommend far-ranging changes in American policies were not representatively selected commissions of American citizens. Rather, they were study groups representing the wealthiest and most powerful organizations of American society, that class of individuals who have the most to gain or lose by overseas investment opportunities and by new directions in military research, development, and procurement.

One such committee was a study group from the Council on Foreign Relations. The Council is a nonpartisan research and discussion group, founded in part by contributions from large corporations and in part by grants from the Carnegie, Rockefeller, and Ford Foundations, which are in turn governed by representatives from similar large corporations. Its 1,400 members (half from New York) form a national foreign policy elite that provides not only the ideas for long-term policy change, but the journal (*Foreign Affairs*) that disseminates these ideas and the personnel who will be appointed to key government positions to implement them. In the late 1950s one of the Council's private study groups was led by Henry Kissinger, a Harvard professor who has since been appointed President Nixon's key advisor on foreign policy. The committee included high-ranking officials of the Atomic Energy Commission, the Defense Department, and the CIA, and its private deliberations led to the publication of Kissinger's *Nuclear Weapons and Foreign Policy,* a book which suggests that nuclear deterrence, while necessary, must be augmented by a host of other military operations and military threats.

A second example of political movement from the power centers of American society to enlarge the scope of foreign military and paramilitary activity was the Gaither Committee. Such special blue ribbon citizens' committees or task forces are liaisons between corporate interests and government officials. H. Rowan Gaither, head of the committee, was a banker and Ford Foundation official. Largely through his efforts, the Douglas Aircraft Company and the United States Air Force were able to make their offspring military research operation, the RAND Corporation, a semiautonomous and influential agency (Friedman 1963). Gaither's Committee included another trustee at RAND, a vice-president of the Carnegie Corporation, the director of research for Bell Telephone, and a Defense Department consultant. The eleven-man group was provided technical services by the RAND Corporation and the Institute for Defense Analysis, and advice by a panel of corporate and military leaders. The final report (which is still secret) was presented at a special meeting of the National Security Council. Those present included influential financiers Robert Lovett and John J. McCloy. The report was highly critical of the government's emphasis on nuclear weapons and its deemphasis of conventional ground forces. McCloy predicted sound support from the business community for increased military expenditures. President Eisenhower remained cautious, but President Kennedy took the proposals seriously and appointed three members of the Gaither Committee to his staff.

It should be noted that similarly composed committees were arriving at similar conclusions around the same time. A prominent example is the series of Rockefeller-financed panels, *Prospect for America,* which included five future appointees of President Kennedy (Domhoff, in Horowitz 1969).

A far-reaching extension of military power promised also that superiority in nuclear weaponry and weapons delivery systems would not be forsaken—only deemphasized—in favor of bolstering all manner of conventional warfare and of developing novel means to fight against wars of national liberation. While all but a few military leaders in the Soviet Union (under Khrushchev) apparently welcomed a detente in the missile race, it was clear that the Soviet Union still intended to claim credit for any wars of national liberation and thereby gain a sphere of influence in Africa, Asia, and Latin America. Kennedy assessed, with apparent accuracy, that the Soviet Union would not be willing to undergo great costs in championing the interests of poorer nations. If the United States could outmatch Soviet expenditures, if it could raise the ante through counterrevolutionary military assistance, and if it could create an alternative model for revolutionary development along American lines, then the new frontier would be transformed in the American image. The populations of these countries would be won over to the support of stable pro-American governments and the hard-core revolutionaries would be isolated, discredited, and if necessary, exterminated. Through effective use of the political, economic, ideological, and military techniques of counter-insurgency, Kennedy judged it possible to keep small wars from escalating into large ones.

In Vietnam the type of war President Kennedy wished to avoid has occurred, even though Vietnam has been an unlimited testing ground for the new techniques. To understand why the war has grown out of hand, it is useful to examine the bureaucratic machinery that was created, or expanded, to do the job.

The Instruments of Counter-insurgency

Implementation of the broader strategy gained momentum when a period of detente between the United States and the USSR followed the harrowing Cuban missile crisis. The Soviet Union and the United States clearly respected each other's property, and both assumed that the balance of retaliatory terror was the ultimate guardian of that respect (in the event arms control talks should fail); thus it became possible to focus the struggle on the underdeveloped nations. For these nations the methods of counter-insurgency were developed. So broad were the civilian and military components of counter-insurgency that a "Special Group" of government officials from many agencies had to meet regularly to survey the tasks and assign them to the most appropriate government agency. The efforts of the Special Group led to large and continuing counter-insurgency programs in Vietnam, Laos, Thailand, Congo, Iran, Bolivia, Colombia, Ecuador, Peru, and Venezuela.

In each of these countries a unique balance is struck between the military and civic action components. The civic action side of counter-insurgency is run by the Agency for International Development, which works closely with the Central Intelligence Agency. A major portion of its work is the training of military personnel in public works, occupying them with socially useful tasks through which they may win the support of the population. Its activities may involve road building—as in Thailand, where the military needed better access to reach and subdue tribesmen of dubious loyalty—or dispensation of rice, medicine, and bubble gum (for the children) after air strikes on rural villages in Vietnam.

The military side of the counter-insurgency program is carried out mainly by the Army's Special Forces, a teaching corps in the new tactics of warfare. In Vietnam and Bolivia counter-insurgency is taught on the spot. In addition, some 24,000 foreign military men were receiving training in the United States in 1964. Still others train in the United States Jungle Warfare School in Panama or at counter-insurgency schools in Okinawa and West Germany. Every branch of the United States armed services is involved in counter-insurgency in projects ranging from underwater demolition work, aerial reconnaissance, and air commandos to the uniform inclusion of counter-insurgency training for all Marines. The Defense Department plays the major role in counter-insurgency research through its Remote Area Conflict programs, but each branch of the service also has its own counter-insurgency research program. The Department of Defense is also in charge of covert operations, such as the development of a guerrilla force within a communist state. Knowledge of such operations is not even shared with the American ambassador, so that his denials of such activity will have a ring of truth.

Four other programs are worthy of special notice. The Public Safety Program trains police forces in foreign countries. It works through two Interamerican Police Academies, one in Panama, the other in Washington. The programs have two thrusts, to win popular support and to gather intelligence on insurgent movements. Through an operation of this type the United States was able to negotiate a large contract between Michigan State University's Departments of Public Administration and Government and Ngo Dinh Diem, the man groomed by the United States to take over the temporary rule of South Vietnam in 1954 (Nicolaus 1966).

The least visible and least accountable part of counter-insurgency is the CIA's activities. Its skill in the arts of espionage makes it capable of infiltrating revolutionary groups, training exiles for an invasion, generating mob actions, and bribing officials. The CIA and the State Department will be examined again in chapter 4. Let us simply note here that the State Department runs for its foreign service officers and ambassadors a course on "Problems of Development and Internal Defense." The State Department is very sensitive to the use of the term *counter-insurgency*, which sounds like unwarranted meddling to internationalists and isolationists and to the peoples of poor countries in need of revolutionary change. The public relations label for the term, therefore, is "Overseas Internal Defense" (Hagan, Aug./Sept. 1965).

The Army Chemical Corps and its related operations is still another agency with a major role in counter-insurgency (as well as potentially in larger warfare). It has long been stockpiling lethal biological and chemical weapons, at Fort Detrick and the Edgewood Arsenal in Maryland, Rocky Mountain Arsenal in Colorado, Pine Bluff Arsenal in Arkansas, Dugway Proving Grounds in Utah, and the Newport Chemical Plant in Indiana. Little is said about these arsenals, and the United States remains a signatory to the Geneva Protocol of 1925, which prohibits the use of "asphyxiating, poisonous or other gases, and of all analogous liquids, materials or devices." Because of this ban, little information has been released to the public on the actual use of such substances in counter-insurgency fights; such knowledge might never have emerged without the persistent inquiry of the Physicians for Social Responsibility (which has since evolved into the Medical Committee on Human Rights). The military used extensive deception to conceal the facts of its contract with Traveler's Research Corporation of Hartford. The carefully worded denials were released not only to the physicians, but to those snoopy congressmen and senators who pressed the inquiries of physicians in their areas. In the meantime, Traveler's was producing large quantities of the dangerous tularemia and plague bacilli and was studying the use of air currents for delivery of toxic clouds over targets in Vietnam. It was even studying the attitudes of United States government leaders and the potential public reaction to the actual use of biological weapons. The rationale for the use of incapacitating chemicals has since been worked out: they can reach an enemy whose location cannot be pinpointed; they are not always lethal, and hence are more humane than bullets, explosives, or nuclear bombs; they are a means of using modern science to control an enemy and win the uncommitted to our side. Dr. Rassweiler, a chemical advisor to the Pentagon, suggests:

> We must hurt them badly enough to deter them from interfering with us or our allies, but not as badly as they know we would hurt them if they retaliated with actual warfare. The damage on them would be of the type for which we could provide relief and restoration—once the country concerned changed its attitude. (Quoted in Brightman, June/July 1966, p. 38)

The "Compensation for Crop Losses" leaflet that is dropped over large areas from one to 24 hours before an attack explains to peasants that the United States government will repay them for any damage done; but the seven-step procedure involves an elaborate shuffling of forms through the bureaucracy, and farmers rarely use it. Instead, the wide use of chemical defoliants by United States forces in Vietnam has proven an effective form of anti-food warfare, of separating the enemy from his vital commodities. By inducing famine our forces have driven entire districts into government refugee camps, or at least have made them unable to feed the Viet Cong. Such measures are highly effective against certain particularly vulnerable segments of the population. Around Quangngai Province it has been common to see packs of four- or five-year-old orphans roaming the countryside, begging for food or stealing it where they can. Teenage group suicides have been another response to famine.

In response to charges of indiscriminate killing through chemical warfare, the Deputy Assistant Chief of Staff for Force Development indicated that the herbicides were merely a form of commonly used weedkillers, "...a relatively mild method of putting pressure on a ruthless enemy" (quoted in Brightman, June/July 1966, p. 39). Dr. John Edsall of Harvard responded that the original charges had greatly understated the case, that anti-food warfare was not indiscriminate killing since it could be expected to select "young children, the old and the ill who are the first victims and the first to die." This selective sensitivity to children is also characteristic of heavy doses of the 2,4–D and 2,4,5–T "weed killers," which cause pulmonary constriction, digestive malfunction, and bleeding from the mouth. Other chemicals used in Vietnam, such as vomiting gas and nerve gas, produce both temporary incapacitating effects and permanent disability, particularly to infants.

The major agency for development of this "more humane" warfare has been the University of Pennsylvania's Institute for Cooperative Research. By the summer of 1966 it had two major contracts for the aerial dispersal of arsenic and cyanide compounds, and the deputy secretary of defense admitted that such programs were actually being carried out in South Vietnam. In 1967 Michael Klare uncovered major projects dealing with chemical and biological warfare in 57 American universities (Klare 1968). While CBW is often concealed, it is a major ingredient of the counter-insurgency network.

The Rationale

Trying to understand how this vast arsenal of destructive counterrevolutionary machinery can be squared with the principle that guerrilla wars are won or lost by the support of the populace is a difficult task. Obviously, espionage, nerve gas, and security behind barbed wire prison encampments do little to win the admiration of a peasant population. There is, of course, a competing theory which places less emphasis on popularity and more on coercion; this theory will also have to be dealt with. But it must first be pointed out, much to the disillusionment of scholars, that the roots of foreign policies lie deeper than the justifications proposed for them.

One form of military preparedness may be justified by a theory of finite deterrence, another by a theory of graduated response or limited war, a third by one of several theories of counter-insurgency. These theories are not all logically consistent and certainly they must compete with each other for the dollar outlay needed to implement them; but scholars are plentiful and their services are readily purchased through research contracts. While the theories they provide help to rationalize one policy or another, the outcome of a policy choice represents mainly the relative political power of the factions involved.

With this proviso it is possible to turn to theories which minimize the role of popular support and emphasize coercive power. The first theory is proposed by W. W. Rostow, a key advisor to two contemporary American presidents. The Rostow thesis is that economic development along the lines of American or other Western capitalistic societies represents the natural process by which poor nations become wealthy democracies. At the early stages the natural process may need assistance in the form of the infusion of large doses of foreign capital, but once self-sustaining growth is achieved, the country is incontrovertibly on the path toward economic stability, increasing productivity, and parliamentary government. At the critical "take-off" phase everything accelerates; the stock of capital rises, a skilled labor pool forms, technology advances, and a class of entrepreneurial merchants and managers develops. After the take-off, according to Rostow, economic progress continues under its own power, accompanied by the development of parliamentary democracy. The only thing that might thwart such a natural evolution, however, is the intrusion of a "disease," that is, communism, before the take-off stage is secure. Because the end is so clearly prescribed by the historical process, it is necessary to only force-feed the poorer nations with capital and to maintain the stability of their governments through the difficult period of transition.

Communist or romantic revolutionary movements, however popular they might be, are to be stifled, and the methods used to stifle them are those of counter-insurgency. General Maxwell Taylor was one of the first, and perhaps the most influential, military leaders to describe the revision of military tactics needed for the task.

Another theorist of similar leaning is RAND Corporation economist Charles Wolf. Wolf's thesis is as follows:

1. Americans tend to be more sympathetic to a revolutionary hero (like Castro) than to the government he opposes (like Batista). Although this sympathy for an alleged defender of the common man may at times be well directed, the main point is that our emotional reactions cloud our views and make us too self-righteous in demanding that the governments we support be popular.
2. The revolutionaries do not need popular support; they need key inputs such as food, recruits, and information.

3. The population is a pawn in the struggle, it must be prevented from supplying such inputs to the insurgents.

Wolf illustrates the process:

> Confiscation of chickens, razing of houses, or destruction of villages have a place in counter-insurgency efforts, but only if they are done for a strong reason: namely, to penalize those who have assisted the insurgents. If the reason for the penalty is not sufficient, explicit, and known to the people, exaction of penalties is likely to harm rather than help the counter-insurgency effort. Military discipline must be tightened and brought under firm control so that whatever harshness is meted out by government forces is unambiguously recognizable as deliberately imposed because of behavior by the population that contributes to the insurgent movement. (Wolf 1967, p. 66, quoted in DuBoff, January 1968, p. 16)

Wolf suggests the full range of coercion, threats, bribes, rumors, and subterfuge as tactics to be employed. His theory remarkably resembles measures which have actually been used by the United States in Vietnam and is well described by a remark attributed to one American general: "Grab 'em by the balls and their hearts and minds will follow" (DuBoff, Jan. 1968, p. 15).

The U. S. and the U. N.

Counter-insurgency is not the only•earmark of the contemporary American role in international conflict. The terror and the astronomical costs of nuclear weaponry, missile delivery and guidance systems, antiballistic missiles, and the new designs in military aircraft have become a mainstay of our economy as well as a part of our national ideology and foreign policy. In counter-insurgency the populations of the poorer countries are considered expendable; in nuclear deterrence, the population of our own country is offered as hostage, made to accept the coercion of conscription, the discipline of civil defense, or the squeeze of the limitless costs of an arms race. But one theme underlies the various strategies: the application of the social and physical sciences and of technology to the development of increasingly sophisticated systems of social coercion and human destruction.

Is ours an adequate analysis? Is it possible that the analysis concentrates too heavily on military and paramilitary aspects of the American role in international conflict and too little on diplomatic process, on the American role in the United Nations, and on the hostility of the international arena in which the American military and counter-insurgency procedures are but one response?

To answer such questions it is essential to note that the United States is not merely one country among many bargaining for its interests through the diplomatic channels or through the formal peace-keeping apparatus of the United Nations. Rather, until 1958, informed professionals at the U.N. Secretariat recognized that the political context of the U.N. assured that any proposition favored by the United States could become U.N. policy. The situation since 1958 (the time of the Lebanon crisis) has been slightly different. Now the professionals recognize only that if the United States *opposes* an action, the entire U.N.—the Security Council, the General Assembly, and the Secretariat—will refrain from taking that action. The corollary of this situation is that any action taken by the United Nations must fit into America's estimation of its own political interests. Since 1958 the United States has not been able to get by with the safe votes of its NATO allies and its political satellite nations, but has had to contend with the large new Afro–Asian bloc. While this does induce some healthy bargaining, with the United States playing a sometimes precarious role between the old colonial powers and their former colonies, American domination of the U.N. remains almost as pervasive as before. This is because the United States itself has considerable and possibly increasing say in the foreign affairs of less developed nations. Behind the vast counter-insurgency arsenal the United States maintains a widespread network of diplomatic and technical aid missions, and continues to exercise pervasive influence through its great financial, commercial, and industrial corporations dealing with the third world.

The power of the United States over the U.N., while not absolute, is great indeed. In 1950, the communist government of North Korea decided to use force to reunify Korea. The Truman administration judged it expedient to resist this attempt militarily and took advantage of an ill-advised Soviet absence from the Security Council (where the five permanent member nations have veto powers) to push through a resolution to send in U.N. (that is, mostly American) forces. When the Soviet Union representative hastily returned to obstruct any more extensive implementation of the action, the United States was able to take the unprecedented step of transferring the issue to the General Assembly, where a safe majority permitted the American-directed action to be continued under the U.N. flag.

In 1956 when Soviet troops prepared to enter Hungary to crush the Nagy government, the United States had again to make a decision. Even a modest U.N. presence such as a visit by the secretary general or his aides might have induced the Soviet Union to accommodate rather than risk a new Korea. However, such an action might also have risked armed conflict in Europe involving the United States and the USSR. The United States decided against such a risk, and an American delegation under Henry Cabot Lodge spread word though the U.N. corridors that Nagy was as bad a Communist as Khrushchev and unworthy of support. Only after the new Hungarian government was crushed did the United States hail Nagy's supporters as heroes and martyrs. Now, the Eisenhower–Dulles administration which had promised to roll back communism could explain to its public that it was the U.N. which had failed to take action. Thus the United States has used the U.N. for its own diplomatic and public relations purposes. It has sacrificed the concept of the U.N. as an independent superordinate agency, transcending narrow national interests, with a morality and a set of sanctions of its own. The agency was originally founded as an impartial organization with the power to discover and to prevent or punish occurrences of international violence. Instead the U.N. has become largely an instrument, like the United States counter-insurgency school, to be used when needed for American political purposes. Instead of an instrument to replace the anarchy of sovereign states we have acquired a diplomatic weapon.

Chinese "Aggression"?

The vast array of American diplomatic and military weapons cannot be explained by the presence of aggressive foreign nations. The American charge of aggressive intentions on the part of either the Soviet Union (especially during the late forties and the fifties) or China (more recently) must be examined against the historical record.

While the U.N. charter condemns aggression, it does not define it; and the United States has consistently rejected the Soviet partial definition —the armed invasion of a state by the military forces of another state. In the absence of a definition the U.N. considers aggression to be any act condemned as aggression by a majority vote in the U.N. In practice this meant an act, committed by a communist state, which the West disapproved. Three instances of alleged Chinese aggression have been charged. The Chinese military actions in Korea, in Tibet, and at the Indian border are facts; whether they were also aggression is an interpretation that must be based on additional facts of the case.

The temporary division of Korea into Soviet and American zones after World War II proved permanent when no agreement could be reached on a government to unify the country. The United States insisted on keeping its man, Syngman Rhee, at the head of the regime. The USSR insisted on a coalition which would include Korean communists, but Rhee refused to allow communists in his government. In May 1950 Rhee's party was badly defeated in an election in South Korea even though it had taken the precaution of arresting hundreds of suspected Communists before the balloting began. Rhee refused to resign, however, and Secretary of State John Foster Dulles flew to Korea to address the South Korean National Assembly. Dulles pledged continued American aid, but only if Rhee's minority government remained in power. After a period of disorder, anti-government demonstrations, and border incidents, with charges and counter-charges made as to who struck first, the North Korean army crossed the 38th parallel. The equally large South Korean army showed little willingness to fight to save Rhee. Within two weeks the capital city of Seoul and most of the South Korean land area had surrendered without a fight. The action was apparently taken without Soviet knowledge; Russian delegates chose that inappropriate time on June 25 to boycott the Security Council because Taiwan was occupying the Chinese seat.

With the Soviet veto absent, the Security Council passed by the absolute minimum of seven votes two resolutions, one calling for North Korean troops to withdraw, and the other asking member nations to help secure such withdrawal and to refrain from giving aid to North Korea. The communist Yugoslavian delegate voted for these resolutions, but his own motion to permit a North Korean delegate to present his case before the council was defeated.

Very quickly foreign armed forces, almost exclusively American, arrived and drove the North Korean troops back toward the 38th parallel. The conflict might easily have been terminated at that point, but on October 7 the U.N. General Assembly approved a new resolution far exceeding its own constitutional authority. The U.N. troops were authorized to continue northward to conquer North Korea and reunify the country under a non-communist government. Within three more weeks, the U.N. forces had taken over much of North Korea, reached the Yalu River, and begun destruction of bridges to the Chinese mainland. Moreover, General MacArthur, the American commander, had announced that North Korean fugitives would be pursued into China. Only at this time did Chinese troops enter the conflict to fight the U.N. force back to a standoff at the 38th parallel in a war which cost the lives of more than two million Koreans. This loss plus the devastation of the land and the maiming of countless numbers of people made the U.S.–U.N. "liberation" of Korea a painful process. Since then, an American-supported military force of 600,000 men has maintained the succession of military regimes in South Korea. These facts are not in dispute. But Chinese officials resent the charge at the U.N. (where their seat is occupied by the unpopular government they overthrew more than 20 years ago) that it was the Chinese who committed an act of aggression in Korea.

The Chinese action in Tibet is even more decidedly not an example of international aggression. Tibet is internationally recognized as a province of China. After ten years of rule under the new Chinese government the province had not yet conformed to national laws requiring land distribution, the liberation of serfs and slaves (the majority of Tibet's population), and the modernization of family law to prohibit the sale of wives and children.

When the Chinese central government began to enforce the new laws in 1959, it met with a brief revolt, which was quickly subdued. Except for the fact that the action lasted only a few weeks and was mild in its execution, the situation is similar to United States Civil War. A team of reputable and experienced British journalists that later investigated thoroughly and traveled throughout Tibet concluded that the rebellion involved only a small minority and was put down with little loss of life or destruction of property.

The third example of Chinese "aggression" is not even a matter of interpretation. It is mythology. The Peking government in 1949 reached amicable and indeed generous boundary settlements with Afghanistan, Nepal, Burma, and somewhat later with Pakistan. India, however, rejected several invitations for direct negotiation, and the Chinese began to construct a road out of an old caravan route through the towering mountains from Sinkiang to western Tibet. Part of this road ran through Ladakh, a barely inhabited area which both the official Indian and British maps listed as unsurveyed and of undefined national origin. The road was in uncontested use for four years before several incidents occurred between Indian and Chinese border patrols. In the diplomatic exchange that followed, India based her claim on unofficial maps, demanded withdrawal of Chinese patrols from the road, and in 1962 attempted to expel them forcefully.

The Chinese readily overcame Indian forces, capturing a number of prisoners and a quantity of military equipment. When India halted its attacks on Ladakh, Chinese troops were withdrawn behind the McMahon line and the prisoners were returned. Even the captured tanks and artillery were repaired and returned. There was almost no battle, no cessation of diplomatic relations or of trade, and no declared attack or ceasefire in the entire incident (Burchill 1965).

Apart from its actions, the Chinese government speaks in hostile terms about and to the United States government. We may understand its terms better if we reverse the shoes for a moment, as did a Canadian historian:

> It is the United States of America in the year 1969. The thousand Chinese military personnel are billeted on Long Island, and another Chinese contingent maintains a base on Hawaii. Off the shores of California and in the Atlantic from New York to Florida, the Polaris submarines of the People's Republic patrol ceaselessly back and forth. Planes based on Long Island, bearing the Communist star, appear suddenly over inland cities and towns, making casual observations. Meanwhile, the American Ambassador to the United Nations waits outside, barred from his seat by the power of the Chinese contingent. (Lin 1967, quoted in Burnell, ed., 1969, p. 105)

The Chinese theory of revolution and the model it provides must have great appeal for third world people driven to desperation by poverty and bad government. Yet neither Chinese propaganda to encourage such revolt nor American propaganda to discourage it is likely to be effective. Revolution is born of certain conditions which can hardly be accelerated or retarded by the advice of foreigners. In any case China, since its revolution, has not been an aggressive nation, and the huge American arsenal cannot be explained by the presence of a clear military threat from China or from any other country. To understand why the United States has generated its fantastic military and paramilitary programs we must look elsewhere—at those whose interests are being protected or promoted by this machine and at the forces that shape American public policy in the area of international conflict. This is the task of the remaining chapters of this book.

References

BRIGHTMAN, CAROL
    1966   "The 'Weed Killers.' " *Viet-Report* 2 (June/July): p. 9.

————
    1968   "The Science of Control." *Viet-Report* 3 (January): p. 2.

BURCHILL, CHARLES S.
    1966   "Chinese Aggression: Myth or Menace?" Text of a speech given in Victoria, B.C., December, 1965. Vancouver, B.C.: The Study Group on China Policy.

BURNELL, ELAINE H., *ed.*
    1969   *Asian Dilemma: United States, Japan and China.* Santa Barbara, Calif.: Center for the Study of Democratic Institutions.

DOMHOFF, G. WILLIAM
    1969   "Who Made American Foreign Policy, 1945–1963?" in David Horowitz, ed., *Corporations and the Cold War*, pp. 25–69. New York: Monthly Review Press.

DUBOFF, RICHARD
    1968   "U.S. Policy: Third World." *Viet-Report* 3 (January): pp. 15–18.

FRIEDMAN, SAUL
    1963   "The RAND Corporation and Our Policy-Makers," *Atlantic* 212 (September): pp. 61–68.

GORDENKER, LEON
    1965   "The View from the 38th Floor." *The Correspondent* 34 (Spring/Summer): pp. 79–87.

HAGAN, ROGER
    1965   "Counter-Insurgency and the 'New' Foreign Relations." *Viet-Report* 1 (August/September): pp. 24–27.

HERMAN, EDWARD S., AND RICHARD B. DuBOFF
    1966   "American Counter-Diplomacy in Vietnam: Part II." *Viet-Report* 2 (June/July): p. 19.

HOLSTI, OLE R.
    1962   "The Belief System and National Images: A Case Study." *Journal of Conflict Resolution* 6 (September): pp. 244–52.

KLARE, MICHAEL
    1968   "CBW Research Directory." *Viet-Report* 3 (January): pp. 25–36.

LEAGUE OF WOMEN VOTERS OF THE U.S.
    1967   *The China Puzzle.* Washington, D.C.

NICOLAUS, MARTIN
    1966   "The Professor, the Policeman and the Peasant." *Viet-Report* 2 (February): pp. 16–21.

O'BRIEN, CONOR CRUISE
    1965   "Conflicting Concepts of the U.N." The *Correspondent* 34 (Spring/Summer): pp. 19–34.

Chapter 2

THE THIRD WORLD

American policy toward the third world operates to reshape less fortunate peoples into the parameters of our modern, Westernized economic and political systems. We will see that such treatment is blind to the highly diverse needs of third world peoples, and in many areas, it is actually harmful. This treatment includes a false attitude of superiority in several spheres whereby we attempt to thrust on others our values and systems under the guise of aid or advancement. As an itinerant holy man from the Iraqi village of Umm al-Nahr expressed it so well:

> ...our goals are different. We want to preserve the way of life which God ordained for us, while you wish to destroy what is known to be good and bring about something which you hope to be better, but which is usually worse. (Quint 1967, p. 59)

In our world the attempt to sell a product, an idea, or a candidate has become largely a task of packaging, labeling, and then promoting it by its most appealing name. The impoverished hungry mass of colonized people have been at different times the colonies, poorer nations, the undeveloped or underdeveloped nations, and are now the developing nations. The last is a sad misnomer, since there is no indication that these nations are, in any absolute sense, developing any greater capacity to feed, house, or educate their numbers. The implication of the new term *developing* is that a nation which travels in the Western orbit, shuns communists, crushes guerrilla movements, minimizes domestic corruption, and advertises for foreign investment capital will eventually reach the take-off stage in economic development which transformed the Western world from an agrarian to an urban, manufacturing society in less than a century.

Whatever hopes are provided by this image are likely to be dashed by an examination of the status of the countries concerned.

Worldwide Poverty

There is ample evidence now that people are going hungry in the world's richest country, the United States (Drew 1969). But the problem is qualitatively different in the poor countries. These include all of Asia (with the exception of Japan and Siberia), all of Africa, and Latin America (possibly excepting Argentina). Southern and Eastern Europe are in the middle range. These countries contain three-fourths of the world's population, and conditions in them differ greatly from those in the developed Western societies. This difference persists even when we compare the contemporary poor countries with the developed Western countries *not* as they are now, but as they were before their industrial development. These differences are summarized by Kuznets:

> The comparison shows that the developed countries in their preindustrial phase enjoyed a per capita income several times higher than that of most underdeveloped countries today; that unlike the latter, they were at or near positions of economic leadership, and had already experienced a long period of growth and expansion under conditions of political independence—growth initiated much earlier by the intellectual (Renaissance and Reformation), political (formation of national states), and geographical revolutions (discovery of the New World) ... many underdeveloped countries today show much higher rates of over-all population growth—traceable partly to higher birth rates, partly to lower death rates, and partly to negligible loss by emigration. (Kuznets 1964)

The poor countries are diverse in many important ways. In some, like Greece and Chile, the average per capita income, while still at subsistence levels for much of the population, is markedly higher than in others, such as Indonesia. Some, like China and India, are national entities of long standing and represent cultures which reach back over 2,000 years. In others, for example Nigeria and the Congo, tribal cultural identities compete with the existence of the newly formed nations. Some are barren desert, some fertile jungles; some have individual land holdings, others some form of communal tenure. An important aspect of the problem of investment capital is the great disparity in the natural resources of these poorer countries. Equally important to the problem of income distribution are their differences in population density. Some of these countries have active revolutionary or radical reform movements, others do not. A serious attempt to help administer any form of assistance to these countries would require a thorough appreciation of these and other differences which is lost in a more global look at the problem.

It is the more general view, however, which helps to expose the staggering proportions of the problem. Particular cases can reveal instances of the inhumanity and unconcern often shown by those with power for others less fortunate. The more general features of international poverty suggest a collective tampering with those forces of nature which could lead to the extinction of the human species.

The Population Explosion

Before their industrial revolution, none of the currently modern countries had more than 30 million people. Their population growth came after, and largely as a result of, increasing area to settle and increasing ability to feed and attend to the health of their citizens. A revolutionary change in population, wrought by this new technology, has been affecting both developed and undeveloped countries since the turn of the century. In this time we have discovered highly effective ways to reduce the rates of infant and adult mortality. The methods are simple and inexpensive. More important, they can be applied by small numbers of modestly trained technicians. The result has been a spectacular population explosion. Where high birth rates were once balanced by high death rates, the number of people who die in a year per hundred thousand population has been halved. The number born continues high and the number surviving infancy has shown an astounding increase.

One illustration is the case of an attack on malaria which, through the use of chemical insecticides, was largely and quickly eliminated in 1950. The same chemical insecticides killed other disease carriers, and when they were accompanied by modest efforts at water purification, there was a sharp drop in mortality, particularly infant mortality. This has meant that in some of the poorer nations the population as a whole is extremely young. In most, more than half the population is under twenty. In some, the number of teenagers is double that of the number of persons in their twenties (Boulding 1965, p. 38). One consequence of such rapid growth is a small work force relative to the number of people who must be fed, clothed, housed, or educated by its efforts. A second consequence is the exodus of teenagers to the urban centers. In several cities a growth of 12 to 15 percent per annum (a resident population doubling every five or six years) has led to severe social disorganization with high rates (20 to 25 percent) of urban unemployment and corresponding increases in crime.

An effective accommodation to the new numbers has not yet been found. Previous population increase had been gradual—it took sixteen hundred years for the 250 million humans who lived at the beginning of the Christian era to double their numbers. Today the three thousand million people on earth will become six thousand millions by the year 2000. Twelve times as many people as were alive at the year one are about to double their numbers in one-fortieth of the time.

A sharp rise in the Indian birth rate several decades ago has subsided, but still a population growth rate of 2.3 percent per year promises a doubling of its giant impoverished population several years ahead of the schedule for the world in general. China will have one billion people to feed by 1980. Where the rate of growth is 3 percent as in Ceylon, Egypt, and some parts of Latin America, the doubling occurs approximately every 23 years.

The most dramatic consequence of the greater population is an increase in death through starvation and malnutrition. Infants who once died at birth now live, many (in annually increasing numbers) only to die of hunger in childhood. Still others live to reproduce offspring who will be no better off than themselves.

The plight of the poor countries today defies our imagination and strains our powers to rationalize our own continuing affluence. It is difficult, perhaps impossible, to empathize with suffering on so large a scale. For a fleeting moment an advertisement for one or another of the helping agencies calls attention to a particular case, of some Korean or Philippine child, destitute and orphaned perhaps by war.

It is difficult to deal with the reality that the fate of such children might well have been the fate in store for one's own child, or for oneself. It is even more difficult to bear in mind that such individual cases are the true meaning of statistical computations showing that two-thirds of the world's population live in countries which collectively produce less than one-sixth of the income of the world. A United Nations study, whose data were collected in 1949, showed the average annual per capita income in these countries to be about $50. The per capita income in dollar purchasing value has not changed materially since then.

In a country which lives at the subsistence level there is no surplus capital for use in industrial development. In each underdeveloped nation the striking observation is not the distinction between socialistically or capitalistically developed industry, but rather absence of industry. This means that with a substantial majority of the population at work trying to feed its ever increasing numbers, there is insufficient trained labor and no funds to pay such labor to engage in the work of housing, clothing, and schooling those who survive the struggle for basic nutrition. Eugene Black, a former president of the World Bank, has asserted that the rate of population increase more than nullifies any annual gain in capital resources for industrial development on the part of the have-not nations (Huxley 1963). The belt around the mass of the people (excluding small elite groups) in many undeveloped countries is pulled as tightly as it can be. Even under the most totalitarian discipline or the most inspired spirit of nationalist self-sacrifice one cannot squeeze blood from a stone. Capital, education, housing, services, and in some cases food are not keeping pace—much less increasing with the number of people.

The Myth of Foreign Aid

Where capital has been made available through loans and gifts the picture is not changed. There are several reasons for this. The first is that the amount of aid has been skimpy. During the period of Marshall Plan aid to war-torn Western European nations, the American donation was $5 per capita. The corresponding figure to Asian nations receiving American aid has been $.25 (Kolko 1969). Another way to view the contribution of foreign aid to development is to examine it in relation to world commodity prices. Since the end of World War II the market prices of raw materials such as sugar, hemp, rubber, and tin have dropped (in current dollar value). At the same time the cost of manufactured items which the poorer nations must import has risen sharply. The result has been a form of subsidy of the rich nations by the poorer ones. The total amount of gifts and loans given to the poorer nations would barely offset this loss, *even if there were no rise in populations.*

There is much exaggeration in this country about the extent of American beneficence in assisting economic development abroad. Michael Brower's analysis of a typical year, by deleting military assistance, helps to clarify the picture.

> ... For the fiscal year 1965, the Congress appropriated funds totalling about $3.6 billion for this purpose, including $510 million for the Alliance for Progress, $980 million for development loans and technical assistance ... , $104 for the Peace Corps. To this we can add about $1.46 billion out of the total Food for Peace shipments. ... Administrative costs and miscellaneous small programs added $73 million more, for a total U.S. bilateral development assistance program of about $3.1 billion in fiscal year 1965. Adding about $500 million for U.S. development aid through multilateral channels brings the overall total to $3.6 billion. This represents only a little over one-half of one percent of our Gross National Product. ... Or, subtracting the Food for Peace program, which is paid for by our domestic agricultural support programs, the burden was only one-third of one percent of our GNP. (Brower 1965, p. 53)

Brower goes on to suggest the magnitude of a program which might actually have served in that year to promote the development of the poor nations. Excluding the communist nations of the third world (which is perhaps an unwise manner of accounting) Brower estimates a combined GNP for the poor countries of $225 billion. An additional $34 billion per year would be required for an average economic growth rate of 5 percent per year. Something over half of this might be achieved if the nations involved saved 8 percent of their GNP. A remaining $16 billion would have to be saved each year in foreign capital. If private foreign investment were to reach $4 billion per year the remaining $12 billion would have to be met by government assistance. The United States, richest of the industrialized countries, accounting for 60 percent of their income might then, following our own principle of progressive taxation, be responsible for up to 75 percent of $9 billion per year. The amount could be reduced to $6.9 billion by withholding assistance from nations unwilling to comply with necessary domestic reforms. Other industrialized nations would probably follow suit in offering assistance.

If the amount seems large, the figure is roughly in line with costs associated with putting a man on the moon (and beyond) ; and the military budget exceeds this amount by over seven times.

Foreign assistance fails also because its administration and policies bear the mark of its purposes, which are political rather than humanitarian. Economically, the United States is the world's leading specialist in all forms of modern weaponry. A substantial portion of assistance to poor nations takes the form of credits to their governments for the purchase of American-made military equipment and training service. Such aid provides a federal subsidy for the defense industry to enter competition for a no-risk sales market. Further, it fits the strategic objectives of American foreign policy: to prevent any form of development which would be unfavorable to investment potentialities. This is sometimes phrased as opposition to dictatorial rule and defense of freedom, but the evidence shows assistance to numerous dictatorial regimes, for example in Spain, Pakistan, and Greece. And in some cases, as in Greece and Guatemala, assistance to the anti-democratic or military faction actually facilitated the destruction of democratically or constitutionally elected governments. Sometimes the policy is phrased as opposition to communism. This also stands up poorly, since Yugoslavia has received our assistance, and other non-communist countries, like India, have had funds cut when they were used for state-owned enterprises. The only consistent thread appears to be assistance to fortify and promote the opportunities of the American economic empire.

Aspects of Economic Development

There are many theories of economic development. Each selects a single critical distinguishing factor between rich and poor nations and assumes that a change in that critical factor will affect the rest. The factors often cited are exploitation, inequality, capital, cultural backwardness, education, achievement values, a middle class, and population density.

It is certainly clear that population control is necessary if development is to occur. It is not clear, however, that population density per se is a major factor in national wealth. The Netherlands and Great Britain are examples of densely populated nations with high standards of living. Moreover, there are vast impoverished areas, for example in Brazil, which are sparsely populated but extremely poor. Even when we concede that, on the world scale, population growth makes capital accumulation impossible, we are left with few guides for action. Compared with the machinery that led to the great decline in mortality, methods of birth control are expensive and extremely difficult to administer on a large scale. Even the intrauterine device, which is relatively low in cost, requires professional assistance and education for use, both of which are in short supply in the poorer nations. More important, they require that the user choose to have fewer children. Such a decision may be wholly alien to cultural values. Children frequently are a source of pride, status, reverence, security in one's older days, and continuity of the extended family. In the poorest areas it is not even certain that two children will fare any better than seven children would have fared. It is not even clear that the two children will be any less immune to death from malnutrition or from the resultant high susceptibility to illness. The frequency of higher birth rates among the poor suggests that where people are treated like animals they will breed like animals. Hence, while population control is an immediate necessity, we cannot really say that it is likely to prove successful in the absence of changes in technical training, in education generally, or in material progress.

The Error of Applying American Standards to Other Nations

ECONOMIC APPLICATIONS

A common assumption is that nations are poor because they lack an industrious, hard-working middle class, a group of entrepreneurs motivated to achieve, to produce for long-term benefits, to save, and to invest. In one instance a program applying our best techniques of inspiring such motivation in Indian merchants has been tried with some success (McClelland 1965, p. 333). There is great danger in the paternalistic assumption that the values of another culture are inferior to our own, and there is great cost associated with attempts to change deeply held individual values. It is also not definite that a goal-directed urban middle class is what the poor countries most need. Perhaps this would be so if the older feudal aristocratic sectors of the poor countries were in conflict with the modern sectors. But for many reasons modern and feudal sectors are at peace. The dynamic mercantile centers have from the beginning based their localized growth and prosperity on the use of cheap labor and cheap produce from the feudal centers. Sometimes their growth has been at the expense of extreme oppression or slavery in the feudal sector. The development has traditionally been oriented to foreign markets and has rarely led to permanent gains among the impoverished. In Brazil one after another of the major industries grew and then declined: first the primitive extraction of wood, then sugar production on large slave plantations, then mining, then rubber extraction, and most recently coffee. Each produced a flurry of economic activity and then declined, leaving an area more depressed than it had been before as the foreign market conditions shifted. The poverty of these areas and their archaic social structures were worsened rather than improved by entrepreneurial activity (Stavenhagen 1966).

In fact the middle class tends to be a small and not very potent force in the poorer nations. Moreover, it has not always been a force for progress. Its urban development has taken place largely at the expense of the traditional society, channeling labor and raw materials from places of great poverty. The wealthy aristocracies in the poor nations have had far greater power than the fledgling middle class, and to a large extent the interests of both the aristocratic ruling elite and the miniscule middle class have coincided. Both have a stake in averting revolutionary reforms, both benefit from maintaining domestic colonialism, and both, at least in Latin America, have been supporters of the military.

American character values fit well with the requisites for economic productivity: pragmatism and materialism. The measure of a man is what he can command in the marketplace, and "to make good" is far more easily understood and appreciated than "to be good." That image is suspect in much of the undeveloped world. Many Latin Americans view the American dedication to work, efficiency, and productivity as a disdain for the moral substance or inner life of the human being. The image of their northern neighbors who walk, eat, read, worship, and even have fun on clock schedule is repugnant to many Latins. Maury Baker, in an article entitled "Dam Yankeeism in Latin America," writes:

> One thing should be understood: the Latin Americans consider the people of the United States as less moral than they are. They consider the civilization of the United States to be inferior to theirs. . . . Latin Americans fear contamination by North American culture, fear what some call "cocacolaza-tion." They fear that along with North American automobiles and refrigerators and television sets will come vices, corruption, false horizons of life and progress. (Baker 1963)

A number of studies have related the rise in achievement motivation in the population to the rate of economic development (McClelland 1961).

Such studies cleverly apply the methods used to score achievement motivation in projective psychological tests on individuals to cultural products such as societal myths and textbooks used in the schools. In this way a country, like an individual, can have its achievement motivation scored by examining the content of the textbooks read by its school children. The data show that countries high in achievement motivation do, in fact, undergo a rapid rise in their rates of economic growth as seen by such indices as the production of hydroelectric power. The finding corresponds with an old thesis of the relation between the Protestant ethic and the rise of capitalism (Weber 1930). The same method of study has led to other findings that support the Latin stereotype of the Yankee. When nations higher in achievement motivation (including the United States) were examined not for development but for individual stress, the findings showed a clear pattern. Using U.N. statistical data on death rates from illnesses closely related to psychic stress, for example duodenal ulcer, essential hypertension, and cirrhosis of the liver, the high-achievement-motivation societies scored significantly higher even when the observations were restricted to those economically developed nations for which statistics on causes of death were most reliable and comparable (Rudin 1965). Since such disorders probably require a physiological or constitutional susceptibility, it seems likely that the stresses indicated in this measure are even more widespread results of a cold, competitive social system. It is typical that the mainstream American attitude disregards the destructive aspects of a highly competitive value system and sees the have-nots, in this country or in foreign lands, as deficient in our virtues. This attitude is a curse on the hopes of the poor for any sort of development.

The American attempt to remodel other peoples and social systems in our own image is not a matter of cultural arrogance alone. Leading American industries are successful and the United States is affluent precisely because its economic policies impoverish other nations. Some economic background will support this statement. By 1960 the United States was importing over half of its required metals and almost 60 percent of its wool. It imported all tropical foodstuffs such as cocoa, coffee, and bananas and well over half of its sugar supply. In 1963 iron and steel industry imports combined (including the manganese vital to steel production) were valued at $22.3 billion, aluminum at $3.9 billion, metal cans at $2.1 billion, copper at $3.1 billion, asbestos and zinc at $0.5 billion each, coffee at $1.9 billion, sugar and chocolate at $1.7 billion. Since these imports came from the poor countries and were critical to both domestic and military productivity in the United States, one might surmise that the poorer countries gained by furnishing their raw materials to the United States. That is not the case, for while America depends on access to these materials to maintain its economic affluence, it is also in a position, as is the European Common Market, to acquire these materials under conditions highly unfavorable to the poor nations.

Three factors are basic to those unfavorable terms of trade. First, Europe has increased its share of world industrial exports at American expense. In fact, only in military exports has the United States kept far ahead of the field. Second, America's production as we know it depends on continuous access to raw materials from the third world. Third, the United States has a significant agricultural surplus which it must market to underdeveloped nations.

The terms of trade—the costs of goods imported by a region compared to its exports—have been shifting continually toward low prices for raw materials and higher prices for manufactured articles. The loss to poor nations from this shift cancels out our foreign aid to them. The poverty of the third world assures that it cannot purchase its own oil and mineral raw materials and thus drive up the price to the United States.

Measured as a percentage of world production, the manufactures of the third world decreased from before World War II to the period 1961–1965. Per capita food production in these countries actually declined, particularly in Latin America. The American policy, which contributes to the economic stagnation of the third world, is to maintain the stability and continuity of our low cost imports and our high cost exports. The actions that implement this policy are foreign aid, diplomatic and economic pressure, trade exclusion, and—where economic measures fail—military assistance and military intervention. Official agricultural export subsidy programs of about $3 billion annually (between 1957–1967) help support the large commercial farmers in the United States. Often, as in India, the conditions attached to agricultural exports assured vital concessions to American industry. Such concessions include agreements to keep costs of raw materials low, special tax incentives for American investors, and use of American-owned shipping facilities. Perhaps the most common and most devastating string attached to foreign assistance is that it must be put into controlled accounts of "counterpart funds" in local currency. These are earmarked for purchase of American goods at high prices, and create a permanent economic servitude; for example, poor third world countries have been obliged to buy American cotton when cheaper cotton was available from other nations (Kolko 1969). Military goods constitute another major American export to poor countries. In some cases the nation may "purchase" a development service, paying American investors for developing tourism or conducting mining explorations which will eventually pay off in American profits. When highly conservative small business interests were complaining that foreign aid was a giveaway, President Kennedy reminded them of the economic facts of life:

> I wish American businessmen who keep talking against the program would realize how significant it has been in assisting them to get into markets where they would have no entry and no experience.... And the importance of this aid to our exports is increasing as our developing assistance is increasing, now almost entirely tied to American purchases. (Kolko 1969, p. 3)

The United States has successfully opposed proposals by poorer nations for a more beneficial commodity price exchange. In conference after conference at Caracas, Bogota, and Buenos Aires the line was held, mineral and coffee prices stayed low, and American corporations and consumers were protected at the expense of hungry people.

POLITICAL CONSIDERATIONS

The key assumption among most American students of the process of nation development is that there exists a continuum between the poor, backward, under-educated state beset by problems and the modern Western industrialized state which has solved them. Where the missionary once believed that the third world could be saved by bringing the church to it, the contemporary social scientist believes it can be saved by bringing to traditional societies the fruits of modernization. Most American social scientists assume without question the usefulness of this goal. They assume that there is a logical, orderly set of moves which will transform newly independent states into self-sufficient, educated, parliamentary democracies which are a part of the Western ("Free World") area of trade. It is impossible to determine the extent to which the funding policies of government and private foundations, which hold the purse for development research, have contributed to this widespread consensus among social scientists. It is clear, however, that consensus in the sciences always presents a danger to truth. Nothing else so well obfuscates the need for a breakthrough in our thinking. If one knows, in advance, both the desired end state and the means to work toward it, then there is little likelihood of learning what alternative ends might be more beneficial or more desirable to the people in question. To put this problem in still other terms, every social scientist who studies the methods of nonviolent urbanization, capitalization of industry, or protection of unstable government structures on behalf of some federal or private funding agency is engaging not only in an intellectual enterprise but also in a political one in favor of the existing consensus about the modernization process. Research on Latin America, for example, has mostly been a part of official American policy toward Latin America, which assumes that foreign trade, stable governments, and a strong middle class are needed and that the simple peasant culture of the countryside, the tactics of armed revolt, and expropriation of foreign holdings are not.

While modernization programs have been dutifully promoted in Chile and Argentina, the result has been largely economic stagnation. The idea that development from traditionalism to modernity is a cumulative process was dealt a severe jolt in Latin America, where the piecemeal reforms just did not add up. The U.N. Economic Commission for Latin America (ECLA) reports that Latin American problems of urban poverty, rural unemployment, slow industrialization, inequalities of income and living standards, dependence on foreign capital, foreign indebtedness, and slow expansion of foreign markets have all become *more* critical during the last ten years. The average growth rate during the 1960s was lower than that of the previous decade.

Disregarding the inability of slow changes to reach the majority of the world's underfed people, social scientists have still assisted United States government policy in its emphasis on stability and order as the sine qua non for change.

> What is the testimony of the developing world regarding expanded political participation and order? In the Congo, in Vietnam, in the Dominican Republic it is clear that order depends in some measure upon compelling newly mobilized strata to return to a measure of passivity and defeatism from which they have recently been aroused by the process of modernization. At least temporarily, the maintenance of order requires a lowering of newly acquired aspirations and levels of political activity. (Ithiel de Sola Pool, cited in Bodenheimer 1970, p. 101)

Besides the crass manipulativeness it reveals, the statement asserts that, however great may be the consensus among Americans about how orderly Latin American change should occur, at least some Latins are not happy with the model. The extent of their unhappiness is proved by the presence of American military assistance teams in at least 20 Latin American countries. They are surely not there to protect the United States from a foreign attack; rather, they are to protect governments of little popularity from their own people.

The most benign interpretation possible for the American presence is the argument that we are giving to the landed, commercial, industrial, and military elite who rule these countries (and who are friendly to American interests) the time to enact significant reforms out of their own enlightened self-interest (that is, fear of communists). If this was the intent, it has not occurred. Large landowners have resisted land reform, industrialization has not been accompanied by equalization of living standards or of income, and average per capita income for the poorer half of the Latin American population is $120 per year. In contradiction to the claim set in Rostow's take-off theory of development, studies now indicate that the developed sectors have advanced materially only at the expense of, and through exploitation of, the "backward" areas (Stavenhagen 1968, cited in Bodenheimer 1970).

Funds are immediately needed by Latin governments and the preferred American mode is investment capital. Interestingly, an inverse relationship exists between capital imports and growth—greater foreign capital
imports are correlated with *lower* rates of economic growth. When we consider the poor terms of trade forced on Latin America by the United States
and other industrialized nations, the reasons become clear. Profits taken out
of the country have far exceeded the input of foreign investments. The
Latin American share of world trade shrank from 11 percent in 1968. The
drop indicated that foreign investment by major powers into the poor countries has had the effect of reducing the host country's ability to profit from its
own exports. By tying aid and loans to the purchase of American goods we
have achieved a situation in which the interest and amortization on Latin
debts to the United States more than exceed the amount of new loans
(U.N.–ECLA 1969). This debt represents colonial dependence in the form
of poverty and economic servitude for the indefinite future.

APPLICATION AT A LOCAL LEVEL

Against a background of poverty made worse by population increase,
it is not uncommon that the idea of progress (at least as an ideal) has crept
into even those villages most remote from Western technology. Poverty,
disease, and ignorance of the technological order were the rule in the village
Umm-al-Nahr (in Iraq) when Malcolm Quint completed his enthnographic
study of the area. Umm-al-Nahr, an area of fertile rice lands and natural
beauty, has a population of hereditary families whose members have traveled
only rarely to the urban centers of Baghdad or Karbala. The market town
is four hours by cart and Amara, the nearest town with a doctor, is twice
as far. The cost of such a trip, much less the medical costs, are prohibitive,
and medical attention is not sought for the distended, worm-filled abdomens
or the gaping fly-covered infections of the children. Ninety-five percent of
the villagers have at least one endemic disease, 80 percent have at least two,
60 percent at least three. Four prevalent parasites infest the villagers while
bone and lung tuberculosis, yaws, and even leprosy are common.

Amid tropical temperatures that rise above 140 degrees Fahrenheit
in the shade (and there is none), the same wooden tools are used for agriculture, and the women carry the same 200- or 300-pound bundles of cut
rice on their heads as they did in this area 5,000 years ago. The Arab social
structure and supporting value system of this Middle Eastern village are,
as in most peasant communities, tradition-oriented. An illiterate father
commands absolute authority over an educated son. Birth and kinship
rather than achievement are the basis of social status. Peasant life is demanding and unchanging; the precedents of the elders leave little room for
deviation. In the village Umm-al-Nahr, the *rajal khayr* (the good and wise

man) is one who conforms absolutely to the traditional standard. He is pious, hospitable, and usually truthful. Above all, he is loyal to his immediate family, clan, village group, and tribe, in that order. Matters of crime or bloodletting are settled immediately with assistance from one's family, and the abstract concept of judging the merits of the case is never raised. *Ayb*, or shame, is the supreme sanction. It is the first word a child learns and the basis for guarding against transgressions of the norms of the kin group and the clan ever after.

When the villagers hear of a new government in Iraq and of progress, they envision it as something that will be given to them by some beneficent government without any essential change in the social order.

Soviet, American, and United Nations technicians, the Iraqi government, the educated classes of the cities, and the peasants of Umm-al-Nahr all define progress differently. For the urban educated minority, progress means the promise of material success: cars, refrigeration, air conditioners, houses with television sets. Some social analysts feel that the cultivation of such an urban, entrepreneurial, Western-oriented middle class is the key to modernization. The evidence shows, however, that such a group has developed at the expense of the peasantry, exploiting both their tribal lands and their cheap labor as they flock to the cities (Baran 1952).

The peasant in hundreds of thousands of villages like Umm-al-Nahr around the world sees progress in terms of land distribution, schools which teach his children (without destroying their tradition), free medical facilities close by, and above all, an increased income.

The fear that progress or modernization may effect an awesome change in the established social order is well founded. Yet a complete substitution of capitalist market rationality and material betterment would, in spite of all the pains of transition, be a progressive step beyond the rigidities of semi-feudal servitude. The great tragedy of the development of the third world is, however, that disruption of his social order has not helped the peasant. Rather, his traditional misery has been augmented. "The superimposition of business *mores* over ancient oppression by landed gentries resulted in compounded exploitation, more outrageous corruption, and more glaring injustice" (Baran 1952, p. 76). When capitalism or mercantilism first took root as one outgrowth of the enlightenment, its option for rapid growth created a strong foil which shook and toppled the feudal traditions of Europe. In the new world its strength was virtually sufficient to obliterate alien cultures. It was a culture of rugged, anti-monopolistic, egalitarian individualism. The contemporary entrepreneur in an underdeveloped country, however, works from a base of tradition and support. His traditions tell him that it is best to make political and economic deals with domestic overlords. Hence effective land reforms are yet to occur in Iran, Greece, Thailand, the Dominican Republic, and elsewhere. Still more important, the new entrepreneur's base of support is closely tied to the American and European businesses with which he has dealings, to American and European churches whose religion he espouses and whose aid he accepts, and to the American and European military which has trained an armed elite, a police corps, and armies of their own to protect his interests, which are, not coincidentally, their own.

In rare cases the educated classes provided leadership to the peasant mass. (Che Guevara was a physician, Makarious of Cyprus an archbishop; and the leaders of the South Vietnamese National Liberation Front include an attorney, an architect, a mathematics professor, and a physician.) Most often, however, the Western-oriented entrepreneur has, through his dread of a communist reform, left the mass of the population to find radical leadership in leftist liberation movements.

Apart from his political preferences, the businessman in Iraq has no real economic incentive to help his impoverished countrymen. People living at the bare subsistence level can consume only the least expensive necessities. There is no investment opportunity. The aristocracy and the newly rich provide a small market, but their tastes are for imported "snob" goods, Cadillacs, and other luxury items. Whatever limited demands remain for machinery or equipment investments, these are more lucratively gotten in exchange for what the local entrepreneur really can and does deliver—raw materials, oil, metals, and certain agricultural products. With virtually servile labor costs and limitless investment assistance from foreign capital the local entrepreneur, however much his Western-educated son may speak to him of progress for the masses, is caught in the role of middleman (in business) and puppet (in government) for the great Western powers.

While monopolistic market structures, low savings, and poor investment incentives are large obstacles to investment, there is yet another strong though less tangible impediment. It is the general fear of chaotic and revolutionary upheaval present in the people of every country where poverty and injustice are the rule. This fear, real or imagined, creates the coalition among military, entrepreneurs, aristocracy, foreign settlements, embassies, and military missions that control the rumblings which in turn motivate the coalition. Social and political tensions are not thereby eliminated; they are merely repressed. Governments representing a coalition of special interests cannot enforce (even if they can create) the blueprints of realistic reform. Progressive taxation would be met by a stoppage of business investment. Who would enforce high capital levies on the luxury goods of the aristocracy, and who would willingly accede to land reform affecting his own land holdings? Who in such a government could renegotiate foreign military and domestic contracts and establish strict controls on exchange? The record of toppled reform governments that have tried is legion. When there is any threat of reform, the coalition tightens its repressive reins.

The keepers of the past are not the builders of the future. If there is hope in the poor nations it is only through a break in the coalition of exploitative rulers and a new spirit of collective good. This ethos of collective effort, of placing the interests of society as a whole over the interests of a few, could have several sources. For the developed nations it could begin with a dismantling of foreign military bases and a use of the savings to phase out exploitative industries. Foreign powers must replace economic assistance with unselfish help and let die those governments which rest upon the exploitative coalition. One way or another the transition will occur. Land not legally given to the peasants may be forcibly taken by them. High incomes not confiscated through taxation can be absolutely expropriated. Corrupt officials may be retired and given asylum or shot before firing squads. The issue is not socialism versus capitalism. An extremely high level of socialist-type planning is inevitable, but it will wither in a corrupt, unproductive bureaucracy unless it is accompanied by the credo of the new humanitarian man. The danger to all of us who share in the coalition of the exploiters is that we may cling too long to our advantages and thereby doom not only millions of underfed sick peasants the world over, but ourselves as well.

Possible Change in Economic Systems

It is inaccurate to imagine that peasants are all of one mind. Most villages have their own ruling class which would be the first to sabotage any form of progress that did not assure existing distinctions of status for themselves. Yet on the village level, poor and moderately well off may be kin and the same individual may be an owner, a sharecropper, and a seasonal worker for his neighbors or for a large plantation. If the dramatic economic changes necessary to reduce the suffering of the third world are to win acceptance, there will have to be a recognition of the reality of cultural differences. The process of technical and economic development must be based originally on the existing village system and must fit the historical needs of the particular area. The agents of change in any given area must not only comprehend but also respect these traditions.

The pace of peasant life does not permit the luxury of time to leave the fields to conduct a revolution. The revolutions of the twentieth century that have involved the participation of the countryside have come at great cost and after great provocation. Yet when all resources, military, economic, and educational, are tied to the coalition whose daily activities augment the suffering of people, the population itself is all that remains to fight the oppressor. Hence, according to Mao Tse-tung's theory of revolutionary war, "It is impossible to win a war, especially a civil war, if the people are not on your side." Both guerrilla and counter-guerrilla theorists accept this precept as a given. The process by which the population can be won was described in Chakotin's *The Rape of the Masses*. Wolf summarized the thesis:

> The processes of organization and psychological conditioning were to go forward simultaneously through army action in quadrillage, forcible reloca- tion, interrogation, the occasional use of torture and through military-spon- sored social work and persuasion. Such an approach has enormous appeal to military technicians and social scientists who think of their findings primarily as techniques for human control. (Wolf 1970, p. 45)

This doctrine was followed with religious fervor by French officers in Algeria. The great flaw in the vision was that it adopted the technique to win a revolution, that is, to win the people, without any understanding of how these people, their history, their culture, and their economic interests were at variance with those of the French colony. Mao's theory of revolu- tionary war falls short because it does not specify who are the people who need radical change in order to survive and who it is that blocks this change. Emptied of its cultural and economic specifics, the practice of Mao's thesis by the French degenerated in Algeria, as it has in Vietnam under American auspices, into an attempt to produce simple obedience to naked power im- posed from without.

Frantz Fanon's concept of revolution goes beyond Mao's: it specifies the need for colonial peoples to rid themselves of foreign oppression. In fact, Fanon believes that the overthrow of colonial rulers is the necessary pre- condition for psychological independence. Violence and disorder are neces- sary to overthrow the repression and control of the state. While Fanon's analysis provides insights into the psychological mechanisms of colonial oppression and submission, it still fails to reveal the critical factor in revolu- tionary efforts. Extensive violence in Algeria has not led to the changes required by the peasants. A shorter period of violent revolt has produced far greater success in Cuba. The difference may lie in the responsiveness and relevance of the revolutionary leaders to their people. In Cuba a native army fought and lived among the people. However, an army of Algerians in Tunisia and Morocco was effectively barred from helping the Algerian native rebel forces and came in only after the French withdrew.

American Idealism in Vietnam

The great fallacy of American foreign policy in Vietnam is the assumption that Americans and their puppet appointees can be more responsive to the revolutionary needs of the Vietnamese than can the Viet- namese people themselves. Major General Landsdale, the architect of American strategy in Vietnam, spelled out the doctrine in the influential journal *Foreign Affairs*. For Lansdale, as for Mao, it is people, not armies or weapons, who are decisive. Purely military responses to the Vietnamese situation would fail because they " ... fall short of understanding that the Communists have let loose a revolutionary idea in Vietnam and that it will not die by being ignored, bombed or smothered by us."

General Lansdale's analysis of what happened in Vietnam is incomplete. He recognizes that the Vietnamese, north and south, are willing to give their lives for national independence. He claims that in the early years after the 1954 French withdrawal from Vietnam the Diem government scored victories for independence but then grew distant from the people. Communist terror was thus able to weaken the psychological bonds between people and government, bring success to the communists, and cause the overthrow and death of Diem. Lansdale does not mention that Diem was selected and appointed to his office, after voluntary exile in Japan, by agents of the United States government. Diem arrived in Vietnam after spending time at Michigan State University under a project secretly supported by the Central Intelligence Agency (Nicolaus 1966). Lansdale does not mention that Diem was part of the wealthy elite Catholic minority in a very poor, war-torn Buddhist country. Never does General Lansdale's article mention the reign of terror under Diem or the weapons sent to Diem's police in violation of the Geneva Accords by the United States government, which made this terror possible. Neither does he mention that the National Liberation Front was organized by persons whom Diem had, for his own political reasons, subjected to harsh imprisonment.

Nevertheless, Lansdale's analysis suggests that since the Vietnamese lack the power to stave off the communists, the United States must take responsibility for finding them an alternative base of power and ideas.

He does recognize that his program " ... involves exporting American principles" in order to provide South Vietnam " ... with a dynamic political answer with which to meet and overcome the foreign ideas introduced by the communists as the political base of their attack." For the general, and for many Americans, ideas which originate in the American experience cannot be foreign anywhere in the world. Lansdale could have substituted the name of any other undeveloped country in his article. His history of Vietnam begins in 1954 with the American involvement, rather than in 1883 when the Vietnamese struggle for national independence began, in 1914 when that movement took inspiration from the idealism of President Wilson's Fourteen Points, or from its ability in World War II to overthrow both the French and the Japanese conquerors.

For General Lansdale it is the American's task to find for the Vietnamese a cause that will rally the people behind a stable government for which they willingly pledge "their lives, their fortunes, their sacred honor. ..." Americans should also promise free elections, find some role for political leaders out of office, direct the AID program to the villages, and encourage their military to take more "civic action," to win the popular support it lacks.

General Lansdale does not specify just what will be the cause which will rally the Vietnamese. By contrast, the NLF program is both more concrete and more relevant to the cultural problems of South Vietnam. One example is the problem of land. In South Vietnam it is concentrated in large holdings, leaving over half the agricultural population at or below the subsistence level. Traditionally, the difference between subsistence and starvation for an estimated 15 to 20 percent of the rural population was the rental to the poorest farmers, at very low rates, of communal lands owned by the village. In 1956 the American-supported Diem government replaced the traditionally elected village councils with appointees from Saigon. Under American pressure to improve local finances Diem ordered the councils to rent out land at the highest rates possible, a move that created sudden havoc and untold misery in Vietnam. Hence Point III of the NLF program calls for a redistribution of communal lands. The same point deals as well with the various elements of a highly complex rural society inhabited by other groups besides peasants. Its appeal, more reformist than revolutionary, raises the problems of accession rights, of land deserted by its owners, and of refugees who were forcibly evacuated from their lands to "strategic hamlets" —an earlier creation of General Lansdale's planning. The NLF program recognizes the negative effects upon urban Vietnamese of the American Import Subsidy Program, which reduces the incentive for domestic manufacture and trade and makes the country permanently dependent on the United States. Further, the NLF program offers participation in elections to the many religious and nationalist sects which comprise Vietnam. It even proposes an autonomous zone for the ferociously independent traditionalist Montagnard tribesmen. The Front, itself a coalition among various communist and non-communist elements in South Vietnam, is determined to achieve absolute independence and eventual reunification after approval by the peoples of the two divisions. In keeping with the long history of Vietnamese nationalism, the NLF will not accept the colonial tutelage of a foreign power administered through a domestic dictatorship. It is legitimate, therefore, to ask whose ideas are foreign in Vietnam: those of the NLF or those of the American military.

Lansdale is also keenly aware that United States assistance without United States political tutelage may well result in dictatorship. This is an excellent point, for it is American aid that enables the rulers of a poor nation to remain propped up by American wealth, protected by their American-trained army and police, and deaf to domestic protest. Hence, Lansdale recommends that economic and military assistance be augmented by "political advice with a higher content of American idealism in it." The precise nature of this higher content is found in the American pacification program. William Ross summarizes from several accounts in the *New York Times* early in 1966.

> There it is indicated that plans already are far advanced to train 42,000 Vietnamese—in 80-man teams—for pacification of the rural areas. The training is being carried out by the CIA. Each team includes an "armed propaganda platoon" which will provide security in the hamlet in question and then undertake "agitation and propaganda." "Meantime, the census grievance team—described by one source as the 'key to the whole idea and the major vehicle to achieve control of the population'—will go into action." (*N.Y. Times*, 1/21/66) The same news story goes on to relate that the team will "... undertake a systematic interrogation of everyone in the hamlet." The villagers will be asked to list their grievances and then to tell all they know about the Vietcong. Some of the villagers will be pro-Vietcong and these will be "asked" to renounce their allegiance or even to become double agents, spying on the Front for Saigon. "Or, if the man in question is an important cog in the Vietcong machine and stubborn, another source said 'he might just have an accident—you could assassinate him.'" (*N.Y. Times*, 1/21/66)
> Interrogations will continue, reaching "each peasant in the hamlet once every 10 days. The project will work something like a dental clinic; the peasant will be given his next interrogation appointment as he ends his first session." (1/24/66) The project, which is "advised" by General Lansdale (1/24/66), plans to issue identity cards and set up family registers (1/23/66). "A map of each hamlet will be prepared, with red markings to show the houses of known Vietcong sympathizers or of citizens with relatives in the guerrilla movement." (1/23/66) In addition there will be an attempt "to organize every group of four to eight houses into an 'inter-family group.' One family head in each neighborhood grouping will be appointed as the group head." (1/23/66) There is some public relations talk of building "democracy"; we should take it with a grain of salt. For the project "will also organize a system of interlocking organizations—one for youths, one for women, one for farmers—to try to make every member of the hamlet a member of some kind of Government-sponsored organization with some discipline and control over him. 'It's a little bit totalitarian,' a source remarked, 'but the idea is to tie each person to some kind of controlled organization.'" (1/21/66) (William Ross, "If History Behaved." *Viet-Report* 2, 1966, pp. 27–32.)

The program has not worked in Vietnam. Things would be far worse if it had. When one group of people take for themselves the right to determine the political well-being of another people, they exhibit the type of social arrogance that legitimized the concept of national or racial superiority. Such feelings have led to the most dangerous totalitarian excesses of the twentieth century, in Germany and the USSR in the thirties and in South Africa today. The American plan for Vietnam is a blueprint for totalitarian control unmatched in history and yet conducted in the name of freedom. It is carried on behind an undeclared war conducted in the name of peace.

The conclusion to be gleaned from this example of American policy toward the third world must take into account the larger economic and political picture. The policy is a product, not an accident, of a world system which distributes the resources of the world most inequitably. People who live in the poor countries are part of the same world system as those living in affluence. Some people live near starvation precisely because others have great concentrations of power.

It is rather striking that few Americans know very much about American intervention in Vietnam or elsewhere. The chapters which follow attempt to locate the origin of United States policy in international conflict.

References

ANDERSON, CHARLES W., FRED R. VON DER MEHDEN,
AND CRAWFORD YOUNG
> 1967 *Issues of Political Development.* Englewood Cliffs, N.J.: Prentice-Hall, Inc.

BAKER, MAURY
> 1963 "Dam Yankeeism in Latin America." *Social Science* 38 (October): pp. 195–204.

BARAN, PAUL A.
> 1952 "On the Political Economy of Backwardness." *Manchester School of Economics and Social Studies* 20 (January): pp. 66–84.

BAUER, PETER T., AND BASIL S. YAMEY
> 1964 "The Economics of Underdeveloped Countries" in Otto Feinstein, ed., *Two Worlds of Change: Readings in Economic Development.* New York: Doubleday and Co., Inc.

BODENHEIMER, SUZANNE
> 1970 "The Ideology of Developmentalism: American Political Science's Paradigm—Surrogate for Latin American Studies." *Berkeley Journal of Sociology* 15: pp. 95–137.

BOULDING, KENNETH
> 1965 "Population and Poverty." *The Correspondent* 35 (Autumn): pp. 38–40.

BROWER, MICHAEL
> 1965 "U.S. Aid: A Prescription for Change." *The Correspondent* 35 (Autumn): pp. 53–60.

CARPENTER, WILLARD
    1964 "Latin America: The Return of the Military." *New University Thought* 4 (Summer) : pp. 3–13.

DREW, ELIZABETH
    1968 "Going Hungry in America: Government's Failure." *Atlantic* 222 (December) : pp. 53–61.

FEINSTEIN, OTTO, *ed.*
    1964 *Two Worlds of Change: Readings in Economic Development.* New York: Doubleday and Co., Inc.

FRAPPIER, JON
    1968 "Guatemala: Military Camp under Liberal Command." *Viet-Report* 3 (April–May) : pp. 15–20.

FRIEDLAND, WILLIAM H.
    1968 "Traditionalism and Modernization: Movements and Ideologies." *Journal of Social Issues* 24 (October) : pp. 9–24.

GALANTER, MARC
    1968 "The Displacement of Traditional Law in Modern India." *Journal of Social Issues* 24 (October) : pp. 65–92.

GERASSI, JOHN
    1967 "Latin America—the Next Vietnam?" *Viet-Report* 3 (January–February) : pp. 5–8.

GORDENKER, LEON
    1965 "The View from the 38th Floor." *The Correspondent* 34 (Spring/Summer) : pp. 79–87.

GUSFIELD, JOSEPH R.
    1968 "Tradition and Modernity: Conflict and Congruence." *Journal of Social Issues* 24 (October) : pp. 1–8.

HUXLEY, A.
    1963 *The Politics of Ecology.* Santa Barbara, Calif.: Center for the Study of Democratic Institutions.

JACOBY, NEIL H.
    1969 "The Progress of Peoples: Toward a Theory and Policy of Development with External Aid." *A Center Occasional Paper* 2 (June) : pp. 3–23.

KLING, MERLE
    1964 "Towards a Theory of Power and Political Stability in Latin America," in Otto Feinstein, ed., *Two Worlds of Change: Readings in Economic Development*, pp. 183–203. New York: Doubleday and Co., Inc.

KOLKO, GABRIEL

    1969   *The United States and World Economic Power*. San Francisco: Bay Area Radical Education Project.

KUZNETS, SIMON

    1964   "Underdeveloped Countries and the Pre-Industrial Phase in the Advanced Countries," in Otto Feinstein, ed., *Two Worlds of Change: Readings in Economic Development*, pp. 1–21. New York: Doubleday and Co., Inc.

LEVINE, DONALD N.

    1968   "The Flexibility of Traditional Culture." *Journal of Social Issues* 24 (October): pp. 129–42.

MCCLELLAND, DAVID C.

    1961   *The Achieving Society*. Princeton, N.J.: Van Nostrand.

    1965   "Toward a Theory of Motive Acquisition." *American Psychologist* 20 (May): pp. 321–33.

MCDERMOTT, JOHN

    1966   "Two Programs for South Vietnam." *Viet-Report* 2 (February): p. 3.

MUNDY-CASTLE, ALASTAIR

    1968   "The Development of Nations: Some Psychological Considerations." *Journal of Social Issues* 24 (April): pp. 45–54.

NICOLAUS, MARTIN

    1966   "The Professor, the Policeman and the Peasant." *Viet-Report* 2 (February): pp. 16–23.

O'BRIEN, CONOR CRUISE

    1965   "Conflicting Concepts of the U.N." *The Correspondent* 34 (Spring/Summer): pp. 19–34.

POOL, ITHIEL DE SOLA

    1967   "The Public and the Polity," in Ithiel De Sola Pool, ed., *Contemporary Political Science*, p. 26. New York: McGraw-Hill.

QUINT, MALCOLM

    1967   "The Idea of Progress in an Iraqui Village," in Claude E. Welch, Jr., ed., *Political Modernization*, pp. 49–63. Belmont, Calif.: Wadsworth Publishing Co.

ROSTOW, W. W.

    1964   "The Take-Off into Self-Sustained Growth," in Otto Feinstein, ed., *Two Worlds of Change: Readings in Economic Development*, pp. 293–327. New York: Doubleday and Co., Inc.

RUDIN, STANLEY A.

    1965   "The Personal Price of National Glory." *Trans-Action* 2 (September–October): pp. 4–9.

RUDOLPH, LLOYD I., AND SUSANNE H. RUDOLPH
  1968 "The Political Modernization of an Indian Feudal Order: An Analysis of Rajput Adaptation in Rajasthan." *Journal of Social Issues* 24 (October) pp. 93–128.

SHEREFF, RUTH
  1967 "How the CIA Makes Friends and Influences Countries." *Viet-Report* 3 (January–February): pp. 15–20.

———
  1968 "Revolution in the Hemisphere." *Viet-Report* 3 (April–May): pp. 4–8.

STAVENHAGEN, RUDOLFO
  1966 "Seven Erroneous Theses About Latin America." *New University Thought* 4 (Winter): pp. 25–37.

U.N. ECONOMIC COMMISSION FOR LATIN AMERICA (ECLA)
  1969 *El Segundo Decenio de las Naciones Unidas para el Desarrollo: Aspectos Básicos de la Estrategia del Desarrollo de América Latina*, p. 7. Lima: ECLA. Summary of the report, *New York Times*, April 20, 1969, cited in Suzanne Bodenheimer, "The Ideology of Developmentalism: American Political Science's Paradigm—Surrogate for Latin American Studies." *Berkeley Journal of Sociology* 15 (1970) pp. 95–137.

WEBER, MAX
  1930 *The Protestant Ethic and the Spirit of Capitalism.* New York: Scribner.

WOLF, ERIC
  1970 "Algerian Peasant Revolt." *Trans-Action* 7 (May): pp. 33–46.

Chapter 3

WAR AND THE MINDS OF MEN

The Preamble to the Charter of the United Nations asserts that wars begin in the minds of men. One common interpretation of this rather general assertion is that war is a form of aggressive behavior that expresses deep hatreds and aggressive needs which are, in turn, an inherent part of the human condition. A second interpretation is that war, along with other forms of international conflict, is simply a form of human behavior, subject only to the same general laws of psychology that govern all beliefs, attitudes, and behavior. It is certainly possible to document the idea that people express basic hatreds through institutionalized violence. It is more difficult to find direct support for the proposition that human aggressiveness is the primary cause of war. The purposes of this chapter are twofold: first, to explore the psychological factors relevant to forming international policy, and second, to examine the more difficult proposition that human aggressiveness is the prime cause of war.

There are several ways in which our knowledge of the causes of individual perception and behavior may illuminate international policy. An individual's appreciation or understanding of a given situation depends on the way he combines information and complex stimuli into perceptions and beliefs. From his perceptions the individual makes projections about the future consequences of current actions. He evaluates these consequences (and the events themselves). His beliefs, attitudes, and projected consequences provide the individual's basic construction of international reality.

People do not merely hold views of international conflict, or of anything else, because of the way things, in some existential sense, really are. Rather, ideas about remote national and international events are based on information which is filtered, screened or elaborated, and cast into gross categories and cliches by the media, which are anything but impartial.

This predigested fare is reduced again in similar fashion by the perceptual, cognitive, and memory processes of the individual. Beliefs and images serve people's attempts to order a stable picture of the world which is compatible .with the fulfillment of their own needs. Because the process is inherently selective, distortions are likely to occur. When the distortions are systematic they reflect either the personality of the individual or the culture in which he operates. These basic psychological processes are the same for the president of the United States, the Chinese premier, and your next-door neighbor. But the effects on policy of attitudes and beliefs held by the president or by elites differ greatly from the effects of "public opinion." Therefore, we shall treat leaders and public opinion separately.

The Personality of the Decision Maker

The personality of a government official contributes to his official interpretations of international events and to his official reactions to them. However, the contribution of personality factors, compared to the effect of organizational pressures, is generally small. Certainly much is said of the paranoia of Adolph Hitler, the equivocation of Adlai Stevenson, and the drive and daring of John F. Kennedy. But these are easy images which help us to personify and simplify the policy process. People harbor images, like that of a courageous Churchill or of a fanatical Castro, which they derive from news reports and editorial commentary. These personifications may be grossly oversimplified, and they may even have little to do with the individual's true personality. *The Selling of the President* (McGinniss 1968) shows how an image of presidential candidate Richard Nixon was consciously designed and advertised by an agency using means much like those used to sell a car or a deodorant. Some aspects of the image were deliberately chosen to counteract actual characteristics of the real man which might prove unpopular. Enough people bought the image of Richard Nixon to elect him president.

Perhaps not all but certainly a great portion of the individual policy maker's behavior is dictated by his role in an organization. In some sense, then, it is the organization which perceives events and reacts to them. For this reason the chapter will suggest only briefly how the individual psychological factor in foreign policy has been studied.

De Rivera (1968) cites several studies which attempt to demonstrate how personal qualities of leaders influence their political behavior. One such study tries to show how President Woodrow Wilson's unconscious attitudes toward an overbearing father related to his conscious desire to champion the cause of victims of injustice and to his uncompromising idealistic stands on various issues, including American membership in the League of Nations.

De Rivera also cites Rogow's case study of emotional instability in an individual statesman, Secretary of Defense James Forrestal, whose high-level policy decisions were distorted, Rogow contends, by his emotional problems. Forrestal's interpersonal contacts, including those with his own family, were shallow and unrewarding. He depended heavily for his self-esteem on success in the accumulation of power. According to Rogow, his business and political judgments reflected his personal needs. As a financier, he engineered the merger of Dodge Motors and Chrysler. As undersecretary and then as secretary of the Navy he fought for the extensive buildup of the Navy. When World War II ended, Forrestal did not want the country to demobilize, but rather to consolidate and extend its power. He was extremely suspicious of communists and sought to build up worldwide defenses against them and to investigate their activities in the United States. His opposition to the formation of the state of Israel also arose from his fear for American security; he felt it necessary to maintain good relations with the Arab states to insure the supply of oil for defense needs. As some of his aspirations to augment the national defenses were thwarted, Forrestal began to feel that Zionist and Soviet agents were following him. His paranoia continued to increase until it culminated in emotional breakdown. Finally, in despair for his country, he committed suicide (Rogow 1963).

But Forrestal's paranoia was by no means the only cause of his policy decisions, if it was even a major one. Anyone with the perseverance to stay in political life long enough to reach a position of great power is likely to have a desire, perhaps a need, for power for its own sake. In this respect Forrestal was probably not so different from other politicians. Also in his fear of communism Forrestal was not alone in the postwar years. For some reason, there was a general overreaction to the exaggerated fear of communist expansion. If we were to examine more closely all the organizational pressures exerted on Forrestal, we might well find that he made substantially the same decisions, within the limited range of choices open to him, that anyone else in his position might have made.

Another instance cited by De Rivera is George Kennan's analysis (1960) of Soviet Premier Joseph Stalin. Stalin, a man of simple origins, felt inferior to the more cosmopolitan and better educated Bolsheviks. After he took power, he continued to fear the resurgence of Communist factions opposed to him, many of which were now in exile. His increasing suspicions and mental instability led to a public argument with his wife, shortly after which she was found dead, a victim either of murder or of suicide. Within a few years Stalin had begun drastic purges of the Seventeenth Party Congress. He justified these measures by exaggerating the threat of Western attack and asserting the need for national unity in the face of this grave danger. Yet his pact with Hitler showed that it was international communism (of a strain he opposed), rather than international capitalism, that he feared most. In Stalin's case domestic policy was affected by emotional instability, and foreign policy became a means to justify extreme domestic actions.

Stalin's personality probably did have some and perhaps a sizeable influence on policy. Yet the foreign policy of the USSR was constantly constrained by its status as the single socialist state in a capitalist world. The tremendous external pressures generated by this conflict might well have caused extreme political struggles inside the USSR even in the absence of a personality like Stalin, although the struggles might not have taken the form of wholesale purges.

Personal predilections can sometimes be deduced from the writings of famous men. De Rivera (1968) contrasts the eight famous presidential decisions that President Truman eulogized in his book *Mr. Citizen* with President Kennedy's examples from *Profiles in Courage*. Truman's admiration was reserved for acts of courage in asserting or protecting the power of the federal government. Kennedy's examples, on the other hand, were of people who defended their beliefs in the face of pressure and at the expense of their own power. This comparison between Truman and Kennedy raises the issue of what difference such characteristics will mean in policy decisions.

Certainly a range of factors tend to minimize the differences. Both men, in order to have become president, had gone through a political screening process which assured that they were politicians interested in winning and in manipulating power. Both had passed the tests of placating the various political factions within their own party. Both came to a presidency with its own existing set of government agencies whose administrative practices were already established and were responsive to the needs of certain groups. The Department of Labor responded to the interests of business and labor leaders; the Department of Agriculture dealt with farming interests; the Defense Department called for more and better weapons and troops. Both presidents had to depend on these continuing agencies for information and cooperation. Besides government officials, the presidents also had to maintain the support of campaign contributors, many of whom were wealthy industrialists.

In any situation, then, many external pressures on the president helped to determine policy outcome. In the Cuban missile crisis of 1961, President Kennedy's space of free movement was limited, regardless of how personally courageous he might have been.

The faulty intelligence he had received had already caused him a severe setback in the abortive Bay of Pigs invasion, and the president could not afford to appear weak again. The majority of his staff advocated destroying the missile sites. After an intensive discussion, Kennedy stood up against the majority view and instead imposed a naval blockade. Even this more moderate action was serious enough to cause a direct confrontation between the nuclear powers; for a time the world was in danger. An attempt to run the blockade could have degenerated within days to a nuclear exchange. Kennedy's policy decision, though not as "tough" as his advisors had wanted, was still well within American policy assumptions. He asserted the "right" of the United States to encircle the Soviet Union with bases without allowing the Soviet Union to adopt a comparable strategy toward the United States. Kennedy's policy was constrained by past practice and political pressures. Even had he been so inclined, he was never free to consider such alternatives as admitting that the Soviet missile sites in Cuba were no different from American sites in Turkey and that perhaps the time had come for a mutual retraction.

The point is that the individual political leader is embedded in a set of organizational constraints. The personal motives and inclinations of a leader can affect policy only within the limits of what he considers realistic. The organizational web that helped filter him through his political rise continues to define for him the realistic requirements and limitations for action.

In routine situations the behavior of the decision maker reflects almost exclusively the position he occupies and the role prescription for acceptable behavior. Under conditions of stress and in ambiguous situations, however, idiosyncratic motives and perceptions come to the fore. Yet even then the actual effects are often minor. President Truman's reactions to news that Chinese troops had entered the Korean War afford an example. A fair reading of the evidence presented in Alan Whiting's *China Crosses the Yalu: The Decision to Enter the Korean War* (1960) and particularly of the data in I. F. Stone's excellent *Hidden History of the Korean War* (1952) shows that Chinese entrance into the Korean conflict was provoked by American policy. A force composed largely of United States troops, under United Nations auspices, had been pushed back almost to the southern tip of Korea, and then had rebounded and retaken most of the Korean peninsula up to the Chinese border. Apparently the United States assumed that Chinese forces were too weak to enter the conflict, or that China had enough of her own problems and was not very strongly committed to support North Korea. In any case, when he heard that Chinese troops had entered the war, Truman responded by lashing out at his domestic critics, instead of assuming the responsibility himself. He told his staff:

> "This is the worst situation we have had yet . . . the liars have accomplished their purpose. The whole campaign of lies we have been seeing in this country has brought about its result. I'm talking about the crowd of vilifiers who have been trying to tear us apart in this country. . . . We can blame the liars for the fix we are in this very morning. . . ." (De Rivera 1968, p. 190)

In this case President Truman's loss of emotional control made him project the responsibility for a failure in his Korean War policy onto his domestic critics. Yet Truman's outburst had little effect on policy; a less emotional president would probably have kept the United States in Korea, just as Truman did. Truman reflected the prevailing military ideology and anti-communist political pressures of the fifties.

In times of crisis the probability that a loss of control will precipitate a calamitous action is the greatest. Under severe emotional tension following the 1914 assassination of the Austrian archduke, the German kaiser made the decision to fight England, despite his knowledge of British military superiority. The kaiser also wanted to believe that Russia was bluffing when she expressed her intentions to support Serbia. The German ambassador to Russia obliged by sending selectively only the information the Kaiser wished to hear.[1] As the crisis deepened the very rate of information exchange among heads of state and their ministers approached overload proportions, a process which itself leads to further restriction of information input and to increasing strain on the policy makers. The frightening thing to contemplate is that it is just such periods of crisis which lead to the hardening of positions and to plunging into conflicts without regard to costs. At one point in the 1914 crisis the kaiser indicated in desperation that if Germany was to "bleed to death," she would at least make England pay in the process (Holsti 1963, pp. 611–13).

The personality of the leader does not exert a completely idiosyncratic influence on his decisions; rather, some generalizations can be offered about the type of man who is likely to enter and succeed in the struggle to get and to hold power. And as Jerome Frank comments, "The qualities which enable a person to gain power are not identical with those which enable him to exercise it wisely" (Frank 1967, p. 169). He must be concerned with maintaining his image and with satisfying diverse constituencies, particularly those from whom he receives support. He is likely to love adulation, to be personally ambitious, and to be readily suspicious of the motives of his adversaries. Such a psychologically defensive orientation is likely to effect his decision making. Studies of risk-taking have shown that the more defensive subjects—those more anxious about their image—were most likely to stick to early judgments which were proving wrong. Conservative, anxious, defensive subjects would rigidly maintain a path of behavior even in the face of failures. Among some male subjects this meant falling deeper into patterns of excessive and irrational risk-taking which could not be modified by a realistic appraisal of their experience (Kogan and Wallach 1964).

We should be cautious in extrapolating these results to the world

---

[1] Note the similar pattern of CIA misintelligence in reporting popular support for Tshombe in the Congo, for Diem in Vietnam, and against the Castro-led revolution in Cuba.

outside the psychological laboratory, however. Although in some sense a politician may be a risk-taker, he certainly will not get far if he takes many irrational risks. Political skill includes the ability to gauge correctly one's support from different quarters and to act in a way that insures and enhances that support. In taking risks, a politician cannot afford to be very far off the mark.

Furthermore, there are strong sociological reasons why a politician might stay within past policy limits rather than venture into unknown territory. New programs are generally more controversial than old ones whose opposition has subsided. If a political officeholder has a choice between making controversial news and making no news at all, he often finds it more expedient to make no news.

While some authors postulate that politicians are basically unable to change their own policies, others depict the successful political leader as ever ready to change his policies to sail with the winds of political pressure. It is difficult to generalize about political decision makers' personality traits. Their position necessitates that they have some competence to deal with power and some interest in the exercise of power, but beyond that there is ample room for personal variation.

Similarities among political figures stem more from the requirements of the politician's role than from basic personality traits. Both elected and appointed officials must pass a series of screening tests before they are serious candidates for office. They are screened by interest groups whose support they will need. A public official, whether city manager or United States president, has a very narrow range of free movement. He has been pre-selected as one who considers policies only within the range acceptable to various interest groups. Once in office he takes the role of mediator of these same pressures. He depends on ongoing agencies beneath him for a supply of information on which to base his decisions, and these organizations have deeply vested interests.

The personal motives, ideology, or political style of a leader may affect national policy within the range of the leader's free movement. The illustrations which have been offered to show a relationship between personality (whether or not acting under duress) and policy decisions are not particularly compelling. In no case do the policies De Rivera and others say are affected by personalities represent new or radical departures. By and large policy is embedded in the practices of the organization responsible for carrying it out. While on rare occasions a leader's traits have changed the course of history, on the whole personality factors play a minor role in the trend of historical events. Even a leader with a sharply deviant personality (assuming that such deviance could survive the screening process) has little room to move policy in directions other than those reflecting the powerful interests of his society.

Public Opinion and International Affairs

People are frequently polled on matters of particular foreign policies—whether to enlarge or constrict an area of conflict, whether to continue or stop testing nuclear weapons, whether to expand or reduce foreign aid. The results of such polls are printed in newspapers and are sometimes considered to be the opinion of the general public. Such an assumption is not always well founded.

Is there, in fact, such a thing as general public opinion on foreign affairs? If so, can it be reflected by this type of poll? These questions are rarely raised and are difficult to answer. Human beings are capable of holding a wide range of casual opinions that reflect little real concern, particularly in areas where they have been made to feel that their concerns do not lead to policy change.

There is, however, a further question raised by public opinion studies, namely, whether either the opinions or the polls do in fact play a role in the determination of actual foreign policies, and again, whether the role played by such opinion is helpful or detrimental to the formation of intelligent policy. As an approach to answering these questions, Rosenberg cites three possible functions for public opinion about foreign policy, namely, opinion as (a) a source of policy innovation, (b) a resource in the execution of policy, and (c) a constraint in policy consideration.

In a democratic society, where ideally people can and should assist in the formulation of policies which greatly affect their lives, there should be some way for deeply felt opinions on foreign policy to function as a source of new ideas. However, opinion is rarely an immediate source of new directions in foreign policy. Indirectly, select groups make their opinions known through lobbyists, and social movements sometimes create pressures to highlight the need for new policies. What such groups accomplish, however, is likely to be only a modest broadening of the agenda from which permissible policies are considered.

More often opinion is seen by national leaders as a commodity, a moderate amount of which is required for maintenance of their own preferred policies. They see opinion as an active and manipulable resource. For example, when the Kennedy administration was seeking Senate ratification of the limited ban on the testing of nuclear weapons, the administration nurtured autonomous groups of "respectable" scholars and peace movement activists as a means of furthering the impression of support for its policies. In this case, it is clear also that these groups were used to create a sense of legitimacy for the test ban treaty.

Another example of the use of opinion in the execution of policy is the civil defense controversy. Many military strategists favored the development of a massive civil defense program because they felt such a program would convey to the Soviet Union the intentions of the United States to go to the brink of total war, and thereby would make credible the threat of nuclear retaliation. The military strategists could not by themselves say to the Soviet government that the United States was ready to rush to the brink of destruction; it was necessary instead to provide visible evidence—in this case, the willingness of the population to participate in a shelter program—to indicate that the American population would support such an extreme policy.

The conscious manipulation of opinion has been a recurrent issue in the question of news management. It is sometimes asserted that the best interests of the United States are served by a restriction of information about its military intentions and activities. While this restriction is purportedly intended to deceive only potential enemies, the price of such policy is that information obviously is concealed from the American public as well. Whether such concealment is useful is another question. Lewis Coser, in "The Dysfunction of Military Secrecy," suggests that violent conflict is more likely to occur when the parties do not have accurate information about each other's military strengths. However, modern nations keep secret a great deal of military information.

Spokesmen for the Department of Defense have made clear their intention to manipulate the release of information in ways consistent with their judgment of the national interest. For example, correspondent Morley Safer reported a 1965 meeting in Saigon with Assistant Secretary of Defense for Public Affairs Arthur Sylvester. The occasion of the meeting was an attempt to re-establish an understanding with members of the press corps, who were subject to constant pressure to follow the government line and to constant criticism if they did not. Reporters were particularly annoyed by recent Pentagon releases regarding B-52 raids which directly contradicted what had actually occurred. Safer's account of Sylvester's performance is illuminating:

> "I can't understand how you fellows can write what you do while American boys are dying out here," he began. Then he went on to the effect that American correspondents had a patriotic duty to disseminate only information that made the United States look good.
> A network television correspondent said, "Surely Arthur, you don't expect the American press to be the handmaidens of government." "That's exactly what I expect," came the reply.
> An agency man raised the problem . . . about the credibility of American officials. Responded the Assistant Secretary of Defense for Public Affairs:
> "Look, if you think any American official is going to tell you the truth, then you're stupid. Did you hear that—stupid!" (Safer 1966, pp. 9–10)

This outburst was followed by a vindictive threat by Sylvester that he did not even have to talk to reporters, since he could deal with them through their editors. Such control over the release of information can be a powerful tool in maintaining popular support or in restricting popular criticism of the activities of government agencies.

The issue of whether public opinion should serve as a constraint on policy has been raised by Tocqueville and others, who have noted Americans' vast indifference to matters of world affairs. This indifference frequently combines extreme ignorance with complete insensitivity to the intricacies of modern international life. The issue is currently raised: If the public is in fact unconcerned about foreign affairs, then why not leave such affairs in the hands of an informed elite? Is it necessary to burden the general populace with problems that do not interest them? The issue is obviously critical to the future of democratic institutions. Citizens of large countries now create, either through action or apathy, conditions that directly affect large numbers of people in their own and many other countries. Collectively, we determine which nations may industrialize, which may have weapons, which may have enough to eat. If we relegate this responsibility to others, in what sense can we still be considered participants in the democratic process? Of course, it is not just the fault of the people if policy does not follow their opinion. Politicians who treat opinion as a manipulable commodity discourage political activists who do try to influence policy.

Opinion, as a constraint on policy, is usually considered a force which acts against fine political differentiation and contributes to a loss of government flexibility. In other words, the government is considered better informed, more progressive, and more sensitive to policy needs than the public. This argument is sometimes used by government officers as an excuse for their unwillingness to explore new directions in foreign policy.

The argument that opinion is a major constraint on the direction of foreign policy is based on certain assumptions. One such assumption, that the public official must satisfy public opinion in matters of foreign affairs to keep his office, is not well supported. The evidence shows that there is almost no correspondence between the roll call votes of a congressman and the opinions of his constituents in matters of foreign policy (Campbell et al. 1966). Even the more modest assumption that public officials actually know the opinion of their constituents is suspect. Only about 10 percent of the American public in any one year write letters or send delegations to influence elected officials at any level of government. Congressmen do, however, tend to pay a great deal of attention to what newspapers and television say, and this does include the polls being reported (Lane and Sears 1964).

In addition to the evidence that congressmen neither know well nor vote according to their constituents' opinions on foreign policy, there is some new evidence to show that opinion has negligible effects on international behavior. The study in question related "positive" and "negative" American and Soviet actions reported by the *New York Times*, with opinion poll data collected in the time periods just preceding the actions. The findings show little or no relationship (Walton et al. 1969).

Opinion on foreign policy tends to resist the reality of events. Even the vast publicity given to the My Lai massacre of Vietnamese civilians by American servicemen was unable to convince a majority of the public that something wrong had been done by their country. An extensive review of the literature on the effects of events on people's international images and beliefs led to the following summary:

> Almost nothing in the world seems to be able to shift the image of 40% of the populations of most countries, even within one or two decades. Combinations of events that shift the images and attitudes of the remaining 50–60% of the population are extremely rare [occasions requiring] mutual reinforcement of cumulative events and substantial governmental efforts as well as the absence of sizeable cross pressures. Most of the spectacular changes of politics involve a change in the attitudes of between one-fifth and one-third of the population. (Deutsch and Merritt, quoted in Frank 1967, p. 103)

There are also, as Rosenau states, some elites whose opinions are more frequently heard. But by and large what we commonly know as public opinion has apparently very little demonstrable effect on international policy. Conversely, while the public *interest* is profoundly affected by the priorities given certain international policies, public *opinion* does not seem to be much affected at all.

A third assumption underlying the possible constraining effect of opinion on policy is that the opinions really do exist: that they are distinct and stable (rather than stemming from a momentary crisis), and that they are strong enough to indicate a real concern over policy. The alternative assumption that the public knows little and lacks differentiated attitudes about world affairs could mean either of two things for the policy maker. He is either constrained to follow very simpleminded policy or, on the other hand, he has extreme freedom to follow policies of his own design.

In 1959, Alfred Hero compiled an extensive summary and analysis of studies made to that date of American public opinion about world affairs. More recent work has not been so comprehensive. Much of Hero's data and analysis have bearing on the question of the depth of interest, knowledge, and involvement of Americans. He makes several distinctions which are helpful in describing data about foreign policy attitudes and sets criteria against which the depth of intelligent involvement can be judged.

The first criterion is sustained interest in major long-term international issues faced by the United States. The assumption is that an intelligent, participating citizen should be not only interested in an issue, but also able to relate it to problems which have preceded it.

The second criterion is the amount of information the American citizen possesses about his own country and other parts of the world. Frequently, where information is very weak, the attitudes associated with a particular position are vague, unstable, and susceptible to change under pressure of irrelevant propaganda appeals.

The third criterion of involvement is whether the individual subjects such information to logical analysis and infers what realistic American policies should be. Ideally, his analysis should take into account opinions that differ from his own.

The last criterion is the measure of action taken by the individual in support of his foreign policy beliefs. Obviously, an intelligently concerned citizen's action is based on a reasonable level of achievement in the other three criteria; action based on ignorance or belligerent generalizations would be detrimental to meaningful participation. Active involvement could range from a minimal awareness of representatives' positions on foreign policy matters and a use of this awareness to determine one's vote to more active involvement through participation in voluntary organizations and, for some in favored positions, through direct channels of communication with policy makers.

Hero's analysis shows that very few Americans measure up to a high standard on all four of the criteria. Even those high on one criterion are usually lacking on the other criteria. Hero divides the population into an attentive minority and a vast, inattentive majority. There are, of course, differences within the population. We find a large group of poorly educated people who tend to be poorly informed on international matters. These people are also, by and large, authoritarian in their personal outlook and patriotic in a selfish and destructive way. Certain institutions accentuate the authoritarian and chauvinistic approach of the larger population. Fundamentalist religious groups and some veterans' organizations exemplify the more overtly institutionalized sources of super-patriotism which nurture the militant chauvinism of the uninformed majority. While education is a major contributor to increasing the individual's attentiveness to world affairs, even among the educated there are numerous instances of highly xenophobic attitudes toward foreign policy.

All groups probably have some xenophobic tendencies. Studies frequently find that people base their dislike for other groups of people on differences they perceive among the other groups. The more different it is from oneself and from one's own group, the more disliked is the foreign group.

People who are highly xenophobic tend to anticipate war and to expect that it will be initiated by the belligerents of other countries. For American citizens the alleged source of belligerent action since World War II is frequently the Soviet Union or China; for Soviet and Chinese citizens, it is probably the United States.

Studies by Bronfenbrenner and by Oskamp and Levinson illustrate how perceptions are distorted between hostile nations. Bronfenbrenner reports on his brief stay in the Soviet Union in 1960. Talking at length with Soviet citizens, he realized how striking were the parallels between American perceptions of the Soviet Union and Soviet perceptions of the United States —virtually mirror images of one another. For example, the Soviet people sincerely believed that the Americans were basically good people who were lied to and manipulated by a tyrannical, oppressive government. They believed further that Americans would want to escape their country and government if they were to see how much better life is under communism. Americans, of course, believe substantially the same of the Soviet people. Bronfenbrenner notes that such belief systems are extremely hard to penetrate; any information which seems to contradict the belief system is quickly reinterpreted to fit existing perceptions. Thus when Bronfenbrenner returned to the United States with his findings, his friends and colleagues assured him that Soviet citizens had been unable to reveal to him their "real" sentiments, since they were so closely watched by their oppressive government (Bronfenbrenner 1961).

The more recent Oskamp and Levinson study separated a college sample into two groups, "doves" and "hawks," on the basis of their positions on the Vietnam war. Both groups were asked to evaluate two identical lists of actions, one attributed to the United States and the other to the USSR. The double standard prevailed, but was more pronounced for the hawks. While the doves demonstrated a degree of openmindedness which made possible some criticism of American foreign policy actions, doves and hawks were equally critical of Soviet actions (Oskamp and Levinson 1969).

While the tendency to like or dislike other nations depending on how similar or dissimilar we perceive them to be to our own may be universal, it affects some people considerably more than others. People who have a strongly xenophobic view of world affairs tend to favor military buildups, to oppose conciliatory overtures, and to view the "enemy" as strong and malevolent, but not invincible.

Whatever we may say about public opinion, it is clearly not an important source of public policy. Given the xenophobic tendencies of some and the centralization of news dissemination, opinion seems to be a force which can be easily manipulated to preserve old directions of policy. These directions have periodically permitted the outbreak of open warfare.

War and Human Destructiveness

We turn to a more far-reaching question: Is there something basic in man's psychological makeup, some fundamental human hatred or aggression, which is the major cause of war and makes war inevitable?

In studying this question it is essential to look at the major ways in which human aggression can be expressed, either directly or symbolically. The clues to symbolic meanings of aggressive activities are sometimes found in psychoanalytic theory.

Psychoanalytic thought on problems of war and peace deals largely with ideas, feelings, and adaptations of which people are not themselves aware. Aggressive destructiveness is one of the motivational states frequently concealed from an individual's consciousness and expressed in devious ways. Some students of the problem consider aggressiveness to be a natural drive of the human species, one it shares with certain other animal species, which also engage in fighting. Others consider aggressive behavior the most natural response to frustration. The choice of this response from among others such as regression to simple behavior, fleeing, or flight into fantasy is thought to depend on the nature of the frustration or on the individual's background.

Whatever the source of hostile feelings, they are clearly expressed in public opinion during periods of international crisis. At such times, feelings tend to polarize into primitive extremes. There are accusations of cowardice, calls for a willingness to fight, rejections of compromise, intensive self-justification of one's own nation, and an assumption of malevolence on the part of other nations. At such times the alternatives are frequently stated as "war" or "surrender." In the case of nuclear war, neither of these alternatives seems acceptable; in fact the results of the two might be interchangeable, or at least considered equally bad by many people. The condition of the unacceptability of nuclear war creates in people's minds an inability to conceive of such war. Atomic war seems more and more impossible in almost direct proportion to the quantitative degree of destructiveness imagined.

When we think of the Nazi extermination of six million Jews, the figure itself helps to immunize us against the horror and inhumanity of snuffing out six million individual lives. The idea of fifty million or 100 million people killed in a nuclear exchange is virtually unimaginable. As people develop an immunization to death statistics, they seem also to develop an immunization even to vivid descriptions of the horrors of an intolerable catastrophe; the horrors become clichés. Neither the warnings of an impending holocaust nor the daily reports of battle fatalities arouse our revulsion. Yet the actual presence of a single child severely maimed in an auto accident may make us feel sick with horror and sadness.

The effects of nuclear attacks of varying strengths have been calculated with some precision. The Scientists' Committee for Radiation Information (1962) described the effects of a single 20-megaton bomb dropped on Columbus Circle in midtown Manhattan. The initial explosion would create a bluish-white glare causing damage to the retinas of anyone looking in that direction. Tests with rabbits show retinal burns from a high-air burst 340 miles away. A fireball four and a half miles wide would rise rapidly, dispersing quantities of vaporized earth and debris. An air burst on a clear day would ignite a man's clothing 21 miles away and produce second-degree burns to exposed skin up to 31 miles from the point of impact. Unless medical supplies and personnel were miraculously spared, most of these burns would result in infection and death.

An intense pressure wave traveling faster than sound would spread from the center, crushing everything in its path. A mass of fresh air would move into the resulting partial vacuum, fanning flames and creating a firestorm. Significantly smaller explosions from prenuclear bombs created a firestorm in Hamburg, Germany, with temperatures as high as 1,500° Fahrenheit and wind velocities exceeding 150 miles per hour. Heat was sufficiently intense to ignite oxygen in bomb shelters, cremating occupants. Heat stroke and carbon monoxide poisoning contributed to the toll of 60,000 persons killed, still fewer than the loss at Hiroshima from a blast of only 20 kilotons.

The Scientists' Committee estimates that in addition to direct ignition of flammable materials, the blast effects would cause fires by destroying stoves, electrical circuits, gas lines, and oil storage tanks, creating an estimated two million fires within the city limits.

A surface blast itself would create a hole 240 feet deep and half a mile across. Shock waves would extend through the tunnels of the subway system to the entire city. The effects of the blast in the inner city (the area within a 7.7-mile radius of Columbus Circle) would include almost total demolition of all housing. People would be severely injured by flying fragments of glass and debris and by being lifted by the displacement effects of the blast up to a 15-mile radius.

Outside assistance to New York would depend on what other areas were hit, but transportation would be completely clogged within a 15-mile radius and most bridges and tunnel entrances would be unusable. Water storage and purification equipment would be broken, and food stored under normal conditions would be consumed by fire. Fuel would be destroyed, leaving no source of heat for homes which remained standing.

Hospitals not destroyed would soon exhaust their emergency sources of auxiliary power, curtailing their lighting, their machinery, and their refrigeration of important drugs, while the millions dead would include large numbers of medically trained personnel. The survivors would be faced immediately with the threat of epidemic from uncollected refuse, sewage, uncontrolled vermin, contaminated food or water, and the accumulation of corpses.

Radiation exposure would be gravest in its long-term genetic effects of increased stillbirths, congenital malformations, reduced mental and physical vigor, feeblemindedness, and sterility. Other somatic effects would include increased incidence of leukemia and other forms of cancer, of degenerative diseases, of cataracts, and of damage to embryos. The short-term effects of radiation, including weakness, uncontrolled vomiting, and susceptibility to infection would further diminish any chance of recovery for the city, as would the likely simultaneous attack on other coastal cities.

The vast extent of this destruction requires a psychological defense mechanism which may reduce our awareness of the danger and contribute to the risk that nuclear war will be permitted to occur. Bernard, Ottenberg, and Redl describe the mechanism of *dehumanization* as "defense against painful or overwhelming emotions [which] entails a decrease in a person's sense of his own individuality and in his perception of the humanness of other people." Its prevalence results not only from awe of modern weapons but also from the nature of our modern technological society, which exposes people to the consequences of change, whether good or bad, but leaves them feeling impotent to do anything about it. One national survey showed clearly that although 42 percent of the population agreed that there was at least a reasonable probability of nuclear war within five years, hardly anyone saw anything that he himself might do toward preventing it (Withey 1962). As we increasingly see problems of modern warfare through the eyes of the military strategist, we are increasingly able to speak of pre-emptive attack, overkill capability, counter-insurgency, civil defense, and tolerable losses as if human beings were no longer involved. We increase our degree of detachment from some alien or enemy group and simultaneously decrease our own capacities for affiliation and concern.

In addition to the quantitative change in destructive capability, the new weaponry has brought about a qualitative change in people's image of war. Especially for Americans, war has been something fought by other people in other places and won or lost with moderate cost. Nuclear war implies instantaneous death to oneself and one's family. In a strange way, the very real possibility of one's own death emphasizes the unreality of the image of war. There is a belief that nuclear war, because it is so devastating, is really too frightful to occur. No one would be insane enough to bring it about; therefore it cannot happen. On the other hand, the same individual can believe that if nuclear war did occur, life would be worthless. Both these beliefs produce the same kind of reaction in the individual—a fatalistic view of the world and a yielding to one's own passivity and inability to do anything about the possibility of war. This passivity and helplessness is in a certain way comforting, for it removes from the individual not only the responsibility to do something that might avert war, but also the need to think about what will happen if he does not (Gifford 1962).

In summary, we see in the public attitude a primitivization of complex international affairs, an aura of unreality about the prospects of war, and a feeling of personal helplessness regarding the possibility of its onset. These are examples of psychological defenses against the realization of the horrors of nuclear war.

It is interesting that the defenses used to protect oneself from confronting the potential horrors of nuclear war are the same types of defense mechanisms we see operating in both public and private attitudes toward one's own death. Much of the literary concern with death represents an attempt to deny its reality. Much of the thematic matter of religion and philosophy deals with the immortality of the individual. A good deal of artistic and scientific legacy is related to the desire to believe that some aspect of one's self, in the form of one's own creation, is continuous beyond the end of one's life. The need to feel immortal can be seen in the importance people attribute to any actions they feel might make history and in the satisfaction people find in their children's and grandchildren's achievements. Interviews with patients who have a terminal illness reinforce the interpretation that individuals cannot conceive of their own personal extinction, and so believe that some aspect of themselves is continuous. (See Eissler 1955 and Deutsch 1936.)

It was Freud's view that the unconscious mind is incapable of conceiving of its own dissolution. Consciously, it may be very easy to view one's end as a biological organism, but this is a relatively abstract and intellectualized concept with little or no emotional concomitant. If we examine the phylogenetic development of the species, we find no strong evidence of a fear of death in animals or in children. However, infants do have strong fears: they fear hunger, helplessness, and separation from parents or guardians. Because the infant has so few capabilities for adaptive care of himself, these fears are sufficiently extreme to be driven out of consciousness. As the child matures, the fears prove intolerable to consciousness and are driven into unconscious processes. Psychoanalysts see the extreme preoccupation with fears of death on some abstract cognitive level as an unconscious representation of earlier infantile fears of separation and helplessness (Deutsch 1936).

It is important to distinguish between death as a biological end to the organism and death as a state of weakness and dissolution of the ego. This distinction helps us to understand the choices made by patients between progressive cardiac invalidism on the one hand and a risky operation on the other—between a willingness to live with an incurable cancer and the permitting of drastic surgical resection or castration. Consciously, the choices are different; unconsciously, both choices represent states of infantile helplessness (Weisman and Hackett 1960).

In Western society particularly, certain forms of helplessness and weakness are considered worse than death itself. The Western image of the masculine hero is a defense against feelings of weakness and passivity. Sometimes the public equates peace, or surrender with losing masculinity, possibly even unconsciously with a fear of castration. Peace is considered a danger, and the "peacenik" weak and cowardly; unconsciously he also poses the threat of arousing one's own feelings of helplessness and passivity.

When we talk about primitive thinking, about the denial of death, about feelings of infantile helplessness—even when we talk about destructive impulses—we are considering images that are not wholly conscious, images that affect the individual's behavior but not always in ways that he himself can understand or appreciate. Because these feelings are largely unconscious, they are not easily subject to debate, nor are they readily changed by attempts at education.

In an exchange of letters between Albert Einstein and Sigmund Freud, Einstein asked whether people had some innate destructive impulse that led them to fight periodic wars. To Einstein it seemed easy to blame militant and hostile leaders, but unless the population itself was willing to follow their leadership, there would be no war. Freud's answer to Einstein involved a description of his highly controversial concept of a death instinct, people's destructive inclination toward themselves and others (Freud 1959).

Before we define the Freudian death wish, it will be useful to examine the evidence on why soldiers fight. Note first that not all do. The glory of warfare is often outweighed by its dangers and degradation, and history is full of refusals to serve, resistance against military conscription, and desertions. The circumstances under which the famed Company A of American infantrymen in Vietnam refused to follow an order to enter a dangerous area were striking. The company, made up largely of 19- and 20-year-old draftees with only a short term of duty remaining, was the remnant of a group which had been pushing for five days through enemy-held territory in an effort to recover the bodies of eight Americans shot down in a helicopter. With half their men, including platoon leaders, already casualties, the group at one point simply refused to follow an order to continue the hunt down a rocky mountain slope (AP, August 26, 1969). When we examine the circumstances and the disillusionment with the Vietnam war among soldiers and civilians alike, it is not difficult to understand why these men refused.

The harder question to answer is why soldiers fight. One view holds that the patriotic esprit and the enforced discipline of military socialization are critical to the decision of the individual soldier to risk his life in combat. It is probably true that both dependence on military discipline and ideological inspiration provide some motivation. Still other analyses suggest that soldiers fight because of close ties and loyalties created among the men in their small combat units. This analysis, in fact, has been the main line of research on World War II (for example Stouffer 1949). The argument is that within a small group of men working together there develop loyalties so intense that they may override both civilian and military goals of the conflict and even the individual's own basic drive toward self-preservation.

A more recent study by Moskos (1969) of American infantrymen in Vietnam gives insight into the basis for cohesion within combat groups. Moskos's findings suggest that group loyalties are a strategy—a social contract—to deal with more basic dangers and deprivations of the combat situation. The horrors of combat are real, and self-interest dictates a tie to other members of the group. Moskos points out that a soldier rarely performs at his best when stationed at the highly dangerous "point" on patrol operations, since good performance would mean sacrificing his own safety for the good of the group. Moskos notes also that close ties rarely outlast the combat situation and soldiers rarely write to or try to see the men they have been close to in combat.

Moskos's data also support earlier findings about the absence of an ideological commitment to fight. Infantrymen react to slogans about defending democracy with "What a crock" or "Be serious, man." Almost all the men responded to the question of why they were there with an individualistic frame of reference: "My tough luck in getting drafted," "My own stupidity for listening to the recruiting sergeant." Upon further questioning over half the soldiers indicated that the United States is in Vietnam to stop communism. Those who could furnish a reason to oppose communists stressed an image of social regimentation. One man said, "Communism is something like the army." The G.I.s had come to think of their South Vietnamese allies as parasites, profiteers, and cowards, so they certainly were not fighting to save the South Vietnamese. Even their image of the United States was primarily that of a place that offered material advantages, and each soldier's entire being centered around his personal "DEROS" (Date Expected Return Overseas).

The desire to be masculine and tough withers rapidly after combat experience. Yet after making the sacrifice, the soldier, like most of us, reduces the dissonant feelings he may have by increasing his justification for the sacrifice. For this reason the typical infantryman opposes the peace demonstrations. They represent to him a type of activity which his own frame of reference, his own long history of subservience to authority, tell him is basically wrong. He envies the peace demonstrators for their privileged status in being out and is no less resentful of the "support-the-boys" campaigns. Moskos quotes one soldier as speaking for most in saying, "The only support I want is out."

It seems clear that the contemporary combat soldier is not to be confused with the stereotyped models of Prussian generals or more modern zealots of global military strategy. He may have needs for danger, for experiences that test his masculinity, or for sheer aggressive expression, but these needs cannot alone explain why he is fighting. He is fighting because he feels he must follow orders to perform even objectionable tasks. Yet Company A and the current generation of resisters notwithstanding, he does comply with policies that reflect the power, motivation, and aggressive needs of others. Is Freud's derivation of war from inherent destructive tendencies strengthened or weakened by these observations?

Freud's analysis raises the general biological question of whether there is in fact such a thing as natural death. His concept is to be understood more in biological or ecological terms than in psychological ones. Freud asked whether death is an accident which merely becomes increasingly probable as the organism gets older, or whether death is rather an inherent characteristic of the organism, given in the structural design of its living protoplasm. He favored the latter view (Gifford 1962).

Freud postulated two competing instinctive forces—the life force, Eros, which synthesizes living matter and living organisms into larger and more complex units, and the death force, Thanatos, which is disintegrative and ultimately reduces living matter to a non-living state. The two forces are not considered separate, nor are they manifested purely or directly. The life force is prominent in activities dealing with reproduction, the nurturant care of human beings, and their organization into larger social groups. The death force is inferred from the process of aging and from destructive behavior. The death force is also evidenced by a frequent form of neurotic behavior, that is, repetition of self-destructive tendencies, and in the tendency of groups toward conflict and fragmentation. The death force does serve certain functions, both biological and social, and in contest with the life force it maintains various balances in civilized society. Freud held that destructive tendencies are at the root of legal institutions, of the individual conscience, and to a large extent, of cultural development.

There are many purely biological rhythms: cycles of rest and activity, of hunger and satiation, of sleep and wakefulness. Perhaps life and death are expressions of a kind of biological rhythm on a larger scale. There is, for instance, an ecological periodicity in the populations of various species. When the caribou population expands greatly, it tends to eat much of the available vegetation, leading to a dispersion of and weakness in the herds, which makes them easier prey to the wolves. The wolves can then provide nutrition for their offspring and increase their population until the caribou population is sufficiently reduced to the point where the wolves will be faced with starvation or dispersion. Similarly, there may be a periodicity of war with cycles of active, large-scale violence interrupted by periods of relative tranquillity.

Freud viewed the conflict between life and death forces as one of the ultimate principles of living systems. He contended that while particular wars are terminable, warfare as an institution is likely to recur. With the advent of modern weapons, however, it is entirely possible that the human species may be accidentally exterminated during one of these violent episodes, before balance—in the form of life forces within the civilization or the species—has a chance to reassert itself. Perhaps the human species, like others before it, faces some kind of inevitable termination of its natural lifespan.

We can look at two of the major elements in the problem of war in this age as expressions of the life and death forces of which Freud spoke. One element, overpopulation, is clearly related to forces of life and reproductiveness; on the other hand, extreme population densities have been associated both experimentally and historically with eruptions of destructive violence. A second element, the capability of modern weapons, can be seen as a major extension of destructive forces; yet the same technologies which created these weapons of destruction may well be suited to create a means of sustenance for the world's increasing population. Both developments— overpopulation and nuclear technology—may be considered to express both life and death forces in society. However, both call for a rechanneling of potentially destructive capability to humane ends. Unfortunately, the rapid growth of population and nuclear technology may have outdistanced the capacity of human societies to make the necessary shift in policy. Other species, such as the dinosaurs, had strength and armor markedly effective for the period of their ascendance, but their small brains were ineffectual in learning to adapt to changing circumstances. Perhaps our relatively larger brains will enable us to profit from their experience.

We have tried to deal seriously with the metaphor of an underlying destructive psychic force beneath the extreme variety of surface hostilities so clearly in evidence around us. Clearly, such destructive forces are an abstraction to help explain a persistent phenomenon. Even if they stood for some irreversible tendency among the various cosmic forces affecting people, it would still not be clear that the inevitable manner of expressing aggression need be the institutional forms of international violence which men have devised.

In this chapter we have treated various psychological factors which some contend have significant effects on international conflict and foreign policy. We have found that the personality of political leaders does not have great effect on the final outcome of policy decisions. We have found that governments try to use public opinion as a resource rather than responding to it as if it were an independent force. And while we have discussed the possibility that innate aggression is a prime cause of war, we cannot use this principle to explain any particular war. To understand particular policy decisions, we need to examine the institutional context in which those decisions are made.

References

BERNARD, VIOLA W., PERRY OTTENBERG, AND FRITZ REDL
  1965 "Dehumanization: A Composite Psychological Defense in Relation to Modern War," in Milton Schwebel, ed., *Behavioral Science and Human Survival*. Palo Alto, Calif.: Science and Behavior Books.

BRONFENBRENNER, URIE
  1961 "The Mirror Image in Soviet–American Relations: A Social Psychologist's Report." *Journal of Social Issues* 17 (July): pp. 45–56.

CAMPBELL, ANGUS, PHILIP CONVERSE, WARREN MILLER, AND DONALD STOKES
  1966 *Elections and the Political Order*, pp. 351–72. New York: John Wiley & Sons.

CHMAJ, BETTY
  1968 "Paranoid Patriotism: The Radical Right and the South." *Atlantic* 209 (November): pp. 91–98.

COSER, LEWIS
  1963 "The Dysfunctions of Military Secrecy." *Social Problems* 11 (Summer): pp. 13–22.

DE RIVERA, JOSEPH H.
  1968 *The Psychological Dimension of Foreign Policy*. Columbus, Ohio: Charles E. Merrill Publishing Co.

DEUTSCH, FELIX
  1936 "Euthanasia: A Clinical Study." *Psychoanalytic Quarterly* 3 (Summer): pp. 347–68.

DEUTSCH, KARL, AND RICHARD L. MERRITT
  1965 "Effects of Events on National and International Images," in Herbert Kelman, ed., *International Behavior*. New York: Holt, Rinehart & Winston.

EISSLER, KURT
  1955 *The Psychiatrist and the Dying Patient*. New York: International Universities Press.

ERVIN, FRANK R., *et al.*
  1962 "Human and Ecological Effects in Massachusetts of an Assumed Thermonuclear Attack on the United States." *New England Journal of Medicine* 266 (May): pp. 1127–37.

FRANK, JEROME D.
  1967 *Sanity and Survival: Psychological Aspects of War and Peace*. New York: Random House.

FREUD, SIGMUND
   1959   *Collected Papers.* New York: Basic Books. (Volume 5: correspondence between Albert Einstein and Sigmund Freud.)

GIFFORD, SANFORD
   1962   "Death and Forever." *Atlantic* 209 (March): pp. 88–92.

HERO, ALFRED
   1959   *Americans in World Affairs.* Boston: World Peace Foundation.

HERSEY, JOHN
   1951   "Mr. President, II: Ten O'clock Meeting." *The New Yorker* 27 (April 14): pp. 38–55.

HOLSTI, OLE R.
   1963   "The Value of International Tension Measurement." *Journal of Conflict Resolution* 7 (September): pp. 608–17.

KENNAN, GEORGE F.
   1960   *Russia and the West under Lenin and Stalin.* Boston: Little, Brown & Co.

KOGAN, N., AND M. A. WALLACH
   1964   *Risk Taking: A Study on Cognition and Personality.* New York: Holt, Rinehart & Winston.

LANE, ROBERT E., AND DAVID O. SEARS
   1964   *Public Opinion.* Englewood Cliffs, N.J.: Prentice-Hall, Inc.

McGINNISS, JOE
   1968   *The Selling of the President, 1968.* New York: Trident.

MOSKOS, CHARLES, JR.
   1969   "Vietnam: Why Men Fight." *Trans-Action* 7 (November): pp. 13–23.

OSKAMP, STUART, AND HANNA LEVINSON
   1969   "International Attitudes of Doves and Hawks: The Role of Belief–Disbelief Systems and Involvement." Paper presented to Western Psychological Association, Vancouver, B.C., June.

"Personality and Politics: Theoretical and Methodological Issues"
   1968   *Journal of Social Issues* 24 (July): p. 3.

ROAZEN, PAUL
   1968   *Political and Social Thought.* New York: Knopf.

ROGOW, ARNOLD A.
   1963   *James Forrestal.* New York: Macmillan.

ROSENAU, JAMES A.
   1961   *Public Opinion and Foreign Policy.* New York: Random House.

ROSENBERG, MILTON J.
    1965   "Images in Relation to the Policy Process: American Public
            Opinion on Cold-War Issues," in Herbert C. Kelman, ed.,
            International Behavior, pp. 277–334. New York: Holt, Rine-
            hart & Winston.

SAFER, MORLEY
    1966   "Television Covers the War." *War/Peace Report* 6 (June/
            July): pp. 9–10.

SCIENTISTS' COMMITTEE ON RADIATION INFORMATION
    1962   "The Effects of a 20-Megaton Bomb." *New University Thought*
            2 (Spring): pp. 24–32. Also in Robert Perrucci and Marc
            Pilisuk, eds., *The Triple Revolution*. Boston: Little, Brown &
            Co., 1968.

SNYDER, RICHARD C., AND JAMES A. ROBINSON
    1961   *National and International Decision Making*. New York: In-
            stitute for International Order.

STAGNER, ROSS
    1967   *Psychological Aspects of International Conflict*. Belmont, Calif.:
            Brooks/Cole Publishing Co.

STONE, I. F.
    1952   *The Hidden History of the Korean War*. New York: Monthly
            Review Press.

STOUFFER, SAMUEL
    1949   *The American Soldier*. Princeton, N.J.: Princeton University
            Press.

WALTON, RICHARD E., WESLEY L. GOULD, DON A. STRICKLAND,
AND MICHAEL DRIVER
    1969   *Social and Psychological Aspects of Verification, Inspection and
            Assurance*. (Final Report to the U.S. Arms Control and Dis-
            armament Agency, January.)

WEISMAN, AVERY D., AND T. P. HACKETT
    1960   "Psychiatric Management of Operative Syndrome: I. The
            Therapeutic Consultation and the Effect of Non-Interpretive
            Intervention." *Psychosomatic Medicine* 22 (July–August): pp.
            267–82.

WHITING, ALLEN
    1960   *China Crosses the Yalu: The Decision to Enter the Korean
            War*. New York: Macmillan.

WITHEY, STEPHEN B.
    1962   "Public Opinion on War and Shelters." *New University
            Thought* 2 (Spring): pp. 6–19.

Chapter 4

THE GUTS
OF FOREIGN POLICY
DECISION MAKING

There is a recurrent debate among people concerned with progressive political change over whether to concentrate on building general public awareness or on directly influencing a small elite group of decision makers. The general public often appears apathetic, uninformed, and lacking any effective channels for influencing foreign policy. Thus it would seem more effective to try to persuade officials directly. The degree to which a decision maker may be influenced is limited, however, by the organizations within which he operates. The organization defines not only the limits of his rights and responsibilities in the decision process but the information he reads, the people he must impress, the kinds of discussions he engages in, and to a great extent the beliefs he holds. Sociologists have a long and rich heritage of study of bureaucratic organizations and their effects on the individual. The United States State Department, the organization officially charged with the conduct of this country's international affairs, is an example of a classic bureaucracy.[1]

---

[1] This chapter deals with the organizations that enact foreign policy. Although many organizations are involved, only two have been selected here for illustration: the Department of State and the Central Intelligence Agency. The Department of Defense was not chosen because its size and complexity would make a brief handling of the subject unsatisfactory.

Muddling Through the Department
of State

The State Department has about 26,000 regular employees including 3,520 foreign service officers. Of the government departments, only the Labor Department has fewer people and only the Justice Department has a smaller budget. The State Department operates 117 embassies, 69 consulates general, and 79 consulates scattered about the world (Attwood 1967).

Large bureaucracies exhibit a tendency to slight their original purposes in favor of an emphasis on the day-to-day routines of operation. The natural tendencies of large organizations are to stifle initiative in favor of reliability, to accentuate status differences, to solve new problems by categorizing them in old pigeonholes, and to expend a great deal of effort in justifying the agency and its activities to outsiders. The State Department is no exception.

Because it is so geographically extended, the State Department has traditionally relied on a large amount of paper communication. A major European embassy receives more than 400,000 words per day, the equivalent of an 850-page book. Much of the paper exchange is set up by departmental regulations requiring regular reports on certain matters regardless of how inconsequential they may be. Even the weekly CIA summary—stamped "secret"—rarely contains anything the embassy has not already seen in the *New York Times* Sunday news digest (Attwood 1967).

Travel and expense vouchers provide a good example of the State Department's bureaucratic paper exchange. A diplomat fully entrusted with national security secrets can be hounded over the most trivial details in filing his official travel expenses. One case reported by a former ambassador to Guinea, William Attwood, regards a foreign service officer who returned on order to Washington.

> His mother, who was not on government orders, traveled with him. In making out his voucher, he carefully separated his own from his mother's expenses. But the last item was a taxi from Union Station to his hotel. In Washington, there is a different fare if two people occupy the cab. Back came a query: "Did your mother ride in the cab with you?" His reply made bureaucratic history: "No, I took the cab. My mother walked and carried the bags." (Attwood 1967, p. 46)

Filing routine paper work is deeply satisfying to the ideal bureaucrat. Emptying an overflowing in-box, initialing reams of paper, and deferring action to a committee or a subcommittee are his daily accomplishments. The chief considerations of such a bureaucrat are to abide by the letter of the regulations, whatever the consequences, to keep a clean desk, and never to make waves.

This is not a formula for an agency that should be creating new programs to respond to long-term changes in world affairs. The State Department in fact does not initiate policies and is organized in a manner that
precludes policy changes. There have been some formal attempts to reor-
ganize the workings of the department, but as in all large bureaucratic
organizations the workings are only partly described by the formal procedures. An informal set of practices and beliefs provides the organization
with its informal culture. This unplanned aspect of State Department life
is described in Andrew Scott's study of dominant modes of belief in the
department. An important principle embodied in the beliefs Scott lists is
that the ability to handle foreign policy problems is an art developed solely
through experience as a foreign service officer, rather than through research
into foreign policy problems. Planning and research are useless, since each
new problem that arises is considered unique. Most State Department
officials believe that the department is doing a fairly good job, as well as
can be expected given the complex and difficult problems it faces, and
that nothing is particularly wrong with the department's organization or
procedures (A. M. Scott 1969).

Such a culture is essentially inhospitable to any efforts other than
those designed to meet immediate problems. Since research and long-term
planning are not particularly welcome, the department simply does not
initiate changes in policy. Long-term programs like the Marshall Plan, Point
Four, the Peace Corps, the Fulbright Act, and the Alliance for Progress
have arisen from sources outside the department.

The goal of State Department activity most frequently appears to be
organizational accommodation, that is, handling a problem without causing
a disturbance. Yet it would be precisely a willingness to challenge established
norms and to engage in sharp debate which might result in policy innovation. Pruitt's study of State Department decision making describes the
standard procedures for assigning and resolving a problem (Pruitt 1964).
The typical product of these procedures is bland and uncreative. We can
understand still better how the suppression of initiative gives rise to such
products by looking at Argyris's study of the actual types of interaction
patterns among officials. Argyris found that the foreign service officer tends
to withdraw from any open discussion of interpersonal difficulties and conflict. He avoids openness about interpersonal problems and about substan-
tive issues that might threaten either his superiors or his peers. When faced
with openly competitive and assertive behavior, the foreign service officer's
norm is to withdraw from any active confrontation, to mistrust the other
person, and to judge him negatively but not tell him so (Argyris 1967).

This all fits well into the goal of preserving bureaucratic tranquillity.
Promotion procedures that reward people for a record of trouble-free senior-
ity tend to accumulate deadwood at the upper middle levels, which further

militates against ever putting a creative idea through the hierarchy. Over-sized staffs also stifle initiative and smother ideas before they have a chance to see the light. In Washington and in the traditionally large European embassies it would be possible to dispense with much of the personnel with-out loss, yet many smaller embassies in Africa are heavily overworked and understaffed.

Despite the reams of written reports collected in the department, little use is made of past experience. The subcultural value that regards each problem as unique combines with inept library and data retrieval systems to make the organization operate almost as if it had no memory. New prob-lems are frequently attacked from scratch without the benefit of previous records or prior reports on analogous problems. Furthermore, the practice of routinely rotating people from one service to another prevents continuity and genuine expertise from developing. Retired foreign service officer Smith Simpson relates one incident which caused a furor in 1967. The Minister of Singapore, Lee Kuan Yew, stated that three years earlier the CIA had offered him a $3.3 million bribe. The State Department first denied the charge (an honest error, since the officers who had any knowledge of the offer had been rotated elsewhere). Later the State Department was obliged to admit its mistake when Lee produced a letter from Secretary of State Dean Rusk apologizing for the incident. The author's conclusion is a marked understatement which illustrates the narrowness of the State viewpoint. "A computer," Simpson writes, "would have spared the United States this, and many another humiliation" (Simpson 1967, p. 298).

Of course the State Department should have an active research and planning unit to replace its outmoded Bureau of Intelligence and Research, and of course it should have an excellent library and the latest computer services in data storage and retrieval. But was that the problem? Why was the Singapore minister's accusation not the cause for a major evaluation of whether the United States through its Central Intelligence Agency really should be in the business of offering secret bribes, setting up secret police agencies, or pulling political strings to keep control of leaders in a myriad of "free world" countries? The answer is that such questions are, according to the way the State Department functions, nobody's business. They are the business only of agencies like the CIA and the Department of Defense, which have a vested interest in the answers.

Rationalizing American Foreign Policy

The State Department's business is to justify American for-eign policy, and its organizational morass (the department is affectionately known as "Foggy Bottom") prevents it from doing much else. Of course the department also carries out routine activities: it runs embassies, issues passports, and so forth; but its main incursion into foreign policy is at the tail end, when policy has already been made and only the rationalizations need refinement. Then the State Department issues a white paper to help rally public opinion around the flag. In recent years, however, there has been substantial public recognition that these justifications are not always based on fact (certainly not on all the relevant facts) and do not always represent the real reasons for American actions. This credibility gap has steadily widened over the course of the Vietnam war. The first serious breach came after the State Department's White Paper of February 1965.

The United States announced on February 8, 1965 that there had been a sneak attack on a base at Pleiku, and that in retaliation American planes had begun bombing North Vietnam. Every attempt was made to give the impression that the attack had been of unusual size, that there were indications that North Vietnam was sending a large number of soldiers and weapons to the South, and that there was no indigenous rebel movement in South Vietnam. On February 27, the State Department issued a White Paper which purported to show that South Vietnam was being invaded by the North. Its thesis was that North Vietnam planned to conquer South Vietnam, and that the NLF was merely a puppet organization created and controlled by North Vietnam. A week later, I. F. Stone, an independent journalist, published a critique of the White Paper which reduced its arguments and its evidence to shreds.

The White Paper claimed that thousands of North Vietnamese soldiers had entered South Vietnam each year for six years, but of the 19 individual cases it cited, 16 of the men proved to be native-born South Vietnamese. The White Paper claimed that North Vietnam was supplying large numbers of weapons to the South, but details indicated that less than two and a half percent of the weapons captured from guerrillas originated in communist countries. The White Paper mentioned that the International Control Commission, which was to see that the Geneva agreement of 1954 was carried out, had issued a 1962 report charging North Vietnam with violating the Geneva agreement; but the paper neglected to mention that the same ICC report had revealed serious American and South Vietnamese government violations of the agreement. The White Paper completely ignored the fact that under the Geneva agreement Vietnam was one country and was to have been reunified, and that it was therefore a gross distortion to speak of North Vietnam as a separate country "invading" South Vietnam ("White Paper" and "Reply" in Gettleman 1965, pp. 284–322).

The Vietnam White Paper was about as credible as the apology the State Department gave for the Dominican intervention in April 1965. In the case of the Dominican Republic, the State Department was somewhat more active in promoting policy, but no more adept at justifying it. In April supporters of Juan Bosch rebelled against the ruling military junta, and the

United States sent in marines, who crushed the rebellion. It was claimed at the time that the marines' mission in Santo Domingo was to protect American citizens and evacuate them if need be. It was later claimed that there had been a danger of a communist takeover during the crisis, and that the United States had intervened to forestall it. The most likely explanation that emerges (see chapter 7) is that the United States, in particular the State Department, and the sugar interests to which some of its higher echelon members are closely tied, wanted to prevent Bosch, then a popular reformer, from returning to power. Bosch might have tried to wrest control over the Dominican economy from the hands of American investors (as he had begun to do from the time he took office as constitutionally elected president in February 1963 until he was overthrown by a military coup later that year). This was a possibility the investors would not tolerate.

Protecting American Investments

To the extent that the State Department's massive clogged machinery does contribute to some kind of foreign policy, it tends to be cautious and conservative. Often, its major goal appears to be to protect American overseas investors. One salient reason for this is that many of the top officials of the State Department (and for that matter the rest of the executive branch) are businessmen, or major stockholders, in the most powerful corporations in the United States. They sometimes leave their corporate posts or divest themselves of large blocks of stock to hold government office, but they still tend to maintain the interests and outlooks of corporate executives. In the Dominican Republic case, the American-owned sugar interests controlled key positions within the State Department, and thus the outcome of the 1965 crisis was to their liking. More generally, three of the five secretaries of state from 1948 to 1968 were former corporation lawyers, and the highest posts just below the cabinet level have been occupied largely by industrialists or financiers, or the sons of such men. William Domhoff has documented the close connections among those in power: men who have in common business interests, and good reasons to protect those interests, are the men who occupy the policy-making positions.

Although policy may not be very cogently formulated within the State Department, other institutions in our society do make intensive studies of foreign policy. One of these is the Council on Foreign Relations, an elite club in New York. A second such group, the Foreign Policy Association, engages in similar activities—discussions of foreign policy issues among experts—but it is relatively more plebeian. (One observer has said that the Foreign Policy Association is to the Council on Foreign Relations as the phone book is to *Who's Who*.) In 1958 the council numbered among its members the president, the secretary of state, the director of the CIA, and the board chairmen of three of the country's five largest industrial corporations, two of the four wealthiest insurance firms, and two of the three largest banks. At that time Joseph Kraft described the council as "the most important single private agency conducting research in foreign affairs." To illustrate the extent of its influence, he pointed out that Henry Stimson, who became secretary of war at the outbreak of World War II, was a member of the council. Stimson brought with him a staff of council members who eventually laid the foundations for America's modern defense establishment. John McCloy, Stimson's personnel chief and in 1958 chairman of the council, said, "Whenever we needed a man, we thumbed through the roll of Council members and put through a call to New York" (Kraft 1958, p. 67). Council members continued to be deeply involved in policy making after the war. Averell Harriman, who is a limited partner in the powerful Wall Street firm of Brown Bros., is a council member who has been governor of New York, ambassador to the Soviet Union, and ambassador-at-large. Henry Kissinger, now Special Assistant for National Security Affairs, not only is a council member, but in the fifties led a study group that included men who had been high officials of the Atomic Energy Commission, the civilian defense establishment, and the military. The council sets up discussion groups of this kind on various topics and their deliberations are always confidential. Their decisions, however, can be a major policy force. (Kissinger's group published a most influential book, *Nuclear Weapons and Foreign Policy*.) The groups help to crystallize ideas in the minds of government officials before those ideas are exposed to the glare of public opinion. The council's prestigious and widely read journal, *Foreign Affairs*, also aids its members in the process of policy formulation.

Kraft writes:

> It is undeniable that the Council, acting as a corporate body, has influenced American policy with wide-ranging effects upon the average citizen. Set against the total public, the Council can hardly be called a representative body; its active membership is by force of circumstance, Eastern; and by any reckoning either rich or successful. Its transactions are remote from public structiny, and in fact, refractory to any detailed examination. Thus, in theory at least, the Council comes close to being an organ of what C. Wright Mills had called the Power Elite—a group of men, similar in interest and outlook, shaping events from invulnerable positions behind the scenes. (Kraft 1958, p. 68)

Policy making does not occur as much in the State Department, which was originally set up for that purpose, as in other institutions that have sprung up since. Sometimes policy is shaped by military action, sometimes by actions of the CIA, other times by actions of industrialists. To find out what interests really hold sway over foreign policy we must examine such institutions as the Council on Foreign Relations, the National Security Council, and the Joint Chiefs of Staff. Further, we must examine the corporate connections of those in positions of power and the institutions which provide the continuous personnel for key decision positions regardless of which political party is elected to the White House. The State Department bureaucracy takes little initiative and holds little power. Individual ambassadors may occasionally affect the course of events by their actions, but on the whole the major trends of American foreign policy are molded elsewhere.

The CIA

In contrast to the bureaucratic ineptitude of the Department of State, the Central Intelligence Agency has mastered the art of controlled information transmission, both within its own organization and among the nine agencies of the intelligence community. The others (besides the CIA) are the National Security Council, the Defense Intelligence Agency, the National Security Agency, Army Intelligence, Navy Intelligence, Air Force Intelligence, the Atomic Energy Commission, the Federal Bureau of Investigation, and the State Department's Bureau of Intelligence and Research. In addition, numerous individuals in other government agencies and in a large number of private business firms, financial institutions, and philanthropic foundations operate as part of the intelligence chain, that substantial part of the American government which is wholly unaccountable to American people and almost completely unaccountable to Congress. Its secret budget extends into the billions, its employment rolls are classified, and its activities are fully known only to its own inner circle, the "Special Group." The State Department output consists largely of memoranda justifying government action or inaction. The CIA, however, blows up bridges, threatens people into spying roles, bribes, creates and even overthrows officials of foreign governments, influences elections, stages demonstrations, bombs cities from planes with disguised identification, establishes radio stations for propaganda broadcasts, assassinates political figures inimical to its interests, builds underground tunnels between countries, and provides fraudulent or deceptive information not only to alien governments but to American ambassadors (including our ambassador to the United Nations). But its operations are not available for public review. While the CIA has offices in all major American cities and agents in every country, it is lodged primarily in a $50,000,000 building in Virginia's Fairfax County. Estimating by overall office floor space there are from eight to ten thousand regular employees at the CIA's Langley headquarters in Fairfax. It has 21 acres of parking space, three incinerators (built at a cost of $105,000 to consume all classified wastepaper), and extensive computer facilities for immediate retrieval of information from its large computerized library. This includes not only classified data but the some 200,000 newspapers, journals, and books received each month (Wise and Ross 1964).

The Inner Workings

The CIA has four divisions. The Support Division is the administrative service wing. It takes charge of equipment, security, and communications, including the development of codes that cannot be understood by other branches of the government. The Research Division deals with technical intelligence, including such activities as assessment of foreign scientific and technical advances and analysis of aerial reconnaissance photos. The Intelligence Division is responsible for collecting data on any country in the world and transforming it into "intelligence." More than 80 percent of its raw data come from open sources such as foreign radio broadcasts and published materials. Reports are prepared from these data by men who are by and large academic, "contemplative" types of liberal persuasion (Wise and Ross 1964).

The Plans Division is the locus of the CIA's cloak-and-dagger operations. It collects the agency's covert intelligence through spies, and controls all special operations such as the overthrow of a government or the training of a counterrevolutionary invasion force. It is the division most enveloped in intrigue and most involved in direct action in foreign affairs. Agents of the Plans Division are planted in every United States government branch involved in foreign affairs. This includes, for example, the United States Information Agency, the Agency for International Development, Radio Free Europe, and the State Department. While some of its operations are for the clandestine funding of projects run through private foundations, commercial enterprises, or universities, the agency also runs some of its own commercial and industrial front companies abroad. One of these is Air America, based in Taiwan. Air America among other things delivers supplies to Meo tribesmen fighting the Pathet Lao in the hills of northeast Laos, and transports the Meos' main cash crop, opium (Scott, Feb. 1970).

The Plans Division tends to be more politically conservative than the Intelligence Division, and its politics show through in its foreign operations. When the CIA decided to overthrow the democratically elected pro-communist regime of Guatemalan President Jacobo Arbenz Guzman, it sought out a new government. Its candidate was Miguel Ydigoras Fuentes, who in early 1954 was living in exile in El Salvador. Ydigoras later wrote of the encounter:

> A former executive of the United Fruit Company, now retired, Mr. Walter Turnbull, came to see me with two gentlemen whom he introduced as agents of the CIA. They said that I was a popular figure in Guatemala and that

they wanted to lend their assistance to overthrow Arbenz. When I asked their conditions for the assistance I found them unacceptable. Among other things, I was to promise to favor the United Fruit Company and the International Railways of Central America; to destroy the railroad workers' labor union; . . . to establish a strongarm government, on the style of Ubico. (Wise and Ross 1964, p. 183)

Cuba

The impact of the Plans Division on actual policy is apparently very great. Consider the famous 1961 Bay of Pigs invasion, an unsuccessful attempt to overthrow the Cuban revolutionary government. The entire invasion was conceived and carried out within the Plans Division. Secret reports, apparently based on little more than the wishes of a small group of early defectors from Cuba, suggested that there was widespread popular disaffection with the regime of Fidel Castro. A militia of Cuban exiles, including pilots to man 24 B–26 bombers, was secretly trained in Nicaragua to take part in the allegedly Cuban revolt. During the four-day war disguised planes attacked Playa Giron, a 1,400-man invasion force was landed, and broadcasts urged a rebellion. Secretary of State Dean Rusk and Ambassador to the United Nations Adlai Stevenson lied to the public to deny American involvement. The Soviet premier threatened to help the Cuban government resist the attack, a move which could have escalated into nuclear war. The attack ended in a debacle with half the B–26s lost, the ground force easily beaten, and four American pilots killed. The activity of these four men has been systematically denied even to their widows, who received compensation checks from a corporation which exists only on paper (Wise and Ross 1964).

During the Bay of Pigs operation the Plans Division did not share information on its own operations even with the Intelligence Division. Neither Robert Amory, Jr., the CIA's deputy director for intelligence, nor Roger Hilsman, director of the State Department's Bureau of Intelligence and Research, had been informed. Hence key presidential advisors were virtually ignorant of critically important plans. Only the Joint Chiefs of Staff had a chance to give their qualified approval, and the plan they accepted was changed in important particulars by the time of the invasion.

Some CIA men still believe that President Kennedy's failure to provide more American bombing and air cover for the invasion caused the disaster. Others feel that the fiasco was an error in judgment to be corrected by more effective planning in the future. The president suffered a loss in public esteem that was not reversed until his popular stand during the subsequent Cuban missile crisis.

Because of its grave failure both in estimating the popularity of the Cuban revolution and in executing its invasion plans, the CIA changed some of its operating procedures. Its new director, John McCone, ordered the Plans Division to keep the Intelligence Division informed of its activities. But President Kennedy's chagrin was not enough to bring about any meaningful changes. The great fear was that an agency which both collected intelligence and devised secret plans might be biasing its intelligence to support its plans. Yet revisions in the CIA's operations stopped short of separating these two functions.

Certainly, by CIA standards the Bay of Pigs was a disaster. Not only did the operation fail to overthrow the communist government of Fidel Castro, but the CIA's own hand in the operation was immediately uncovered. This was a far cry from its stunning success in Iran, where it overthrew the popular Premier Mossadegh in 1953 after he had nationalized the Anglo-Iranian Oil Company. And the Bay of Pigs was a less well-kept secret than CIA intervention in overthrowing the elected President Arbenz in Guatemala following his attempt to nationalize certain holdings of the United Fruit Company.

Wherever it sets up shop, the CIA takes a stance far to the right, sometimes even in opposition to the activities of the State Department. It topples reformist governments and replaces them with repressive regimes, often military dictatorships. In utter disregard for the opinions or interests of the populace, it installs unpopular rulers in place of constitutionally elected officials, then finances a propaganda machine and a well-paid army loyal to the new ruler in order to prop up his government. When American business interests are threatened by higher taxes, loss of privileges, or expropriation (even with compensation), the CIA often moves in with its money and talents to turn events in a more profitable direction.

The CIA sometimes causes dismay in more liberal circles by undermining its own goals. The governments it chooses are frequently so reactionary that they drive the people into sympathy with the outlawed revolutionary left. The long-run effect is to thwart the purposes of American foreign policy. The Cuban episode illustrates just this pitfall. The Plans Division, the most conservative quarter of the CIA, gathered intelligence, drew up the plans, trained Cuban exiles, and carried out the Bay of Pigs operation. The more liberal Intelligence Division was completely ignorant of the plans and had no opportunity to counter the Plans Division's estimates of potential support among Cubans, or to put into perspective the calculations of probable success.

The CIA failed, but a decade later the outcome in Cuba is a success by other standards. Unemployment has been sharply reduced. Literacy has, except among the small non-Spanish speaking Haitian minority, become nearly universal, and the educational system has shown the most rapid growth rate of all Latin American countries. Once private and elitist, education is now free at all levels. The economy, once dependent on cane sugar alone, has been diversified by a major development in cattle breeding. Rents have been reduced and housing construction greatly accelerated. Public health programs have provided universal innoculations, and many hospitals have been constructed, particularly in the rural areas. Even the 1,300 middle class doctors who left after the revolution have been more than replaced by newly educated physicians, a majority of whom work in public services in the areas where they are most needed. Recreational facilities once reserved for the wealthy tourist are open to all. Hunger has been eliminated. The large prisons of pre-revolutionary days are empty reminders of a bygone era (*Profile of Cuba* 1965). Moreover, observers note the great enthusiasm of Cubans for their national development and for their leaders, who walk unguarded among an armed population and who work the fields regardless of their political position. The goal of economic development, which the United States claims to promote at great cost in other nations, has been accomplished in Cuba without cost to the United States, and against the will of the CIA and the American government.

Laos

The CIA's role of protector against popular election of leftist or neutralist regimes is clearly evident in Laos. The pro-communist Pathet Lao in 1957 reached a political agreement with the government in which the Pathet Lao received two cabinet posts and were permitted to participate in elections for specially created seats in the National Assembly. In these elections the left showed a considerable increase in strength since the 1954 agreements. Thirty-two percent of all votes and 13 of the 21 contested seats went to the Pathet Lao and an allied left-leaning neutralist group. The premier's half-brother and leader of the Pathet Lao, Prince Souphanouveng, received more votes than any other candidate (Scott, April 1970). Schlesinger describes the CIA response to the Laotians' day at the polls:

> In 1958 Washington decided to install a reliable pro-western regime. CIA spooks put in their appearance, set up a Committee for the Defense of the National Interests (CDNI) and brought back from France as its chief an energetic, ambitious and devious officer named Phoumi Nosavan. Prince Souvanna, who had shown himself an honest and respected if impulsive leader, was forced out of office [by a withholding of U.S. aid and CIA encouragement of a parliamentary crisis, allegedly through the use of bribes]; a veteran politician named Phoumi Sananikoune took his place. (Schlesinger 1965, pp. 325–26, quoted in Scott, April 1970, p. 35)

The United States supported and counseled the Sananikoune regime, and the Pathet Lao were excluded from the new cabinet. Sananikoune then manufactured a crisis by sending armed patrols into a disputed area on the North Vietnamese border, obtained emergency powers from the Assembly, and ordered Pathet Lao battalions integrated into the national army. The CIA continued to find, and to fabricate, evidence that uprisings in Laos were the work of intruding North Vietnamese troops (Scott, April 1970). Predictably, the CIA followed its usual pattern of polarizing the country, overthrowing a legitimate neutralist government and replacing it with a repressive one, and blaming the resultant unrest on foreign (communist) intervention to justify an increased American military presence.

Iran

CIA intervention in Iran further illuminates the power and aims of the agency. Iran has deposits of copper and coal and holds 13 percent of the world's oil reserves, much of which is yet untapped. Its rivers hold an almost unlimited potential for hydroelectric power. It supports a population of almost 30 million people (10 million more than a decade ago) on a large land mass with 1,000 miles of common border with the Soviet Union. Amid these resources the population remains in poverty despite a flow of American assistance to Iran which has run into hundreds of millions of American dollars.

In the early 1900s a European cartel called the Industrial Bank of Persia was organized to finance the Anglo-Iranian Oil Company. One of the partners in the cartel was the German banking house of J. Henry Schroeder and Company, on whose American board of directors sat Allen Dulles, later head of the CIA. The legal counsel for Anglo-Iranian was Sullivan and Cromwell, a New York law firm in which Allen Dulles and his brother John Foster (secretary of state under Eisenhower) were partners.

In 1951 the shah of Iran named as his premier Mohammed Mossadegh, a strong spokesman for nationalism and independent economic development. The popular Mossadegh quickly took action to bring the profits from Iranian oil to the people of Iran. He announced the expropriation of Anglo-Iranian Oil and the nationalization of Iran's oil fields. At stake for Anglo-Iranian were assets valued in the billions, in the form of resources which it had exploited for 50 years. Anglo-Iranian refused to provide its technicians to work the oil fields, and other Western companies joined to effect a virtual boycott of Iranian oil. Iran was helpless, and the economy careened toward bankruptcy. Mossadegh then wrote to President Eisenhower, indicating that unless he received American aid for Iran's financial troubles he would be forced to ask for help elsewhere—meaning the Soviet Union. The president delayed while the CIA put pressure on the shah to oust Mossadegh. An American agent then paid a vist to the shah, who suddenly announced that he was replacing Mossadegh as premier with Major General Fazollah Zahedi, a member of the overly inflated Iranian police force. But by the time the Colonel of the Imperial Guards, whose duty it was to serve notice to Mossadegh, did his duty, Massadegh had gathered an army of supporters. They arrested the colonel, and the shah hastily left for Rome. Undaunted, the American agent supervised the careful spending of more than 10 million CIA dollars in Teheran within the next few days. Within four days a large impromptu circus parade, common in the streets of Teheran, suddenly became an organized mob and began yelling "Long live the shah" and "Death to Mossadegh." The crowd joined in, and at the height of the confusion, troops loyal to the shah attacked Mossadegh's supporters. After nine hours of bitter fighting, Mossadegh's troops were surrounded and forced to surrender. The shah was flown home from Rome and Major General Zahedi became premier. The assistance once sought by Mossadegh now flowed in at an average rate of 5 million dollars per month (Tully 1962).

The shah and other Iranian officials soon became men of extreme wealth, and the shah maintained a standing army larger than that of West Germany. After the coup an international consortium signed a 25-year renewable pact with the Iranian government. Anglo-Iranian Oil Company (which became the British Petroleum Oil Company) got 40 percent of the oil being extracted, and a group of American companies divided 40 percent, with the remainder going to Royal Dutch Shell and Compagnie Française des Pétroles. The details of the contract were not made public because, according to Secretary of State Dulles, such information "would affect adversely the foreign relations of the United States . . . and would almost certainly revive the former antagonisms and derogate from the benefits of the consortium formula" (Nirumand 1969, pp. 100–104). Expectations of benefits to the consortium were, and continue to be, amply fulfilled. The control of Iranian oil and hence of the Iranian economy has remained in its hands. The benefits to Iranians, however, have left something to be desired.

The Iranian government, under popular pressure, introduced land reforms in 1961, but these affected only a quarter of the needy Iranian peasants. Those assisted were saddled with exorbitant mortgages which negated the benefits of land ownership. The landlords, meanwhile, were compensated for the parcels of land taken from them; as a bonus they were given the opportunity to become share-owners in formerly government-owned enterprises. Income distribution and class structure did not change, and the Iranian peasant remained in his miserable condition.

Widespread illiteracy still prevails in Iran, estimated by the Iranian government at 85 percent in 1962. Hunger and malnutrition are critical problems. At the same time political dissent among university students is brutally suppressed, and students have been arrested and beaten by the hundreds, tortured, and murdered for their political views (Nirumand 1969).

American military and economic assistance has continued to Iran. As in Athens, Santo Domingo, and Saigon, American aid is needed to put down the growing number of dissident Iranians who believe that foreign domination of their country through the shah is not in their own best interest.

The 1953 coup exhibits at once the tremendous power and the long-run weakness of the CIA. It can create armies, name premiers, and overthrow governments, but it cannot produce progress. The CIA director was unconcerned that nationalization was a just action of a legally constituted government and could bring Iran out of extreme poverty. American officials had no interest in the thought that aid sent to Iran after the coup might have been given earlier to compensate the expropriated oil company. Neither were American officials interested in urging American interests to break their boycott. American officials feared that Soviet inroads would be used for military advantage and, as the rhetoric goes, to remove Iran from the free world orbit. Increased influence in Iran might have won for the Soviet Union a warm water outlet on the Persian Gulf and a source of valuable oil. Neutrality and independence were not permissible outcomes for two reasons. The first was that the CIA operates closely with large American business interests abroad, and an independent Iran might well choose to seize some of its lucrative oil profits. The second was that the larger goal of protecting the American empire means to the decision makers that they must follow a strict policy of anti-communism.

It is the day-by-day operations of CIA agents (who sometimes work through such businesses and through the embassies) which make policy by feeding anti-communist "intelligence" back to the United States. They implement policy by their regular activities. But at the highest levels the directors of agencies like the CIA are financiers, corporation executives, or attorneys for major corporations. At the time of the 1953 coup the director of the CIA was Allen Dulles, who had been an associate of the law firm of Sullivan and Cromwell, the legal counsel for the Anglo-Iranian Oil Company. The key agent in Teheran who staged the coup was Kermit Roosevelt (grandson of Teddy), who later became Gulf Oil's government relations director and then a vice-president of the company (Wise and Ross 1964).

That CIA directors have included prominent military men like Admiral Radford and prominent industrialists like John McCone (who has extensive interests in steel and shipbuilding) helps to explain some of the direction of that agency.

Producing the Agent

Once it is decided that a nation is not to control the profits of its own resources for its own development, then the issues of anti-communism can be used to provide the essential rationale for whatever operations must follow. While economic domination is a prime mover, it is the "logic" of anti-communism which permits men to degrade themselves in the corruption and subversion of responsive governments. This logic is discussed in the chapter on realpolitik. Here we will look at the process of indoctrinating the CIA agent with this compelling raison's d'etre. We will see what kind of person can be induced to engage in a lifetime of deception, bribery, and illegal actions; how such people are selected; what the compensations are; and what happens to these people in the course of their work.

An aspect of the agency which must certainly be compelling to some is its aura of intrigue. For the immature person in particular, reading a good spy novel is not enough when the lure of participating in a real one is present. The situation combines danger with genuine intellectual challenge. The atmosphere of danger is conveyed by such activities as U-2 flying missions. An example of the challenging intellectual problems that arise is the case in which the refuse from a commercial Soviet airliner was secretly bought, carried away, and examined by an agent. From this refuse, the agent salvaged a bent coat hanger which intelligence reports told him had been made from the metal shavings of a wing on a newly designed Soviet long-range bomber. By use of spectroanalysis and chemical tests the CIA was able to identify the materials of the hanger (and the bomber wing) and, from this, to calculate both the range and bomb load of that particular plane (Tully 1962).

For some men, the challenge and romance of such intrigue combines with a belief that intelligence work is somehow vital to American interests. To find bright people who meet its criteria, the CIA recruits on the college campuses. Its selection procedures are arduous and include aptitude tests devised by Princeton's Educational Testing Service. CIA assessment teams check potential recruits to determine whether their personalities fit the CIA's needs. If a student winces in the dentist's chair or if he is sensitive to kidding, he can be rejected (Tully 1962). The screening process may even include an interview with a psychiatrist with an unzipped fly ("Three Tales," p. 17). A group of junior officer trainees (JOTs) is finally selected for a program of intensive training and indoctrination. The indoctrination is subtle, but from the start the enemy is depicted as so ruthless that any tactics against him, no matter how base, are necessary. Much of the indoctrination relies on an account of horrendous Soviet activities in subversion or military intervention (activities which the CIA itself has copied, improved upon, and vastly expanded). The job the JOTs undertake is not an apolitical one of securing intelligence, but a political one of attacking communism and anything that resembles it. The training materials include a CIA history of the installation and overthrow of governments, with the strength of their anti-communism being the only criterion of assessment. It is implicit that popular democracies can be overthrown, military juntas can take their place—only anti-communism, or immediate usefulness to the larger anti-communist cause, matters.

The scrutiny of the preselection period continues during training. JOTs are observed as they learn to lie automatically about their identities and their occupations, as they bug each other's rooms or try to make each other drop a piece of background information during casual conversation. Extreme security precautions gradually make the individual somewhat distant from friends and colleagues. It is not only lock-picking, wiretapping, microfilming, safecracking, and forgery which comprise the craft of espionage, but also the ability to lie to an enemy, to a friend, and to oneself. To remain effective as an agent in the CIA, one must develop a deep identification with one's craft. Pay is rather low since people overly concerned with money are poor security risks. Personal social life, sex life, and the ability to question oneself must all be subordinated to the image of oneself as a professional spy. Only after this dehumanizing transformation can an agent be expected to perform reliably under stress.

One high official of the CIA confided, "I don't know the names of everyone I deal with at the agency. We often use pseudonyms in case a wire is tapped or a piece of paper gets into the wrong hands. And we never use real names in communications" (Wise and Ross 1964, p. 241).

The CIA's large crop of college-educated, research-oriented scholars, many with Ph.D.'s and many from Ivy League schools, help to put out a magazine called *Intelligence Articles*. While it is primarily a journal for "scholarship" about intelligence work, its articles help to depersonalize the work and to preach the lesson that the craft comes first. The conclusion of one article was as follows: "There is no place for laxness even if it may seem overbureaucratic and ridiculous. The application of security measures has to be executed precisely in every detail. There is no place for overconfidence in friends and old acquaintances" (Wise and Ross 1964, p. 245).

Once his essential trust in people breaks down, the agent can be increasingly useful in intelligence operations. The dehumanization of the training process helps the agent to heighten his caution and to waive his moral judgments. Once he can justify distrusting a long-time friend or killing an alien agent, then he can justify anything, including if necessary killing some of his fellow citizens.

One former agent recalled a story told to a class of JOTs. It involved a man who photographed one of the staging areas in Nicaragua for the Bay of Pigs invasion. The photos showed unremoved markings on American planes. Hitchhiking to New York shortly afterward, he was picked up quite by chance by a CIA man who notified "the company." It became clear that the man was too idealistic to be bought off, the CIA instructor related, so "on his way to the newspapers . . . he was struck by a laundry truck and killed. And those photos just plain disappeared" ("Three Tales," p. 21).

From that point it is only a modest step to accepting a host of weapons which violate the Geneva Convention, such as bullets that explode on impact, self-made napalm for stickier Molotov cocktails, or the "mini-canon," which involves a plastic explosive in a number ten can with power sufficient to destroy an entire bus and its passengers ("Three Tales," p. 21).

The process of dehumanization is unending. When some persons can be regarded as expendable or manipulable, others can be added to the category. Foreign students studying in American colleges are prime targets. They are lured by cash investments and by pressure from agencies like the American Friends of the Middle East and the Asia Foundation, which rely on CIA funds channeled through other foundations. Such agencies also encourage some students and discourage others, as in their refusal to assist Iranian students who oppose the shah. The use of funds to turn foreign students into traitors is matched domestically by the CIA's infiltration of organizations within this country. American trade unions have been given a financial boost from the CIA, which helps to create unions in other countries which will be sympathetic to American foreign policy. The exposure by Congressman Wright Patman of a vast network of CIA funding conduits spread across the country led to the now classic revelation that key officers of the United States National Student Association had also been bought by CIA funds (Stern 1967).

Conclusion

The rigidities of bureaucracy make the State Department much less a foreign-policy making organization than it might be. Hence, the decision options of the social science laboratory to increase or reduce communication, to escalate or de-escalate one's level of armament or military activity, are not real options of the State Department. The department is simply not capable of organizing itself for a major change in policy.

The CIA is also unable to change the major directions of policy. But unlike the State Department, which produces only words to justify policies generated elsewhere, the CIA does create policy, continually shaping certain events of international importance but always adhering to the same gross policy direction. Its size and its secrecy give it a broad license to discover things and to act on its findings. With all its elaborate machinery and skilled personnel, however, the CIA still lacks the capacity to evaluate whether its

most basic goals are really in the broader interests of the American people
(as opposed to the narrower interests of American business). This gives some
meaning to the way Webster's dictionary lists three types of intelligence:
human, animal, and military, in that order. The lowest forms of human
endeavor are those which move with speed and efficiency in the pursuit of
objectives that are degrading to the individual. The CIA is *not* a necessary
compromise with morality; it is a moral monster.

This chapter has concentrated on only two of the agencies reputed to
affect policy in international affairs. Several others bear serious scrutiny: the
White House staff, the Joint Chiefs of Staff, the National Security Council,
and more. These will not be analyzed separately. Instead, we will try to
develop a theory and gain some insight into the ways policy goals are determined through an intensive look at the military–industrial complex.

References

"An Easy Switch to Peacetime"
    1968   *San Francisco Chronicle* (September 25): p. 2.
ARGYRIS, CHRIS
    1967   "Some Causes of Organizational Ineffectiveness Within the
            Department of State." *Center for International Systems Re-
            search, Occasional Papers* 2. Department of State. Pp. ii–ix,
            1–52.
ATTWOOD, WILLIAM
    1967   "The Labyrinth in Foggy Bottom: A Critique of the State
            Department." *Atlantic* 219 (February): pp. 45–50.
DOMHOFF, G. WILLIAM
    1967   *Who Rules America?* Englewood Cliffs, N.J.: Prentice-Hall,
            Inc.
DREW, ELIZABETH B.
    1968   "Washington Reports." *Atlantic* 222 (August): pp. 4–10.
FALL, BERNARD
    1969   *Anatomy of a Crisis.* New York: Doubleday & Co.
GETTLEMAN, MARVIN E., *ed.*
    1965   *Vietnam: History, Documents and Opinions on a Major World
            Crisis.* Greenwich, Conn.: Fawcett Publications. (Especially
            pp. 284–322.)
KISSINGER, HENRY
    1957   *Nuclear Weapons and Foreign Policy.* New York: Harper &
            Row.

KRAFT, JOSEPH
1958 "School for Statesmen." *Harper's* 217 (July): pp. 64–68.

MINISTRY OF FOREIGN RELATIONS OF CUBA, INFORMATION DEPARTMENT
1965 *Profile of Cuba.*

NIRUMAND, BAHRAN
1969 *Iran: The New Imperialism in Action.* New York: Monthly Review Press.

PRUITT, DEAN G.
1964 "Problem Solving in the Department of State." *The Social Science Foundation and Department of International Relations.* Monograph No. 2, pp. i–v, 1–56. Denver, Colo.: University of Denver.

SCHLESINGER, ARTHUR
1969 *A Thousand Days.* Boston: Houghton Mifflin.

SCOTT, ANDREW M.
1969 "The Department of State: Formal Organization and Informal Culture." *International Studies Quarterly* 13 (March): pp. 1–18.

SCOTT, PETER DALE
1970 "Air America: Flying the U.S. into Laos." *Ramparts* 8 (February): p. 39.

———
1970 "Laos: The Story Nixon Won't Tell." *New York Review of Books* 14 (April 9): pp. 35–41.

SIMPSON, SMITH
1967 "Who Runs the State Department?" *The Nation* 204 (March 6): pp. 294–99.

STERN, SOL
1967 "NSA and the CIA." *Ramparts* 5 (March): pp. 29–37.

STONE, I. F.
1965 "A Reply to the White Paper." *I. F. Stone's Weekly* 13 (March 8): pp. 1–4.

"Three Tales of the CIA"
1967 *Ramparts* 5 (April): pp. 15–28.

TULLY, ANDREW
1962 *CIA: The Inside Story.* New York: William Morrow & Co.

WISE, DAVID, AND THOMAS ROSS
1964 *The Invisible Government.* New York: Random House.

Chapter 5

REAL POLITIK
AND THE STRATEGISTS

Scientific thought has apparently been applied to warfare since man first waged war. Its application has changed the nature of warfare and continues to do so. The natural sciences—physics, chemistry, and biology—have made enormous contributions. Psychology and economics have found major applications in modern wars, and the applied disciplines—medicine, aeronautics, and naval engineering, for example—have also assisted immeasurably. Increasingly, war has become a cooperative enterprise in which all forms of creative endeavor are applied to the task at hand. Basically, technical advance serves an analogous function for military and civilian pursuits: it increases the sensory and motor capacities of people. First, through radar, television, range finders, and detection devices of all sorts, it brings the individual decision maker information that is not immediately available to his senses. In war, of course, this is primarily information about the actions of the enemy. Second, technology enables the decision maker to magnify his motor abilities—to fly from place to place, to destroy people with the movement of a finger on a trigger, or to level cities with the push of a button.

Until recently the question of what information to seek and which actions to embark on was more art than science, and it was resolved in much the same way as the aristocracy of old planned their moves and countermoves in preparation for battle. In such circumstances the strategy of warfare was very much an art, and the value of experience in playing such games (even secondhand through the study of history) was immeasurable. In his memoirs of the Allied invasion of the French coast, General Eisenhower recounts that after all the intelligence reports were in, he alone had to decide whether to invade, with only his military experience and talent to guide him in making this critical judgment. Very recently, however, science (in this case mathematics) has come to the aid of the decision maker in his task, with the science of rational choice.

The science of rational choice is derived largely from the mathematical theory of games, which has been finding major applications in business and economic decisions. The possibility that an exact science can govern the making of important decisions is alluring, and seems to promise immense power. This apparently great potential is tempered, however, by an appreciation of what the games can and cannot do.

The theory of games involves a classification system, not of objects but of situations. Each situation to be covered by the theory must involve two or more parties. Each party is capable of making one or more specific moves which are constrained by rules governing the situation. The moves of the several parties determine an outcome of the situation which is translatable into a payoff, either positive or negative, to each of the participants. All situations under this extensive rubric are called games; to these games the theory addresses itself. To the uninitiated the term *games* sounds like a horrible misnomer, since some situations that meet the definition, such as where to invest limited capital in a race with a competing firm, how to wage war, or what to promise one's date, are regarded with deadly seriousness. These situations are games only in the mathematician's sense. The values of the various outcomes are absolutely and definitely given, and the mathematician's only concern is with the logical relationships between the moves and the outcomes.

Games of war have long been fashionable among the aristocracy. Early chess pieces were fine replicas of horsemen, armed and geared for battle. Between the onset of the European feudal system and the Napoleonic wars, royalty played with their tin soldiers in games which were trial runs for their more serious armed battles or wars, which would follow. To the kings who played these war games, the outcome of real battles was a matter of vital concern involving sovereign rule over specific peoples and territories.

By comparison with the stated goals of modern wars, the objectives of that earlier type of conflict were modest, and the limitation of human or material costs in pursuit of such objectives led to a preoccupation with questions of strategy. It was primarily with the art of strategy that Frederic the Great and his counterparts concerned themselves. Each ambitious monarch assumed, and assumed that others would assume, that nations strive to maximize their domains and engage in battles to do so wherever the costs do not outweigh the advantages.

When it was determined that a reasonable exercise of power over the Spanish throne or a territorial redrawing of the Alsatian border might be achieved, a declaration of war was issued. Where the outcome was in doubt, battles were fought by professional warriors leading professional armies of loyal gentry and select professional mercenaries who alone had the right to bear arms. The rules of warfare were observed as a matter of the pride of the professional warrior. As in chess, when the position of one side was no longer tenable, it surrendered. An appropriate ceremony following this surrender arranged for the new conditions of rule until the next battle took place. Retribution following wars such as these was usually mild and was tempered by the familial ties relating the royal families to one another.

Warfare during these times had no ideological basis, but was rather the natural outgrowth of the explicit purpose of sovereign nation-states at the time: to survive and to extend their power and influence. Battles were fought when they could achieve these ends and avoided when they were irrelevant. With the possible exception of the Holy Wars, destroying a demoniacal adversary or fighting to extend the virtues of one's way of life were simply not a part of the way the game was ordinarily played.

There have been some rather obvious changes in the conception of nations and in the conception of war. Nations now allegedly stand for particular ideals, and ideological rationales abound among the declared purposes of warfare. Moreover, the cost of modern warfare often seems incommensurate with its objectives. Wars often seem to extend beyond the point at which any progress toward the nation's ideals—peace, justice, freedom, socialism, etc.—can be achieved by their continuation. Still, wars continue to be played out, with deadly consequences. Why?

The realist school of political science holds that the purpose of nations, which use war selectively as a means to other ends, has changed little through history. Those changes which have occurred have been in superficial phenomena, in the words used to rationalize the pursuit of national interest and in technology and tactics, more than in the fundamental reasons for wars. The basic realist tenet is that high ideals have not replaced the pursuit of national power, nor has ideology replaced the calculation of costs and rewards as a determinant of military foreign policy.

There is little doubt that some aspects of the international scene bear little resemblance to the Europe of the seventeenth century. During the French Revolution and the subsequent Napoleonic era, wars were fought for ultimate purposes, not to be appeased by a minor shift in territorial borders or by changes in the order of succession to the throne. Napoleon was not related to any monarch. He fought with armies of conscript patriots by new rules of warfare, permitting costs to life which far surpassed the accepted conventions of the time. World War I and the United States' war in Indochina are clear examples of wars of attrition in which a calculation of the costs by the parties involved would have terminated the conflicts much earlier. And surely "to make the world safe for democracy," a rallying cry in World War I, is not a matter of pure national interest or of adding to national power and influence. But the realist school can point to numerous instances in which the messianic motives for engaging in warfare appear as epiphenomena to the underlying pursuit of national security and national interest. Certainly, the actions of the Allies in World War II can be seen as designed to protect the security of the various Western nations against the expansionist objectives of Germany and Japan. Moreover, the extension of communism into Eastern Europe following World War II can be seen as a nationalistic act by the Soviet Union to protect its security by providing a buffer zone. The ideological conflict with the United States may be regarded as secondary. Finally, the succession of treaties between major countries, which have been broken by one party when its interest was no longer served, supports the concept of separate national states, each striving to extend its power and influence like the feudal monarchies of the past.

The realist school contends that the same motives adequately describe the actions of both historical and modern nations. Moreover, the realists assert that such purposes are necessary to and inherent in the concept of nation-states, basically because of the power motivations of human beings. They regard the nation-state itself as having a permanence and autonomy which extends beyond the lives of particular nation-states, or of alliances or organizations which bind them to one another. The idealist school, on the other hand, takes a more beneficent view of human nature and a more optimistic view of historical possibilities. This school views the system of nation-states as a transient phenomenon evolving toward international organizations and controls which will ultimately transcend the nation-state and preclude warfare. It should be clear that the differences between the realist and idealist schools have little to do with realism in the sense of scientific validity. The realist in this context accepts as self-evident and inevitable a self-aggrandizing motivation on the part of nation-states.[1]

The realist, or realpolitik, view serves as a model to explain the purposes of the separate players in a game with large stakes. In this game of complex rules governing particular moves and countermoves, the strategists are at least able to agree on objectives of play. Once the objectives of play are clearly defined (as were the objectives of the early monarchs), it is possible for them to engage in trial conflicts on the giant chessboards of simulated conflicts. The study of such trial conflicts has grown into a large and influential enterprise, particularly in the United States. It is known as strategic analysis.

---

[1] For a further discussion of the different views of history see the articles by Haas, Morgenthau, and Organski in James N. Rosenau, ed., *International Politics and Foreign Policy* (Glencoe, Ill.: The Free Press, 1961).

It seems obvious that the costs involved in modern war make the games more complex for the contemporary strategist. When gold or trade with the Orient was at stake, the rewards seemed high relative to the costs of battle. Later, when markets and colonial sources of raw materials were the prizes, it was still possible to weigh the losses of warfare against the advantages of winning. But what advantages could possibly be worth the loss associated with a major modern war? Is any gain worth the obliteration of large civilian populations? What market is worth the destruction of a city? And if the given objectives of the nation-state can no longer be said to be served by the tactics of armed conflict, then what, if any, is the business of the strategy analysts?

Remember that this is not the first time war has been questioned as a rational instrument of foreign policy. Shortly after the Napoleonic era Karl von Clausewitz wrote his often quoted thesis that war was merely a continuation of diplomacy by other means. His emphasis, often missed, was that war must be a rational tool for achieving specific objectives and that it must be fought with the strategic elegance which will restrict the costs to reasonable limits. In a way, Clausewitz's writing helped resuscitate the belief in war for the European monarchs who had not yet fully recovered from Napoleon's brutalization of the noble art. Modern strategists do the same thing for military and civilian decision makers that Clausewitz did for the monarchs: they create a conception of conflict in which warfare may still be used and be said to fulfill a rational purpose.

Paradoxically, the most prominent contemporary military strategists are not military men at all, but are civilian employees of the many large institutes under contract either to the Department of Defense or to one of the service branches. This arrangement facilitates the hiring of civilian scholars from various disciplines at a pay scale higher than they would be able to receive as military officers and significantly higher than they might receive from academic appointments in colleges and universities.

The best known of these military strategists, and perhaps the one whose name is associated most with the controversy over strategic military thinking, is Herman Kahn. In this book *Thinking About the Unthinkable* Kahn warns that people, so frightened by the devastation of modern nuclear weaponry, might cease to believe that anyone would knowingly risk a war and might therefore fail to take the measures necessary for living and conducting policy in the nuclear age. Kahn worries also that people will regard nuclear war as so horrible that its consequences are worse than death, and that they will see the only choices in a modern conflict situation to be total annihilation or total surrender. Kahn believes that these are not the only choices, and that an effective understanding of nuclear capability and the threat of its use can preserve the possibilities for waging conflict at a lower level. Since any effective defense of civilian populations is outmoded by the destructive capabilities nations now possess, Kahn asserts the necessity of maintaining a deterrence: the capacity to strike back, if struck first by an enemy, with such overwhelming force that the enemy population would be decimated. Under such a powerful threat of retaliation, the enemy would be extremely unlikely to take the risk associated with an aggressive strike. With the nuclear powers thus deterred from engaging in an all-out assault against each other (except under the most highly provocative conditions), it is possible for these powers to engage in a number of lesser moves in an attempt to gain marginal advantages over each other. Moreover, if the level of threat is of sufficient magnitude and is given in a manner which makes it seem extremely credible, the threat of the use of nuclear weapons in retaliation may itself be useful in extracting concessions from the other side. Hence the goal of the game of contemporary modern warfare, according to theorists like Kahn, is to be able to threaten, even to threaten nuclear blackmail, convincingly.

It becomes important, therefore, to talk and think as if we are ready and able to withstand even the possibility of major nuclear war. Kahn argues that it is not only necessary but realistic for us to do this, much the same as it is realistic for us to make adequate preparation for the possible occurrence of an earthquake. After all, he argues, like an earthquake, a nuclear war is possible, and according to Kahn it would not necessarily be a total, unmitigated disaster. However, Kahn's analogy to the earthquake or to other natural disasters is weak because of his apparent assumption that a nuclear war is something like a natural disaster, which may happen regardless of the preparations we choose to make or not to make. Unfortunately, however, if nuclear war does occur, it will not be the consequence of some uncontrolled act of nature, but of the decisions of persons charged to carry out policy decisions. Planning for what will happen before, during, and after the use of nuclear weaponry seems very likely to affect these decision makers. The effect might in fact be to increase the likelihood of nuclear war.

The credibility of the deterrent force is a major factor in Kahn's scheme for survival, and he spends some time describing the advantage of both having, and demonstrating to the other side, the technical capability to deliver a retaliatory nuclear strike. This could be done by making the counterattack force in some way invulnerable to a surprise attack by the adversary, for example by hiding the missiles on moving box cars, planting them in protected underground silos, or locating them on submarines at various places in the ocean. Kahn is somewhat less complete in his analysis of the psychological aspects of a credible deterrent threat. An actual instance in which a decision had to be made illustrates the problems involved. Signs of a forthcoming missile attack from an unidentified origin were detected by the radar systems of the United States's early warning stations in Alaska. Should an immediate counterattack be launched? A number of factors prevented the men in charge from initiating an immediate counterstrike against the Soviet Union. One factor was that the Soviet premier happened to be in New York City attending the United Nations at the time, making it unlikely that the Soviets would be launching an attack. But what if he had been in Moscow at the time? We have had several similar close calls (Livant 1961).

These critical decisions, we must remember, are made by human decision makers necessarily acting under great stress. Psychological evidence strongly suggests that decisions made under stress often fail to take into account all available information. When the stress involves group conflict, it sometimes results in a greater number of warlike acts. The decisions to be made in the face of evidence of an oncoming attack are not automatic. In our example of the falsely detected attack, the unidentified object turned out to have been the moon; it had been detected by a radar station with greater capability than had been expected. If the objects had been conclusively identified as missiles, the decision makers would have had to ask another question: what was the origin of the attack? An American retaliation against the wrong nation would only increase the ultimate extent of damages to the United States. What if the attack had been an accidental strike, the result of a testing operation gone haywire? It would then be unwise to retaliate and bring about further destruction. And how could one actually confirm the source of the strike and, even beyond this, its intention? Would the decision maker then, if he could reach the president, have the president call on the hot line to ask the Soviet premier whether the attack was indeed intended? If it was intended, what would the Soviet premier say? If he denied the intended strike, could his words be trusted? And if such trust exists, even under stress, then what is the function of the entire detection system and the extremely costly arsenal of weapons in the first place?

Even if the attack was confirmed to be an intentional attack, and if its source was certain, would the decision maker then decide to strike a retaliatory blow? The entire purpose of the deterrent is to deter such an attack, to prevent the kind of damage that that attack would bring about. Once an attack is launched, the deterrent has already failed. To launch a retaliatory attack would only assure that the other side would then counterattack again and bring about still further devastation to one's own nation. Would it not be better, since the deterrent had already failed, to surrender to the other side, rather than to allow one's own side to be obliterated completely? Could the decision maker, whose job was to assure the protection of his own land, engage in the very behavior which would assure its complete annihilation?

To make the threat of retaliation credible in the first place, the decision maker must play the game to the hilt; he must understand the game is to win, to outdo or prevail over the other party without necessarily regarding the costs or losses involved. The punishment of a hostile enemy must be a positive objective for the person making the decisions—else why would he do so irrational a thing as to destroy himself and all that he values, merely for the sake of retribution? The paradox that Kahn fails to see is that there are unintended consequences if we do in fact convince the other side, and they do in fact convince us, that the decision makers involved are imbued with the spirit of the game and will in fact launch retaliatory strikes at all costs. If it was effectively persuaded that the enemy was bent on its own destruction, a nation might not wait for a real provocation to engage in retaliation. It might build up its own "retaliatory" capability with the idea of using it as nuclear blackmail to extract concessions or even surrender. A nation which is convinced that its enemy has extremely hostile intentions might even decide that it is better to strike first than to risk being caught off guard. Here we go round and round in some of the dangers created by the psychological conditions necessary for a credible deterrent.

Kahn barely deals with the psychology of the decision maker, and deals not at all with his value system. In this sense his thought is very similar to game theory: he is abstracting from the contest only the strategic aspects of the game. What move can be made from among which options, and with what costs or rewards to the party making the moves? Also, as in game theory, Kahn does not question why the objectives of one side or the other should be either fulfilled or thwarted. These questions are not legitimate to the gamester. It is a given that a chess player, for example, tries to win, that a poker player tries to win as much as possible. Nothing in the game theoretician's strategy questions those objectives. While Kahn does not actually use the powerful mathematical tools of game theory to analyze the situations he depicts, the similarities between his approach and the approach of the gaming strategists are extremely important. The scenarios he describes, in which the only concerns are how to maximize one's own advantage, conceal the values for which that advantage is being sought. In this way Kahn can suggest a move "in the national interest" which would in fact destroy a third of the nation's population.

Not all of the moves that Kahn suggests are of this magnitude. The basic idea in his teachings, and the reason for their popularity among military men, lies in the numerous lesser military and paramilitary options which Kahn sees as still feasible behind the deterrent threat. His book *On Escalation* deals with an ordering of these options along the 44 rungs of a ladder ranging from mild diplomatic notes to total destruction.

The concept of escalation is, in simplified form, the game of chicken. Two cars face each other on a highway, each with a tire on the center line, and advance toward each other. The first to swerve is chicken. The strategies are obvious. Give every possible indication of resolve and unconcern for one's own safety. Use high speed, down a fifth of gin, and tamper with the brakes and steering mechanism to hamper their function. This strategy is considered likely to work (except in the case which Kahn does not cover as well, where the other driver has also used high speed, downed a fifth of gin, and tampered with his brakes and steering mechanism) (Rapoport 1965).

At each intensification of the conflict the options are laid out. In an early stage they may involve refusal to facilitate negotiations, or legal harassment against the adversary's prestige. Kahn weighs carefully the advantages of escalating and crossing the nuclear threshold at his seventeenth rung of the escalation ladder, "Barely Nuclear War." Through deception in this phase one could possibly pass off a slight nuclear attack as an accident, by offering to punish the guilty individuals or to provide an indemnification which would indicate one's sincerity but not actually compensate for the other side's loss. Here, as at every other stage, the other side may refuse to back down, and a new level will be reached. Kahn draws one blueprint in which the Soviet Union invades West Germany. The United States retaliates with two or three nuclear weapons, not so much to destroy the Soviet attack as to suggest that, having used two or three, we might use more. The Soviets, of course, might then use two or three nuclear weapons to indicate that they were not frightened by the American strikes. Kahn writes, "One can thus easily imagine a cease fire being called immediately after the Soviet retaliation" (quoted in Rapoport 1965, p. 378). Kahn gives the arguments pro and con for going on, however, and later states that tit-for-tat "reciprocal-reprisal wars of resolve [involving nuclear weapons, Ed.] may be a standard tactic of the future" (quoted in Rapoport 1965). At rung 39 the tit-for-tat exchanges are in the city trading stage. Kahn carefully indicates how long-range planning, for example for fallout shelters or for the evacuation of cities, may provide one with a strategic advantage.

Military strategists like Kahn have dealt with fallout shelters, underground cities, and the like to live out a nuclear attack. While scientific data do not support the effectiveness of such means, the strategists nevertheless are willing to advocate the great effort necessary to make such civil defense as convincing as possible to the other side. If an amount of totalitarian discipline is needed for the rehearsal of urban evacuation, or if military strategists must be given powers exceeding the normally restricted role of the military in a democracy, the strategists appear willing to pay the costs in order to safeguard the national interest. Even the despicable task of deciding whom to save and whom to sacrifice can be undertaken (secretly, so as to avoid too much public clamor) in order to pursue the strategy game.

It must be apparent by now that the national interest Kahn strives to preserve is very little related to the wishes or needs of the American public. Rather, public opinion and morals, where they are useful, are to be mobilized for strategic advantages. Kahn makes clear, however, that public opinion will be little involved in the decision making of a third world war. The national interest here refers not to the wishes of a people to protect or extend the values on which their original allegiance to a way of government is based. Instead, the strategist's national interest is the patriotism of the Prussian soldier or of any other career militarist: the defense of the state as an end in itself. That people object to such pursuits appears as irrational to the strategist as if the pieces in a game of chess were to complain about the sacrifices being made in order to win. But in the real game we are the pieces. It behooves us then to look not only at the way the game is currently being played but also at why it is being played at all.

On the contemporary scene, the strategic ideas of Herman Kahn, Henry Kissinger, and others like them are sought not because they have validity but because they provide a rationale for the expansion of such measures of military preparedness as the Strategic Air Command, the ICBM and IRBM systems, and the ABM. Such multi-billion dollar systems are justified through studies made by certain contract research organizations which conduct research on any problem for which funds are available. Strategy analysis, which we have discussed above, is one kind of study that buttresses military priorities; operations research is another.

In essence, operations research is a method for solving technical problems by calculating the outcomes of various combinations of inputs. By varying the input operations, the scientist can assign probabilities to the range of possible outcomes. The method forces the scientist to attend to specific detail and lets him include large numbers of variables in a single analysis. For the military, the beauty of operations research is that the analysis often rests on basic assumptions that can be stated (and then forgotten) among the mass of technical data and data estimates which are used to solve the problem. But however forgotten these assumptions may be, they still affect the outcome of the research. Let us take the assumption, for example, that a nation capable of using its clandestine facilities for production of a first strike capability will actually do this. Such an assumption leaves only the technical question of how much secret productive capacity and technical skill can be estimated for that country. That question is ideally handled by operations research. The country's potential capabilities can then be presented as a bona fide threat to the United States, based on "research." The Department of Defense and Congress might then approve creation of a force to counter this potential threat. Such a counter-move might well cause the other nation to use its facilities in exactly the assumed way; thus the assumption behind the research becomes a self-fulfilling prophecy. In this way operations research on defense has become the backdrop for the theorists of military strategy.

Like strategic thinking, operations research does not deal with human values or with the process of value change. Typically it does not address itself even to the question of what actions might reduce the need for continued military expenditure. Not all research on national defense, however, has been along the lines of military operations research or of Kahn's strategy analysis. Some research on strategy has emphasized changing values, inducing accommodation, and letting the players choose their goals rather than deciding arbitrarily on competitive goals.

Some researchers in the early sixties attempted to find strategies for achieving disarmament. Psychologist Charles Osgood suggested a means of gradually disarming that might increase international trust and good will. At a time when American and Soviet officials, both with nuclear weapons at their disposal, were locked in an interaction pattern of suspicion and mutual threat, Osgood suggested a pattern of unilateral actions which he thought could reverse the spiraling arms race and begin a movement toward disarmament and tension reduction (Osgood 1962). His thesis was that while suspicions would preclude both an early agreement on arms reduction and a major disarmament by one or both sides, they would still permit a series of small unilateral overtures that would not jeopardize the security of the country making the moves. He predicted that a series of small disarming moves announced in advance and honestly fulfilled would be met eventually by reciprocal behavior on the part of the cold war adversary.

Sociologist Amitai Etzioni has recounted the events which marked a period of thaw after the 1961 Cuban missile crisis, and which supported Osgood's theory. During the thaw the sequence of moves occurred in the following order:

1. President Kennedy announced a reappraisal of the cold war and called for new modes of cooperation. The United States suspended nuclear tests in the atmosphere.
2. The USSR broadcast the Kennedy speech intact on Moscow radio, and Premier Khrushchev made a speech welcoming the Kennedy approach. The USSR stopped production of strategic bombers and removed its objections to the presence of United Nations observers in Yemen.
3. The United States removed its objections to the restoration to full status of the Hungarian delegation to the United Nations.
4. A limited nuclear test ban was signed.
5. Soviet Foreign Minister Gromyko called for a non-aggression treaty between NATO and the Warsaw Pact.
6. Kennedy called for joint efforts to "explore the stars together."
7. Direct flights were scheduled between Moscow and New York.
8. The United States agreed to the sale of wheat to the USSR.
9. Gromyko called for a pact outlawing nuclear weapons in outer space.
10. Kennedy responded favorably, and an agreement was reached on the exchange of captured spies (Etzioni 1967).

This succession of moves is not, of course, a scientific confirmation of the Osgood thesis, although it does suggest that the arms race might be encouraged to spiral downward instead of upward. Other social scientists have tried a more systematic plotting of the interaction of events between nations (Walton et al. 1969; McClelland and Hoggard 1968). Using newspaper headlines to indicate all major moves and countermoves during a specific time period, William Gamson studied the ability of three different belief systems to predict the actual responses of the Soviet Union to American moves. One position (the "tough line") held that the USSR's goal was to destroy the United States and everything it stood for; hence the United States should never compromise or appear conciliatory. The "moderate line" saw the USSR as wanting to replace the Western social system with communism, but held that USSR was not willing to take excessive risks toward that end. The "soft line" held that the Soviet Union was more interested in maintaining and consolidating its position than in expanding. Each belief system implied that certain American actions (tough, moderate, or soft) would result in certain Soviet responses. As is so often the case, the reality is more complex than our simple theories of it. None of the implicit theories—hard, soft or moderate—was able to predict accurately the Soviet response to American moves under both crisis and non-crisis conditions. The tough line predicted best under crisis conditions but the soft line forecast better under non-crisis conditions. The moderate line predictions were less accurate than chance under either condition. But even these findings are inconclusive, dealing only with immediate effects of American moves. The long-term effects of a conciliatory policy (the soft line) have not been seen because they have not been tried (Gamson 1964; Gamson and Modigliani 1965).

All these studies of the historical record drew their data from the chaos of history and tried to fit it into their theoretical categories. Since the precise events suggested by Osgood's hypothesis did not actually occur, there is no way to determine whether they would have worked, short of controlling history. This we cannot do, but we can simulate some very simple controlled situations in a small-group laboratory. Extensive experimental studies have had individuals perform tasks that simulate some aspect of international conflict. A relatively small number of elements are selected for study.

In one laboratory study two players are given the task of making either conciliatory or antagonistic moves by converting their missile tokens to factories or vice versa. Each player, moving secretly, gradually converts some portion of his five missiles and, after both have completed the task, the result is shown. Each player then gets a positive or negative payoff depending on the outcome of the disarming task. The outcomes are arranged so that both sides may win something if both disarm, but a player caught less armed is punished for weakness and the more heavily armed player gains at his expense. If both stay fully armed, neither wins. The particular set of payoffs used heightens the psychological problems of trust and suspicion in disarming. Each player, calculating selfishly, does better to remain fully armed no matter what his partner does. Yet paradoxically, if both players follow the strategy of remaining fully armed, no one wins. Over many trials, it is possible to win only if both players take the risks of disarming. Many players in such a game distrust each other and forgo winning by staying fully armed. The interesting question here is whether there is some strategy a player might use to bring about cooperative or disarming moves on the part of his adversary. By using a preinstructed stooge, the experimenters had one of the two players do precisely what the Osgood proposal requires, that is, make known his moves in advance, continually taking the initiative by disarming just one step more than the other player did during his last turn. The findings showed that consistent unilateral initiatives toward trust tend to be reciprocated (Pilisuk and Skolnick 1968).

While such simulated studies can come close to isolating the psychological factors relevant to the Osgood proposal, they still are not conclusive. The factors that operated in the controlled laboratory may be outweighed by other factors operating in a more complex social environment. What would be the outcome if there were not two actors, but three or ten or fifty? What would happen if the decision maker, before deciding to disarm, had to take into account pressures from the general public or from his military establishment? Even these complications in policy decisions have been studied, with some success, in the laboratory. The technique of simulation is again used, most frequently with some form of the inter-nation game developed by Harold Guetzkow (Guetzkow et al. 1963; Sawyer and Guetzkow 1965). This technique poses a situation in which persons representing certain roles in particular nation-states are able to interact with one another in many of the ways open to actual nation-states. This gives the investigator an opportunity to study specific effects he wishes to introduce, for example the effects of the spread of nuclear weapons, the relationship between the stress of rapid information inputs and tendencies to initiate aggression.

One such study carried out by Raser and Crow (1964) assumed that one nation had an invulnerable retaliatory system, and tested the consequences of that fact on its own behavior and the behavior of other nations. The researchers found that the invulnerable nation "was seen as stronger, was more threatening, lost some of its interest in arms control, was able to deter more effectively, changed its policies so that accidental and preemptive war became less likely, but was much more willing to start wars to gain its national objectives. Other nations' interest in arms control agreements increased, and alliance patterns shifted toward less cohesiveness" (Raser 1965, p. 452, footnote).

Even these more complex simulations may err by omitting certain factors important to the real scene or by overestimating the importance of others. Still, they do provide an exciting laboratory in which to study the operations of individual psychological factors and group interaction patterns in an international setting. The tragedy of academic peace research is not that it has failed to produce the definitive study on how to achieve peace, but that it has provided good evidence about policy paths which ought to lead to peace but which are never really put to the test. Why is this?

The military and executive decision makers are not constrained to try only those techniques which have been effective, either historically or in the laboratory. No study was requested to indicate whether each of a dozen separate escalating moves in Vietnam was likely to yield the anticipated effect of making the opposition disappear (and none of them have). We are faced with a problem that is not a matter of research knowledge alone. When a clever decision maker is committed to a particular course of action, he can find or invent the game with the "right" assumptions—the assumptions that tell him the moves he is making must be the right ones.

Men like Herman Kahn and Henry Kissinger are clever men. Like other intellectuals concerned with defense they are employed under military contracts to find ways not of preventing war, but of preserving it. Herman Kahn can readily envision common interests which might enable the American and Soviet nuclear giants to achieve an agreement to terminate hostilities short of total destruction (even after a nuclear exchange has begun). It is strange, then, that he can dismiss as unrealistic the idea that similar common interests could lead to an agreement to end all war and all war preparations. What actually makes this possibility so unrealistic is that so little effort is expended to achieve it. Peace is not imposible, but it is unlikely so long as the major efforts of researchers and of the government are directed toward finding ever more sophisticated means of waging war. The defense intellectuals devise a game of global strategy and invent the concept of brush fire wars, counter-insurgency, limited wars, and the 44 rungs of the escalation ladder. All this helps maintain the illusion that wars are still suited to the resolution of conflicts and that the military art is something more than the outmoded cancerous growth it has become in modern society. The strategists are playing the wrong game—and we are the pawns.

References

ETZIONI, AMITAI
  1967 "The Kennedy Experiment." *Western Political Quarterly* 20 (June): pp. 361–80.
GAMSON, WILLIAM A.
  1964 "Evaluating Beliefs about International Conflict," in Roger Fisher, ed., *International Conflict and Behavioral Science*, pp. 27–40. New York: Academy of Arts and Sciences.

GAMSON, WILLIAM A., AND ANDRE MODIGLIANI
  1965 "Soviet Responses to Western Foreign Policy, 1946–53." *Peace Research Society: Papers*, III. Chicago Conference.
GUETZKOW, HAROLD, *et al.*
  1963 *Simulation in International Relations.* Englewood Cliffs, N.J.: Prentice-Hall, Inc.
HAAS, ERNEST B.
  1961 "The Balance of Power: Prescription, Concept or Propaganda," in James N. Rosenau, ed., *International Politics and Foreign Policy.* Glencoe, Ill.: The Free Press.
KAHN, HERMAN
  1962 *Thinking About the Unthinkable.* New York: Horizon Press.

  1965 *On Escalation: Metaphors and Scenarios.* New York: Praeger.
KISSINGER, HENRY A.
  1958 *Nuclear Weapons and Foreign Policy.* Garden City, N.Y.: Doubleday & Co.
LIVANT, WILLIAM P.
  1961 "Attack Versus Aggression: How Can We Distinguish?" *Committee of Correspondence Newsletter* 20 (October): p. 22.
McCLELLAND, CHARLES A., AND GARY D. HOGGARD
  1968 "Conflict Patterns in the Interaction among Nations." Mimeographed, Los Angeles: University of Southern California.
MORGENTHAU, HANS J.
  1961 "Power and Ideology in International Politics," in James N. Rosenau, ed., *International Politics and Foreign Policy.* Glencoe, Ill.: The Free Press.
ORGANSKI, A. F. K.
  1961 "The Power Transition," in James N. Rosenau, ed. *International Politics and Foreign Policy.* Glencoe, Ill.: The Free Press.
OSGOOD, CHARLES
  1962 *An Alternative to War or Surrender.* Urbana, Ill.: University of Illinois Press.
PILISUK, MARC, AND PAUL SKOLNICK
  1968 "Inducing Trust: A Test of the Osgood Proposal." *Journal of Personality and Social Psychology* 8 (February): pp. 121–33.
RAPOPORT, ANATOL
  1960 *Fights, Games and Debates.* Ann Arbor, Mich.: University of Michigan Press.

  1962 "The Use and Misuse of Game Theory." *Scientific American* 207 (December): pp. 108–18.

1963 "N-Game: Strategic and Non-Strategic Approaches to Problems of International Security." *Aspect* (November).

1964 *Strategy and Conscience.* New York: Harper & Row.

1965 "Chicken a la Kahn." *Virginia Quarterly Review* 41 (Summer) : pp. 370–89.

RASER, JOHN R.
1965 "Weapons Design and Arms Control: The Polaris Example." *Journal of Conflict Resolution* 9 (December) : pp. 450–62.

RASER, JOHN R., AND W. J. CROW
1964 "WINSAFE II: An Inter-Nation Simulation Study of Deterrence Postures Embodying Capacity to Delay Response." La Jolla, Calif.: Western Behavioral Science Institute.

ROSENAU, JAMES N., *ed.*
1961 *International Politics and Foreign Policy.* Glencoe, Ill.: The Free Press.

SAWYER, JACK, AND HAROLD GUETZKOW
1965 "Bargaining and Negotiation in International Relations," in Herbert C. Kelman, ed., *International Behavior: A Social–Psychological Analysis.* New York: Holt, Rinehart & Winston.

WALTON, RICHARD E., WESLEY L. GOULD, DON A. STRICKLAND, AND MICHAEL DRIVER
1969 *Social and Psychological Aspects of Verification, Inspection and Assurance.* Final Report to the U.S. Arms Control and Disarmament Agency, January.

Chapter 6

IS THERE
A MILITARY-INDUSTRIAL
COMPLEX
WHICH PREVENTS PEACE?[1]

The term *military–industrial complex* appears often in popular books and in the newspapers today. If there exists an omnipotent elite committed to militarism, then there is simply no basis for hope that voices for peace have established, or can establish, an influential channel into inner policy circles. The purpose of this chapter is to examine the theory and evidence which help to clarify this issue.

The New Concern

Not since the thirties has there been such a rash of attention to military–industrial power as there is today. Then, as now, the president himself raised the specter of improper military influence. FDR, on the eve of a Senate investigation of the munitions industry, said flatly that the arms race was a "grave menace . . . due in no small measure to the uncontrolled activities of the manufacturers and merchants of the engines of destruction and it must be met by the concerted action of the people of all nations" (Raymond 1964, p. 262; also *Congressional Quarterly Weekly Report* 1964, 6, pp. 265–78). While Dwight Eisenhower did not sound so

[1] An earlier version of this essay by Marc Pilisuk and Tom Hayden was published in the *Journal of Social Issues* 21, no. 3 (July 1965), pp. 67–117.

militant as Roosevelt, and while he never adopted FDR's 1932 campaign pledge to "take the profits out of war," he did resume a popular tradition with his warning against the "unwarranted influence" of the military–industrial complex. It may be a significant measure of the times that one president could make such warnings in his very first campaign for office, while the other couched it among several other farewell remarks.

The thirties are a prelude to the sixties, too, in the area of congressional investigation of militarism. Then Senator Gerald P. Nye investigated the fabulous World War I profits of United States Steel and Hercules Powder and discovered, with horror, the instrumental role of munitions makers and other commercial interests in beginning the war. Nye revealed, for example, that the American ambassador in London informed President Wilson in 1917 that probably "the only way of maintaining our pre-eminent trade position and averting a panic is by declaring war on Germany" (Raymond, p. 264). As Roosevelt was more aggressive than Eisenhower, so also were Nye, Borah, and other popular senators more aggressive than their counterparts in the sixties. Nevertheless, similar issues are now being raised in congressional committees. The most shocking of these issues may be found in the report of the hearings of Senator John McClellan's committee on government operations, *Pyramiding of Profits and Costs in the Missile Procurement Program*. This report pointed out the likely danger that the government "can be placed in the unenviable position of reluctant acquiescence to the demands and conditions set by the contractor," and that "profits were pyramided on other profits without any relationship at all to the effort being expended by those making the profit." In what might have been front page scandal in any area but national defense, the committee documented two mechanisms by which millions upon millions of dollars of excess profit have been reaped by the defense industries. The mechanisms are (a) claiming profits on work subcontracted to other firms (which in turn subcontract portions of their work to others and charge a profit on the subsubcontracted work, too), and (b) overestimating the subcontracting costs (on incentive type contracts), thereby reaping huge profits by undercutting the original estimates. However, the contrast with the thirties is clear. Senator McClellan only wanted to improve the efficiency of what he called "these necessary monopolies."[2] A more far-reaching investigation under the direction of Senator Clark dealt with the convertibility of the defense empire to civilian job-creating tasks. He claimed first that the new defense emphasis on electronics and on research and development, and the monopolization of defense by a few companies and geographic areas, considerably reduces the potential effect of defense as an economic stabilizer;

---

[2] United States Senate, Committee on Government Operations, report of the Permanent Subcommittee on Investigations, *Pyramiding of Profits and Costs in the Missile Procurement Program*, March 31, 1964.

and second that certain firms, especially those in the aerospace industry, suffer an overcapacity crisis that spurs them to insist on more missiles than the nation needs.[3] Senator Clark's hearings, too, were mild in contrast to those of the thirties. Even milder, however, was the 1962 survey report of Senator Hubert Humphrey, who said it was "nonsense" to believe that American industry is opposed to disarmament.[4]

Another measure of the interest in military–industrial power is the number of popular and technical books published dealing with the subject. In the thirties the widely read books were Davenport's *Zaharoff, High Priest of War*, Engelbrecht and Haneghen's *Merchants of Death*, and Seldes's *Iron, Blood and Profits*. Two decades passed before the work of C. Wright Mills began to attract broad attention to the subject of organized militarism. Including Mills's pioneering books, there have been at least 21 major books published on this subject during the period between Sputnik and the American escalation of the Vietnam war into North Vietnam. Many of them are by journalists (Cook, Coffin, Raymond, Swomley, Wise and Ross); some by economists (Benoit, Boulding, Melman, Peck, Perlo, Scherer); sociologists (Etzioni, Horowitz, Janowitz, Mills); political scientists (Meisel, Rogow); novelists (Bailey, Burdick, Knebel, Sutton); and at least one physical scientist (Lapp).

Whatever the objective referent, if any, of a "military–industrial complex," it is undeniable that the concept now plays an important role in the political consciousness of many persons, on a scale without precedent since the thirties. It is a telling fact that the new literature, with the exception of Mills, Cook, and Perlo, still lacks the bite of the old, and that the proposed solutions are very modest. In the thirties a popular idea, proposed by the Nye Committee but never implemented, was the nationalization of the munitions industries. By the sixties the reverse has happened; most military research, development, and production is done by private companies subsidized by the federal government. Military–political–industrial cooperation is so pervasive and frequent that it becomes a hair-splitting task to identify specifically any "merchants of death." Also, the scale of potential destruction has so increased, the nature of warfare strategy has so changed, and the existence of the military in peacetime is so accepted, that it seems quaint to imagine defense contractors with bloody hands. Furthermore, the assumed threat of communist expansion has become the ultimate justification of the postwar military buildup, whereas in the past such buildups could

[3] United States Senate, Committee on Labor and Public Welfare, report of the Subcommittee on Employment and Manpower, *Convertibility of Space and Defense Resources to Civilian Needs: A Search for New Employment Potentials*, 88th Congress, 2nd session, 1964.

[4] United States Senate, Committee on Foreign Relations, Subcommittee on Disarmament, *The Economic Impact of Arms Control Agreements*, Congressional Record, October 5, 1962, pp. 2139–94.

be attributed more clearly to industrial profit and power motives. Reasons such as these probably explain both the long silence and the modest character of the current resurgence in discussion of these matters.

But these reasons account partially for the inadequacy of analysis as well. The question, "Does there exist a military–industrial complex which prevents peace?" at first seems debatable in straightforward, yes-or-no terms. Indeed, it might have been answerable in the twenties or thirties but not in the postwar period. When there is permanent intermingling and coordination among military, industrial, and government elites, and whenever greater war-preparedness can be justified by reference to the communist movement, the question becomes much stickier. Because of this, the easiest conclusion to support is that a "complex" simply does not exist as an omnipresent obstacle to policy change. Indeed, this belief has become the accepted norm for "informed" discussion of interests vested in the perpetuation of military preparedness. The next most easily supported conclusion would be that we have become trapped in the hell-fires of militarism by a sinister but concealed elite of military–industrial leaders, which through its puppets pulls the strings on every major policy decision. The latter theory is non-conformist, radical, and smacks too strongly of classical conspiracy theory to be palatable to most scholars. Indeed, the dominant attitude (explicit or tacit) in most of the literature of the early sixties was that there exists no military–industrial complex capable of preventing peace. It was claimed that the military–industrial complex operates as a subgroup within the limits of an essentially civilian society. This view sees the complex equating its own interests with those of the nation as a whole; but, it is argued, this tendency toward power aggrandizement is checked by countervailing interest blocs in society. Moreover, the complex is not seen as having a corrosive effect on democratic processes; even if it is conceded that military and technological expertise or well-financed public relations give the complex unusual privilege and visibility, it is argued that this is no different in principle from certain other influential groups, all of which are limited by the web of constraints that comprises a pluralist society. Usually it is added that the internal differences in the complex, such as differences among the separate services or between the military and the industrial procurement sectors, tend to restrict further its ability to impose a policy line on the United States. This point of view appears in scattered form throughout the literature.

Some important examples of this literature include *The Invisible Government* by Wise and Ross, *Power at the Pentagon* by Raymond, *Disarmament and the American Economy* edited by Benoit and Boulding, and *The Weapons Acquisition Process* by Peck and Scherer. Each points to a power bloc important in the determination of foreign policies, in the decision to move toward arms reduction or control, or in lobbying for increased defense expenditure. All acknowledge that some impediments to change are presented by the concentration of power in these groups, but none sees any one group sufficiently dominant to resist all forms of control or counter pressures from other segments of society.

None of these denials of irresponsible military–industrial power marshalls very significant evidence to support their views. Examples are given of specific conflicts between civilian and military groups in which the military lost (for example, the dismissal of General Walker for ultra–right-wing indoctrination of his troops, the refusal to be first to break the moratorium on nuclear weapons testing). Examples are given of heated divisions between the services over what military strategy should be pursued (the arguments over conventional warfare in the late fifties, and the more recent RS–70 controversy). Sociological studies reveal underlying diversities within single corporations, between competing corporations, and within the demographic and institutional character of each branch of the armed services.[5] And, throughout, American pluralism is cited as an automatic check against any elite group.[6]

At a more general level, these fragments of evidence point toward three grounds for denying that a military–industrial complex prevents peace:

1. It is held that the scope of decisions made by any interest group is quite narrow and cannot be said to govern anything so broad as foreign policy.
2. It is held that the complex is not monolithic, not self-conscious, and not coordinated, the presumed attributes of a ruling elite.
3. It is held that the military–industrial complex does not wield power if the term power is defined as the ability to realize one's will even against the resistance of others and regardless of external conditions.

These formulations, to repeat, are made neither explicitly nor consistently in the literature. But they crystallize the basic questions about definition which the literature raises. Moreover, they are quite definitely the major contentions of academic criticism of the power elite theory. The more widely read academic critics include Daniel Bell, Robert Dahl, and Talcott Parsons. Since their critiques are mainly directed at the work of C. Wright Mills, it is with Mills that we will begin to analyze the theories which claim that there *is* a military–industrial complex blocking peace.

[5] See Janowitz for a good sociological study of interservice differences.

[6] For the thesis that a "peacefare state" counterweighs a "warfare state," see Klaus Knorr's review of Fred J. Cook in the *Journal of Conflict Resolution* 7, no. 4 (December 1963). The "pluralist position," which usually says that the social system has semi-automatic checking mechanisms against tyranny, is basic in discussions not only of the military, but of economics and politics as well. See Robert Dahl, *Who Governs?*; John Kenneth Galbraith, *American Capitalism*; Seymour Martin Lipset, *Political Man*; Talcott Parsons, *The Social System*.

The Thesis of Elite Control

Mills is by far the most formidable exponent of the theory of a power elite. In his view, the period since World War II has been dominated in America by the ascendance of corporate and military elites to positions of institutional power. These "commanding heights" allow them to control the trends of the business cycle and of international relations. The cold war set the conditions which legitimize their ascendance, and the decline and incorporation of significant left–liberal movements, such as the CIO, symbolize the end of opposition forces. The power elite monopolizes sovereignty, in that political initiative and control stem mainly from the top hierarchical levels of position and imfluence. Through the communications system the elite facilitates the growth of a politically indifferent mass society below the powerful institutions. This, according to Mills's argument, explains why an observer finds widespread apathy. Only a small minority of the people believe in actual participation in the larger decisions which affect their existence, and only the ritual forms of "popular democracy" are practiced by the vast majority. Mills's argument is addressed to the terms of the three basic issues we have designated, that is, scope of decision power, awareness of common interest, and definition of power exerted.

By scope, we mean the sphere of society over which an elite is presumed to exercise power. Mills argues that the scope of this military–industrial elite is general, embracing all the decisions which in any way could be called vital (slump and boom, peace and war, and so on). He does not argue that each decision is directly determined, but rather that the political alternatives from which the "deciders" choose are shaped and limited by the elite through its possession of all the large-scale institutions. By this kind of argument, Mills avoids the need to demonstrate how his elite works during each decision. He speaks instead in terms of institutions and resources. But his basic evidence is rather negative: no major decisions in twenty years have been contrary to the policies of anti-communism and corporate or military aggrandizement; therefore a power elite must be prevailing. Mills might have improved his claims about the scope of elite decisions by analyzing a series of actual decisions in terms of the premises which were *not* debated. Such analysis could point to the mechanisms (implicit or explicit) which led to the exclusion of these premises from debate. By this and other means he might have found more satisfying evidence of the common, through perhaps tacit, presuppositions of seemingly disparate institutions. He might then have developed a framework analyzing "scope" on different levels. The scope of the Joint Chiefs of Staff, for instance, could be seen as limited, while at the time the Joint Chiefs could be included in a larger elite having larger scope. Whether this could be shown awaits research of this kind. Until then, however, Mills's theory of scope remains open to attack, but, conversely, is not subject to refutation.

Mills's theory also eludes the traditional requirements for inferring monolithic structure, that is, consciousness of elite status, and coordination. The modern tradition of viewing elites in this way began with Mosca's *The Ruling Class* in a period when family units and inheritance systems were the basic means of conferring power. Mills departs from this influential tradition precisely because of his emphasis on institutions as the basic elements of society. If the military, political, and economic institutional orders involve a high coincidence of interest, then the groups composing the institutional orders need not be monolithic, conscious, and coordinated, yet still they can exercise elite power.[7] This means specifically that a military–industrial complex could exist as an expression of a certain fixed ideology (reflecting common institutional needs), yet be composed of an endless shuffle of specific groups. For instance, 82 companies have dropped out of the list of 100 top defense contractors and only 36 "durables" remained on the list from 1940 to 1960. In terms of industry, the percentage of contracts going to the automotive industry has dropped from 25 percent in World War II to four percent in the missile age. At the same time, the aircraft companies grew from 34 to 54 percent of all contracts, and the electronics industry from 9 to 28 percent (Peck and Scherer 1962). Mills's most central argument is that this ebb and flow is not necessarily evidence for the pluralists. He stresses the unities which underlie the procession of competition and change. The decision to change the technology of warfare enabled one group to "overcome" another in an overall system to which both are fundamentally committed. Moreover, the decision issued from the laboratories and planning boards of the defense establishment and only superficially involved public opinion. Case studies of weapons development by Peck and Scherer, in which politics is described as a marginal ritual, would certainly buttress Mills's point of view.

The institution analysis enables Mills to make interesting comments on his human actors. The integration of institutions means that hundreds of individuals become familiar with several roles: general, politician, lobbyist, defense contractor. These men are the power elite, but they need not know it. They conspire, but conspiracy is not absolutely essential to their maintenance. They mix together easily, but can remain in power even if they are mostly anonymous to each other. They make decisions, large and small, sometimes with the knowledge of others and sometimes not, which ultimately control all the significant actions and resources of society.

Where Mills's approach tends to fall short is in its unclarity about how

---

[7] See James H. Meisel, *The Myth of the Ruling Class*, for the best available discussion of this innovation in theorizing about elites. For evidence on this theory see Ben Seligman's *The Potentates* and William Domhoff's *The Inner Circles*.

discontinuities arise. Is the military–industrial complex a feature of American society which can disappear and still leave the general social structure intact? Horst Brand has suggested a tension between financial companies and the defense industries because of the relatively few investment markets created by defense (1962). Others have challenged the traditional view that defense spending stimulates high demand and employment. They claim that the concentration of contracts in a few states, the monopolization of defense and space industry by the largest 75 or 100 corporations, the low multiplier effect of the new weapons, the declining numbers of blue-collar workers required, and other factors make the defense economy more a drag than a stimulant (Melman 1963; Etzioni 1964). Certainly the rising unemployment of 1970 in the midst of expansion of the ABM system and extension of the Vietnam war to Laos and Cambodia show the flaws of relying on defense spending as an economic stimulant. Mills died before these trends became the subject of debate, but he might have pioneered in that debate if his analytic categories had differentiated more finely between various industries and interest groups in his power elite. His emphasis was almost entirely on the "need" for a "permanent war economy" just when that need was being questioned, even among his elite.

However, this failure does not necessarily undermine the rest of Mills's analysis. His institutional analysis is still the best means of identifying a complex without calling it monolithic, conscious, and coordinated. Had he differentiated more exactly he might have been able to describe various degrees of commitment to an arms race, a rightist ideology constricting the arena of meaningful debate, and other characteristics of a complex. More exact analysis has yet to be done; we shall discuss it later in this book.

Mills's theory is most awkward in its assertion that the elite can, and does, make its decisions against the will of others and regardless of external conditions. This way of looking at power is inherited by Mills, and by much of modern sociology, directly from Max Weber. A rather fantastic quality is attributed to the elite: literal omnipotence. Conversely, any group that is not always able to realize its will even against the resistance of others is only "influential" but not an elite. Mills attempts to defend this viewpoint but, in essence, modifies it. He says he is describing a tendency, not a final state of affairs. This is a helpful device for explaining cracks in the monolith —for instance, the inability of the elite to establish a full corporate state against the will of small businessmen. However, it does not change the ultimate argument—that the power elite cannot become more than a tendency, cannot realize its actual self, unless it takes on the quality of omnipotence.

When power is defined as this kind of dominance, it is easily open to critical dispute. The conception of power depicts a vital and complex social system as essentially static, as having within it a set of stable governing components, with precharted interests which infiltrate and control every outpost of decision authority. Thereby, internal accommodation is made necessary and significant change, aside from growth, becomes impossible. This concept goes beyond the idea of social or economic determinism. In fact, it defines a "closed social system." A closed system may be a dramatic image, but it is a forced one as well. Its defender sees events such as the rise of the labor movement essentially as a means of rationalizing modern capitalism. True or false as this may be, did not the labor movement also constitute a "collective will" which the elite could not resist? An accommodation was reached, probably more on the side of capital than of labor, but the very term *accommodation* implies the existence of more than one independent will. On a world scale, this becomes even more obvious. Certainly the rise of communism has not been through the will of capitalists; Mills would be the first to agree to that. Nor does the elite fully control technological development; surely the process of invention has some independent, even if minor, place in the process of social change.

Mills's definition of power as dominance ironically serves the pluralist argument, rather than countering it. When power is defined so extremely, it becomes rather easy to claim that such power is curbed in the contemporary United States. The pluralists can say that Mills has conjured up a bogeyman to explain his own failure to realize his will. Indeed, they have said just that in review after review of Mills's writings. A leading pluralist thinker, Edward Shils, says that Mills was too much influenced by Trotsky and Kafka:

> Power, although concentrated, is not so concentrated, so powerful or so permeative as Professor Mills seems to believe.... There have been years in Western history, e.g., in Germany during the last years of the Weimar Republic and under the Nazis when reality approximated this picture more closely.... But as a picture of Western societies, and not just as an ideal type of extreme possibilities which might be realized if so much else that is vital were lacking, it will not do. (Shils 1961)

But is Mills's definition of power the only suitable one here? If it is, then the pluralists have won the debate. But if there is a way to designate an irresponsible elite without giving it omnipotence, then the debate may at least be recast.

The fundamental question of the definition of power is not answered in the other major books which affirm the existence of a military–industrial complex. Cook's *The Warfare State*, Perlo's *Militarism and Industry*, and several more recent works are good examples of this literature which is theoretically inferior to Mills's perplexing account.

Cook's volume has been pilloried severely by deniers of the military–industrial complex. At least it has the merit of creating discussion by virtue of being one of the few dissenting books distributed widely on a commercial basis. It suffers, however, from many of the unclarities typical of the deniers. Its title assumes a warfare state while its evidence, although rich, is only a compilation of incidents, pronouncements, and trends, lacking any framework for weighing and measuring. From Cook's writing several hypotheses can be extracted about the "face of the Warfare State," all of them suggestive but none of them conclusive: (1) the Department of Defense owns more property than any other organization in the world;[8] (2) between 60 and 70 percent of the national budget is consistently allocated to defense or defense-related expenditures; (3) the military and big business have an inevitable meeting of minds over the billions of dollars in contracts the one has to order and the other to fulfill; (4) the 100 top corporations monopolize three-fourths of the contracts, 85 percent of which are awarded without competition; (5) as much as one-third of all production and service indirectly depends on defense; and (6) business and other conservative groups, even though outside the defense establishment, benefit from the warfare emphasis because it subordinates the welfare state, which is an anathema to them (pp. 20–24, 162–202).

There is no doubt that Cook's data have held up during the years since his book was written. The federal budget of $154.9 billion for fiscal year 1971 assigns 64.8 cents of every tax dollar to the cost of past and present wars and war preparation. Vietnam war costs are concealed in the 48.4 cents per dollar for current military expenditures. Veterans' benefits and national debt interest are also sizeable items. The Nixon administration claims that 41 percent of its budget is for human resources. That figure, however, includes trust funds like social security (for which the government is merely a caretaker), veterans' benefits, and even the Selective Service System. The actual human resources figure is 17 percent, indicating that welfare is still being crushed by warfare (Senator Mark Hatfield, address, Feb. 10, 1970, Corvallis, Oregon).

Cook's work much more than Mills's is open to the counter-argument that no monolithic, semi-conspiratorial elite exists. Even Cook's definitions of vested interests are crude and presumed. Moreover, he suffers far more than Mills from a failure to differentiate between groups. For instance, there is nothing in his book (written in 1962) that would explain the economic drag of defense spending, which Cook preceptively observed in a 1963 *Nation* article, "The Coming Politics of Disarmament." In 1962 he wrote that big business was being fattened off war contracts, but the next year that the "prolonged arms race has started, at last, to commit a form of

---

[8] Swomley (1964) accounts for Department of Defense holdings equivalent in size to eight states of the United States. Kenneth Boulding, using personnel as well as property criteria, calls the Department of Defense the world's third largest socialist state (personal discussion, 1963).

economic hara-kiri." Hara-kiri does not happen spontaneously; it is a culmi-
nation of long-developing abnormalities. That Cook could not diagnose
them before they became common in congressional testimony illustrates the
lack of refinement in his 1962 analysis. Cook's failure is that he visualizes
a monolith, obscuring the strains that promote new trends and configura-
tions.

It is because of his attention to strains that Perlo's book is useful.
Perlo draws interesting connections between the largest industrial corporations and the defense economy, finding that defense accounts for 12 percent
of the profits of the 25 largest firms. He adds that foreign investment
creates a further propensity toward a large defense system, and he calculates
that military business and foreign investments combined total 40 percent
of the aggregate profits among the top 25 firms. He draws deeper connections between companies and the major financial groups controlling their
assets.

Such an analysis begins to reveal important disunities within the business community. For instance, it can be seen that the Rockefellers are
increasing their direct military investments while maintaining their largest
foreign holdings in extremely volatile Middle Eastern and Latin American
companies. The Morgans are involved in domestic industries of a rather
easy-to-convert type, and their main foreign holdings are in the safer European countries, although they too have unsafe mining interests in Latin
America and Africa. The First National City Bank, while it has large
holdings in Latin American sugar and fruit, has a more technical relationship with its associated firms than the stockholder relationship. The Mellons
have sizeable oil holdings in Kuwait, but on the whole they are less involved
in defense than the other groups. The DuPonts, traditionally the major
munitions makers, have "diversified" into the overextended aerospace and
plutonium industries, but their overseas holdings are heavily in Europe.
Certain other groups with financial holdings, such as Young and Eaton
interests in Cleveland, have almost no profit stake in defense or foreign
investments. On the other hand, some of the new wealth in Los Angeles
is deeply committed to the aerospace industry.

Perlo makes several differentiations of this sort, including the use of
foreign-policy statements by leading industrial groups. But he does not have
a way to predict the conditions under which a given company would actively
support economic shifts away from the arms race. These and other gaps,
however, are not nearly as grave as his failure to analyze other components
of the military–industrial complex.[9] He makes no attempt to include politi-

---

[9] In an earlier book, *The Empire of High Finance* (1957), Perlo documented
the close relations of the major financial groups and the political executive. He did
not, however, extend this analysis to congressmen and senators, nor did he offer
sufficient comparative evidence to demonstrate a long-term pattern.

cians, military groups, and other forces in a "map" of the military–industrial complex which he believes exists. Perhaps this is partly because of the book's intent, which is to document profiteering by arms contractors; nonetheless, his book is not theoretically enlightening about the question we are posing. Nor does it refute the pluralist case. In fact, it contains just the kind of evidence that pluralists currently employ to demonstrate the absence of a monolith.

The newer literature, written since 1965, gives a somewhat more penetrating glimpse into the extent of the merger of the military and the defense industry. Lapp, *The Weapons Culture*, Weidenbaum, "Arms and the American Economy," Galbraith, *The New Industrial State*, and Knoll and McFadden, *American Militarism 1970*, all show the heavy involvement of the Department of Defense with the corporate giants. The two most striking recent works which provide the most concrete detail on the operation of this military–industrial network are Seymour Melman's *Pentagon Capitalism* (1970) and Richard Barnet's *The Economy of Death* (1969). Both are well written and a must for any serious student of contemporary policy. *Pentagon Capitalism* describes the network as a giant enterprise controlled by the civilian defense establishment, or "state-management." Through the elaboration of government controls over the firms that carry out defense contracts, the Defense Department's role has changed from that of customer to that of administrator over a far-flung empire of defense production. The Pentagon is able to divert capital and scientific and technical manpower to its own purposes, drawing resources away from productive activity to what Melman calls economically parasitic activity. He holds that the prime goal of the "state-management" is to enlarge its decision power. Thus wars, once begun, tend to expand; "security gaps" are invented, causing weapons systems to grow in size and sophistication; and international arms sales increase.

Barnet (*The Economy of Death*) sees the military–industrial complex as more decentralized, like a machine with several separate parts that run together smoothly. Each institution that makes up the complex acts for its own purposes, and all contribute to justifying and maintaining the irrational and dangerous growth of military capability. Barnet documents the interchangeability of personnel between industry and the military. A major strength of Barnet's work is his willingness to be specific, to give the key names from those in his study of 400 top decision makers who come from a handful of law firms and executive suites "in shouting distance of one another in fifteen city blocks in New York, Washington, Detroit, Chicago and Boston." Many of the names are commonly known (although the extent of their financial-world connections is not)—Charles Wilson, Neil McElroy, Robert Anderson, George Humphrey, Douglas Dillon, John McCone, Adolphe Berle, Averell Harriman, William C. Foster, John McCloy, Robert

McNamara, Roswell Gilpatric, James Douglas, William Rogers, and Nelson Rockefeller. Men such as these are systematically recruited into top cabinet posts and become "National Security Managers." Their common backgrounds, even to membership in the same elite social clubs, assure a measure of homogeneity for their task of defining who or what threatens this nation and what should be done about it. Their views on the national interest reflect their own success in judicious management of risk in the business world. Barnet's assumption about the homogeneity of this "club" is supported by Domhoff's "Who Made American Foreign Policy, 1945–1963?" It is clear that a man like William Rogers, with the right background but no particular knowledge or background in foreign affairs, can be made secretary of state while a civil rights leader, Martin Luther King, was admonished by official spokesmen for taking a position against the Vietnam war.

Barnet believes that the ongoing mechanisms of the system keep it moving in old paths. The evils are not incidental, he says, but built into the system. Military solutions to international problems seem more reliable and "tougher" than diplomatic solutions, and they are backed up by millions of dollars' worth of "scientific research"; so military solutions are preferred even by civilian defense officials. The military, the civilian defense establishment, and defense contractors constantly work together to develop new weapon systems to meet defense "needs"; they feed one another's ideologies, and costlier, more elaborate weapons result. It is difficult and expensive for military contractors to convert to peacetime production, so they have done virtually no planning for conversion, and many have abandoned all interest in such planning. Perhaps most important for Barnet, those in power see America's chief purpose as consolidating and extending American power around the world; military technology is an indispensable tool for that purpose. Whether this collection of civilian managers is really in control or whether it is merely serving a more powerful military bureaucracy is the point at issue; Barnet leans toward the view of the ascendence of the relatively smooth-working military hierarchy. Domhoff, using very similar evidence, places the aristocratic economic elite at the top of the pinnacle.

Melman, in particular, presents a strong case that militarism in the United States is no longer an example of civilian corporate interests dictating for the country a military role in order to produce hardware for profit from the government-consumer and to defend the outposts of capitalism. Instead, he feels that the system is led by the military managers for their own interests in power; it is a state socialism whose defense officials dictate the terms of policy, and of profits, to their subsidiary corporations. Melman supports his case by the observation that not only the personnel but also the actual operating procedures demonstrate that the Defense Department and the corporations that serve it have interpenetrated one another's operations

—to such an extent that there is for all practical purposes really only one organization. The horrible example which comes to mind is that of the rise of Hitler, which was first backed and promoted by industrialists who later lost their measure of control over an uncontrollable military machine. Melman's thesis differs from both the pluralist doctrine, which sees various groups competing for power, and the Marxist doctrine, which sees the greed of the capitalists as the prime mover. In Melman's convincing analysis the military is fast becoming king.

Melman's analysis may yet prove true. For the present, however, corporate capitalism has fared too well to alleviate all suspicions of the hidden hand. The new interlocking industrial conglomerates like Litton, Textron, and General Dynamics, and the main financial houses of the United States, provide an inner core whose interests are permanently protected even as individual corporations prosper or falter. For such centers of elite power, which Barnett shows to be the main source of top Defense Department and other foreign policy–appointed officials, the terms of the military merger have been highly beneficial. The benefits must be seen not only in profits but in the retention of the entire profit-making system against the demands of a hungry and impatient world. Melman speaks of the drive of the new technocratic military bureaucracy to increase its power and control, but deemphasizes the interests this power is protecting. Barnet specifies the community of interest and outlook among the corporate decision managers who are recruited into the inner circles of foreign policy, but does not state explicitly what beliefs lie at the core of the practices which are thereby promoted.

Both Barnet and Melman believe that American militarism is a function of institutions directly involved with defense. It can be argued, on the other hand, that a description of something called a military–industrial complex should include all the power centers of American society. Directorates of the major defense contractors are not separable from those of industries geared primarily to the production of consumer goods. Neither are the consumer industries independent of military and diplomatic actions which protect international marketing advantages. Barnet himself notes that not only that faction of the labor movement directly employed in defense industries, but organized labor in general is a political supporter of military–industrial power. The universities are heavily involved in defense interests, as is the complex of oils, highways, and automotives. Even in education the armed services' Project 100,000 has inducted a large number of former draft rejects for resocialization and basic educational development (followed by two years of applied study abroad in Vietnam for the successful graduates) (Little 1968; Pilisuk 1968).

Barnet and Melman deal incompletely with the relationship of the sector they regard as the military–industrial complex to the rest of society.

Both realize the tremendous power of the military, the civilian defense officials, and the defense industry combined. They are aware that the defense establishment has a powerful hold on public opinion through the public's fear of enemy attack and through defense control over a larger sector of the work force. Yet they seem to hope this power can be curbed by a loud enough public outcry. In the last analysis they too believe that the defense establishment has merely been allowed to grow out of hand, and that now the exercise of some countervailing power may bring sanity back into American policy and make peace possible.

Revising the Criteria
for Inferring Power

We have found fault with so many books and divergent viewpoints that the most obvious conclusion is that current social theory is deficient in its explanation of power. We concur with one of Mills's severest critics, Daniel Bell, who at least agrees with Mills that most current analysis concentrates on the "intermediate sectors," for example, parties, interest groups, formal structures, without attempting to view the underlying system of "renewable power independent of any momentary group of actors" (Bell 1964). However, we have indicated that the only formidable analysis of the underlying system of renewable power, that of Mills, has profound shortcomings because of its definition of power. Therefore, before we can offer our own answer to the question, "Is there a military–industrial complex which blocks peace?" we must return to the question of power itself in American society.

We have agreed essentially with the pluralist claim that ruling-group models do not "fit" the American structure. We have classified Mills's model as that of a ruling group because of his Weberian definition of power, but we have noted also that Mills successfully escaped two traps common to elite theories, namely, that the elite is total in the scope of its decisions, and that the elite is a coordinated monolith.

But perhaps we have not stressed sufficiently that the alternative case supporting pluralism inadequately describes the historical dynamics of American society. The point of our dissent from pluralism is over the doctrine of "countervailing power." This is the modern version of Adam Smith's economics and of the Madisonian or Federalist theory of checks and balances, adapted to the new circumstances of large-scale organizations. The evidence for it is composed of self-serving incidents and a faith in semi-mystical resources. For instance, in the sphere of political economy, it is argued that oligopoly contains automatic checking mechanisms against undue corporate growth, and that the factors of public opinion and corporate conscience are additional built-in limiting forces.[10] We believe that evidence from the field, however, suggests that oligopoly is a means of stabilizing an industrial sphere either through tacit agreements to follow price leadership or through rigged agreements in the case of custom-made goods; that "public opinion" tends much more to be manipulated and apathetic than independently critical; that "corporate conscience" is less suitable as a description than is Reagan's term, *corporate arrogance.*

To take the more immediate example of the military sphere, the pluralist claim is that the military is subordinate to broader civilian interests. The first problem with that statement is the ambiguity of the term *civilian*. Is it clear that military men are more "militaristic" than civilians? To say so would be to deny the increasing trend of white-collar militarism. The top strategists in the Department of Defense, the Central Intelligence Agency, and key advisory positions are often Ph.D.'s. In fact, "civilians" including McGeorge Bundy, Robert Kennedy, James Rostow, and Robert McNamara are mainly responsible for the development of the only remaining "heroic" form of combat: counter-insurgency operations in the jungles of the underdeveloped countries. If "militarism"[11] has permeated this deeply into the "civilian" sphere, then the distinction between the terms becomes largely nominal.

The intrusion of civilian professors into the military arena has been most apparent in more than 300 universities and non-profit research institutions which supply personnel to and rely upon contracts from the Department of Defense. About half these centers were created to do specialized strategic research. One of these, the RAND Corporation, was set up by Douglas Aviation and the Air Force to give "prestige type support for favored Air Force proposals" (Friedman 1963). When RAND strategy experts Wohlstetter and Dinerstein discovered a mythical "missile gap" and an equally unreal preemptive war strategy in Soviet post-Sputnik policy, they paved the way for the greatest military escalation of the cold war era, the missile race.

Civilian strategists have frequently retained an exasperating measure of autonomy from the services which support them. Such conflicts reached a peak when both the Skybolt and the RS–70 projects met their demise under the "cost effectiveness" program designed by Harvard economist Charles Hitch (then with RAND, later Defense Department comptroller,

---

[10] For this argument, see A. A. Berle, *The Twentieth Century Capitalist Revolution*, and J. K. Galbraith, *American Capitalism*. For sound criticisms, but without sound alternatives, see Mills's and Perlo's books. Also see Michael Reagan, *The Managed Economy* (1963), and Bernard Nossiter, *The Mythmakers* (1964), for other refutations of the countervailing power thesis.

[11] We are defining the term as "primary reliance on coercive means, particularly violence or the threat of violence, to deal with social problems."

now president of the University of California). That the opinions of civilian and military planners of military policy sometimes differ does not detract from the argument. What must be stressed is that the apparent flourishing of such civilian agencies as RAND (it earned over 20 million dollars in 1962, with all the earnings going into expansion, and spawned the non-profit Systems Development Corporation whose annual earnings exceed 50 million dollars) is no reflection of countervailing power. The doctrine of controlled response, which dictated the end of the RS–70, served the general aspirations of each of the separate services, of the Polaris and Minuteman stable deterrent factions, of the brush fire or limited war proponents, of the guerrilla war and paramilitary operations advocates, and of the counterforce adherents. It is a doctrine of versatility intended to leave the widest range of military options for retaliation and escalation in United States hands. It can hardly be claimed as victory against military thought. The in-fighting may have been intense, but the area of consensus between military and civilian factions was still great.

Consensus

Countervailing power is simply the relationship between groups which fundamentally accept "the American system" but which compete for advantages within it. The corporate executive wants higher profits, the laborer a higher wage. The president wants the final word on military strategies, the chairman of the Joint Chiefs does not trust him with it. Boeing wants the contract, but General Dynamics is closer at the time to the Navy secretary and the president, and so on. What is prevented by countervailing forces is the domination of society by a group, a clique, or a party. But this process suggests a profoundly important point: that *the constant pattern in American society is the rise and fall of temporarily irresponsible groups.* By temporary we mean that, except for the largest industrial conglomerates,[12] the groups that wield significant power to influence policy decisions are not guaranteed stability. By irresponsible we mean that many activities within their scope are essentially unaccountable in the democratic process. These groups are too uneven to be described with the shorthand term *class.* Their personnel have many different characteristics (compare IBM executives with the Southern Dixiecrats), and their needs as groups are different enough to cause endless fights; for example, between small and big business. No one group or coalition of several groups can tyrannize the rest. This is demonstrated, for example, by the changing status of the major financial groups; for example, the Bank of America, which

---

[12] The term refers to industrial organizations like Textron and Ling–Temco–Vought which have holdings in every major sector of American industry.

grew rapidly, built on the financial needs of the previously neglected small consumer.

However, these groups clearly exist within consensus relationships more general and durable than their conflict relationships. This is true, first of all, of their social characteristics. In an earlier version of this chapter we compiled tables using data from an exhaustive study of American elites contained in Warner et al., *The American Federal Executive* (1963) and from Suzanne Keller's compilation of military, economic, political, and diplomatic elite survey materials in *Beyond the Ruling Class* (1963). The relevant continuities demonstrated by the data suggest an educated elite with largely Protestant, business-oriented origins. Moreover, the data suggest inbreeding with the result that business orientation has probably been at least maintained, if not augmented, by marriage. Domhoff, in *Who Rules America?*, has shown that elites generally attend the same exclusive prep schools and universities and belong to the same exclusive gentlemen's clubs. The consistencies suggest orientations not unlike those found in an examination of the editorial content of major business newspapers and weeklies, and in more directly sampled assessments of elite opinions.[13]

Other evidence for consensus relationships, besides attitude and background data indicating a pro-business sympathy, would come from an examination of the practice of decision making. By analyzing actual behavior we can understand which consensus attitudes are reflected in decision making. Here, in retrospect, it is possible to discover the values and assumptions which are recurrently defended. This is at least a rough means of finding the boundaries of consensus relationships. Often these boundaries are invisible because of the very infrequency with which they are tested. What are visible most of the time are the parameters of conflict relationships among different groups. These conflict relationships constitute the ingredients of experience, which gives individuals or groups their uniqueness and variety, while the consensus relationships constitute the common underpinnings of behavior. Social scientists have tended to study decision making in order to study group differences; we need to study decision making also to understand group commonalities.

Were such studies done, our hypothesis would be that certain "core beliefs" are never questioned. One of these beliefs, undoubtedly, would be that efficacy is preferable to principle in foreign affairs. In practice, this means that violence is preferable to nonviolence as a means of defense. A second belief is that private property is preferable to collective property. A third assumption is that the particular form of constitutional government practiced within the United States is preferable to any other system of government. We refer to that preferred mode as limited parliamentary demo-

---

[13] For some interesting work about the attitudes of business and military elites see Angell 1964; Bauer et al. 1963; Eells and Walton 1961; and Singer 1964.

cracy, a system in which institutionalized forms of direct representation are carefully retained, but with fundamental limitations on the prerogatives of governing. Specifically included among the limitations are many matters encroaching on corporation property and state hegemony. While adherence to this form of government is conceivably the strongest of the domestic "core values," at least among business elites, it is probably the least strongly held of the three on the international scene. American relations with, and assistance to, authoritarian and semi-feudal regimes indicate that the recipient regime is evaluated primarily on the two former assumptions and given rather extensive leeway on the latter one.

The implications of these "core beliefs" for the social system are immense, for they justify the maintenance of our largest institutional structures: the military, the corporate economy, and a system of partisan politics that protects the concept of limited democracy. These institutions, in turn, may be seen as current agencies of the more basic social structure. The "renewable basis of power" in America at the present time underlies those institutional orders linked in consensus relationships: military defense of private property and parliamentary democracy. These institutional orders are, by definition, not permanently secure. Their maintenance involves a continuous coping with new conditions, such as with technological innovation and with the inherent instabilities of a social structure which arbitrarily classifies persons by role, status, access to resources, and power. The myriad groups composing these orders are even less secure because of their weak ability to command "coping resources"; for example, the service branches are less stable than the institution of the military, particular companies are less stable than the institutions of corporate property, political parties are less stable than the institution of parliamentary government.

In the United States there is no ruling group. Nor is there any easily discernible ruling institutional order, so meshed have the separate sources of elite power become. But there is a social structure organized to create and protect power centers with only partial accountability. In our definition of power, we avoid the Weber–Mills meaning of *omnipotence* and the contrary pluralist definition of power as consistently *diffuse*. We are describing the current system as one of overall "minimal accountability" and "minimal consent." We mean that the role of democratic review, based on genuine popular consent, is made marginal and reactive. Elite groups are minimally accountable to publics and have a substantial, though by no means maximum, freedom to shape popular attitudes. The reverse of our system would be one in which democratic participation was the orienting demand around which the social structure was organized.

Some will counter this case by saying that we are measuring "reality" against an "ideal," a technique which permits the conclusion that the social structure is undemocratic according to its distance from our utopian values.

This is a convenient apology for the present system, of course. We think it possible, at least in theory, to develop measures of the undemocratic in democratic conditions, and place given social structures at positions along a continuum. These measures, in rough form, might include such variables as economic security, education, legal guarantees, access to information, and participatory control over systems of economy, government, and jurisprudence.

The reasons why a chapter reviewing the power of a purported military–industrial complex should be concerned with democratic process are twofold. First, just as scientific method both legitimizes and promotes change in the world of knowledge, democratic method legitimizes and promotes change in the world of social institutions. Every society, regardless of how democratic it is, protects its core institutions in a web of widely shared values. But if the core institutions should be dictated by the requisites of military preparedness, then restrictions on the democratic process, that is, restrictions on mass opinion exchange (as by voluntary or imposed news management) or on decision-making bodies (as by selecting participants in a manner guaranteeing exclusion of certain positions), would be critical obstacles to peace.

Second, certain elements of democratic process are inimical to features of a military-oriented society, and the absence of these elements offers one type of evidence for the existence of a military–industrial complex even in the absence of a ruling elite. Secretary of Defense Robert McNamara made the point amply clear in his 1961 testimony before the Senate Armed Services Committee:

> Why should we tell Russia that the Zeus development may not be satisfactory? What we ought to be saying is that we have the most perfect anti-ICBM system that the human mind will ever devise. Instead the public domain is already full of statements that the Zeus may not be satisfactory, that it has deficiencies. I think it is absurd to release that level of information. (Military Procurement Authorization, Fiscal Year 1962)

Under subsequent questioning McNamara attempted to clarify his statement, saying that he wished only to delude Russian, not American, citizens about United States might. Exactly how this might be done was not explained.

A long established tradition of "executive privilege" permits the president to refuse to release information when, in his opinion, its release would be damaging to the national interest. Under modern conditions responsibility for handling strategic information is shared among military, industrial, and executive agencies. Discretion over when to withhold what information must also be shared. Moreover, the existence of a perpetual danger makes the justification, "in this time of national crisis," suitable to every occasion in which secrecy must be justified. McNamara's statement, cited above, referred not to a crisis in Cuba or Vietnam but rather to the perpetual state of cold war crisis. Since the decision about what is to be released and when is subject to just such management, the media have become dependent on the agencies for timely leaks and major stories. This not only gives an aura of omniscience to the agencies, but also gives them the power to reward "good" journalists and punish critical ones.

The issues involved in the question of news management involve more than the controls available to the president, the State Department, the Department of Defense, the Central Intelligence Agency, the Atomic Energy Commission, or any of the major defense contractors. Outright control of news flow is probably less pervasive than voluntary acquiescence to the objectives of these prominent institutions of our society. Nobody has to tell the wire services when to release a story on the bearded dictator of our hemisphere, or the purported brutality of Ho Chi Minh. The devil image of the enemy has become a press tradition. In addition to a sizeable quantity of radio and television programming and spot time purchased directly by the Pentagon, an amount of service valued at $6 million by *Variety* is donated annually by the networks and by public relations agencies for various military shows (Swomley 1959). Again, the pluralistic shell of an independent press or broadcasting media is left hollow by the absence of a countervailing social force of any significant power.

We listed earlier several shared premises unquestioned by any potent locus of institutionalized power:

1. Efficacy is preferable to principle in foreign affairs (thus military means are chosen over nonviolent means).
2. Private property is preferable to public property.
3. Limited parlimentary democracy is preferable to any other system of government.

At issue is the question of whether an America protecting such assumptions can exist in a world of enduring peace. Three preconditions for enduring peace must be held up against these premises. The first is that enduring peace will first require or will soon generate disarmament. Offset programs, or plans for reallocation of the defense dollar, require a degree of coordinated planning for the change that is inconsistent with the working assumption that "private property is preferable to public property" in a corporate economy.

The available projections regarding offset programs, especially regional and local offset programs, necessary to maintain economic well-being in the face of disarmament in this country highlight two important features. One is the lag time in industrial conversion. The second is the need for coordination in the timing and spacing of programs. One cannot reinvest in new home building in an area which has just been deserted by its major industry and left a ghost town. The short-term and long-term offset values of new hospitals and educational facilities will differ in the building and use stages, and regional offset programs have demonstrable interregional effects (Reiner 1964). Plans requiring large-scale worker mobility will require a central bank of job information and a smooth system for its dissemination. Such coordination will require a degree of centralization and control beyond that which our assumption regarding the primacy of private property would permit. Gross intransigence has already been seen even in contingency planning for non-defense work by single firms like Sperry Rand, which have already been severely hurt by project cutbacks. And the prospect of contingency planning will not be warmly welcomed by the new aeroframe industry (which is only 60 percent convertible to needs of a peacetime society) (McDonagh and Zimmerman 1964). Private planning by an individual firm for its own future does occur; however, without coordinated plans, the length of time ahead for which we can accurately forecast market conditions remains smaller than the lag time for major retooling. A lag time of six to ten years would not be atypical before plans of a somewhat over-specialized defense contractor could result in retooling for production in a peacetime market. In the meantime, technological innovations, government fiscal or regulatory policies, shifts in consumer preferences, or decisions by other firms to enter that same market could well make the market vanish. Moreover, the example of defense firms that have attempted even the smaller step toward diversification presents a picture which is not entirely promising (Fearon and Hook 1964). Indeed, one of several reasons for the failures in this endeavor has been that marketing skills necessary to compete in a private-enterprise economy have been lost by the industrial giants who have been managing with a sales force of one or two retired generals to deal with the firm's only customer. Even if successful conversion by some firms were to serve as the model for all individual attempts, the collective result would be poor. To avoid a financially disastrous glutting of limited markets, some coordinated planning will be needed.

The intransigence regarding public or collaborative planning occurs against a backdrop of an increasing army of unemployed youth and aged, as well as of regional armies of unemployed victims of automation. Whether work is defined in traditional job market terms or as anything worthwhile that a person can do with his life, work (and some means of livelihood) will have to be found for these people. Much work needs to be done in community services, education, public health, and recreation, but this is people work, not product work. The lack of a countervailing force prevents the major reallocation of human and economic resources from the sector defined as preferable by the most potent institutions of society. One point must be stressed. We are *not* saying that limited planning to cushion the impact of arms reduction is impossible. Indeed, it is going on, and with the apparent blessing of the Department of Defense (Barber 1963). We are saying that accommodation to a cutback of $9 billion in research and development and $16 billion in military procurement requires a type of preparation not consistent with the three unchallenged assumptions.

Even the existence of facilities for coordinated planning does not, to be sure, guarantee the success of such planning. Bureaucratic institutions, designed as they may be for coordination and control, set up internal resistance to the very coordination they seek to achieve. The mechanisms for handling bureaucratic intransigency usually rely on such techniques as bringing participants into the process of formulating the decisions which will affect their own behavior. We can conceive of no system of coordinated conversion planning which could function without full and motivated cooperation from the major corporations, the larger unions, and representatives of smaller business and industry. Unfortunately, it is just as difficult to conceive of a system which would assure this necessary level of participation and cooperation. The same argument cuts deeper still when we speak of the millions of separate individuals in the "other America" whose lives would be increasingly "administered" by the centralized planning needed to offset a defense economy. Job assignments to distant geographical locations, vocational retraining programs, development of housing projects to meet minimal standards, educational enrichment programs—all of the programs conceived by middle class white America for racially mixed low income groups face the same difficulty in execution of their plans. Unless they can participate directly in the formulation of the programs, the target populations are less likely to participate in the programs and more likely to continue feeling alienated from the social system which views them as an unfortunate problem rather than as contributing members. Considering the need for active participation in real decisions, every step of coordinated planning carries with it the responsibility for an equal step in the direction of participatory democracy. This means that the voice of the unemployed urban worker may have to be heard, not only in city council meetings to discuss policy on rat control in his dwelling, but also in decisions about where a particular major corporation will be relocated and where the major resource allocations of the country will be invested. That such decision participation would run counter to the consensus on the items of limited parliamentary democracy and private property is exactly the point we wish to make.

Just as the theoretical offset plans can be traced to the sources of power with which they conflict, so too can the theoretical plans for international governing and peace-keeping operations be shown to conflict with the unquestioned beliefs. United States consent to international jurisdiction in the settlement of claims deriving from the nationalization of American overseas holdings or the removal of American military installations is almost inconceivable. Moreover, the mode of American relations to less developed countries is so much a part of the operations of those American institutions which base their existence on interminable conflict with communism that the contingency in which the United States might have to accept international jurisdiction in these areas seems unreal. For example, Mexican offers to mediate with Cuba are bluntly rejected. Acceptance of such offers would have called into question not one but all three of the assumptions in the core system. International jurisdictional authority might institutionalize a means to call the beliefs into question. For this reason (but perhaps most directly because of our preference for forceful means) America has been preoccupied, in negotiations regarding the extension of international control, almost exclusively with controls over weaponry and police operations and not at all with controls over political or social justice.[14]

The acceptance of complete international authority even in the area of weaponry poses certain inconsistencies with the preferred core beliefs. Nonviolent settlement of Asian–African area conflicts would be slow and ineffective in protecting American interests. The elimination, however, of military preparedness, both for projected crises and for their potential escalation, requires a faith in alternate means of conflict resolution. The phasing of the American plan for general and complete disarmament says in effect: prove that the alternatives are as efficient as our arms in protection of our interests and then we will disarm. In the short term, however, the effectiveness of force always looks greater.

The state of world peace is affected by people's comparison of themselves with persons who have more of the benefits of industrialization than they do. Such comparisons increase the demand for rapid change. While modern communications heighten the pressures imposed by such comparisons, the actual disparities revealed by comparison promote violence. Population growth rates, often as high as 3 percent, promise that population will double within a single generation in countries least able to provide for their people. The absolute number of illiterates as well as the absolute number of starving persons is greater now than ever before in history. Foreign aid barely offsets the disparity between declining prices paid for the underdeveloped countries' prime export commodities and rising prices paid for the finished products imported into these countries (Horowitz 1962). All schemes for tight centralized planning employed by these countries to rationally accrue and disperse scarce capital are blocked by the unchallenged assumptions on private property and limited parliamentary democracy. A restatement of the principle came in the report of General Lucius Clay's

---

[14] An objective account of the major disarmament negotiations may be found in Frye (1963).

committee on foreign aid. The report stated that the United States should not assist foreign governments "in projects establishing government owned industrial and commercial enterprises which compete with existing private endeavors." When Congressman Broomfield's amendment on foreign aid resulted in the cancellation of a United States promise to India to build a steel mill in Bokaro, Broomfield stated the case succinctly: "The main issue is private enterprise vs. state socialism" (*Atlantic Monthly*, September 1964, p. 6). Moreover, preference for forceful solutions assures that the capital now invested in preparedness will not be allocated in a gross way to the needs of underdeveloped countries. Instead, the manifest crises periodically erupting in violence justify further the need for reliance upon military preparedness.

We agree fully with an analysis by Lowi (1964) distinguishing types of decisions over which elite-like forces seem to hold control (redistributive) from other types in which pluralist powers battle for their respective interests (distributive). In distributive decisions the pie is large and the fights are over who gets how much. Factional strife within and among military, industrial, and political forces in our country are largely of this nature. In redistributive decisions the factions coalesce, for the pie itself is threatened. We have been arguing that the transition to peace is a process of redistributive decision.

Is there, then, a military–industrial complex which prevents peace? The answer is inextricably embedded in American institutions and mores. Our concept is not that American society contains a ruling military–industrial complex. It is more nearly that American society *is* a military–industrial complex. The complex can accommodate a wide range a factional interests, from those concerned with the production or use of a particular weapon to those enraptured with the mystique of optimal global strategies. It can accommodate those who rabidly desire to advance toward the brink and into limitless intensification of the arms race. It can even accommodate those who wish either to prevent war or to limit the destructiveness of war through the gradual achievement of arms control and disarmament agreements. What it cannot accommodate is the type of radical departure needed to produce enduring peace.

References

ANGELL, ROBERT C.
1964   "A Study of Social Values: Content Analysis of Elite Media." *Journal of Conflict Resolution* 8 (December): pp. 329–85.

BARBER, ARTHUR
  1963   "Some Industrial Aspects of Arms Control." *Journal of Conflict Resolution* 7 (September) : pp. 491–95.

BARNET, RICHARD
  1969   *The Economy of Death.* New York: Atheneum.

BAUER, RAYMOND A., I. POOL, AND L. DEXTER
  1963   *American Business and Public Policy.* New York: Alberton.

BELL, DANIEL
  1964   *The End of Ideology.* Glencoe, Ill.: The Free Press.

BENOIT, EMILE, AND K. E. BOULDING, *eds.*
  1963   *Disarmament and the Economy.* New York: Harper & Row.

BERLE, ADOLPH A.
  1954   *The Twentieth Century Capitalist Revolution.* New York: Harcourt.

BLUESTONE, IRVING
  1963   "Problems of the Worker in Industrial Conversion." *Journal of Conflict Resolution* 7 (September) : pp. 495–502.

BRAND, HORST
  1962   "Disarmament and American Capitalism." *Dissent* 9 (Summer) : pp. 236–51.

BURDICK, EUGENE, AND H. WHEELER
  1962   *Fail-Safe.* New York: McGraw-Hill.

BURTON, JOHN
  1962   *Peace Theory.* New York: Knopf.

CARTWRIGHT, DORWIN
  1959   "Power: A Neglected Variable in Social Psychology," in Dorwin Cartwright, ed., *Studies in Social Power.* Ann Arbor, Mich.: Research Center for Group Dynamics.

CATTON, BRUCE
  1948   *The War Lords of Washington.* New York: Harcourt.

COFFIN, TRISTRAN
  1964   *The Passion of the Hawks.* New York: Macmillan.

COHEN, BERNARD C.
  1963   *The Press and Foreign Policy.* Princeton, N.J.: Princeton University Press.

COOK, FRED J.
  1962   *The Warfare State.* New York: Macmillan.

———
  1963   "The Coming Politics of Disarmament." *The Nation* 196 (February 6) : pp. 36–48.

DAHL, ROBERT A.
  1961 *Who Governs?* New Haven, Conn.: Yale University Press.

———
  1963 *A Modern Political Analysis.* Englewood Cliffs, N.J.: Prentice-Hall, Inc.

DILLON, W.
  1962 *Little Brother Is Watching.* Boston: Houghton Mifflin.

DOMHOFF, G. WILLIAM
  1969 "Who Made American Foreign Policy, 1945–1963?" in David Horowitz, ed., *Corporations and the Cold War*, pp. 25–69. New York: Monthly Review Press.

EELLS, RICHARD, AND C. WALTON
  1961 *Conceptual Foundations of Business.* Homewood, Ill.: Irwin Press.

ETZIONI, AMITAI
  1962 *The Hard Way to Peace.* New York: Collier.

———
  1964 *The Moon-Doggle.* Garden City, N.Y.: Doubleday & Co.

FEARON, H. E., AND R. C. HOOK, JR.
  1964 "The Shift from Military to Industrial Markets." *Business Topics* 12 (Winter): pp. 43–52.

FEINGOLD, EUGENE, AND THOMAS HAYDEN
  1964 "What Happened to Democracy?" *New University Thought* 4 (Summer): pp. 39–48.

FISHER, ROGER, ed.
  1964 *International Conflict and Behavioral Science.* New York: Basic Books.

FISHMAN, LESLIE
  1962 "A Note on Disarmament and Effective Demand." *The Journal of Political Economy* 70 (June): pp. 183–86.

FREIDMAN, S.
  1963 "The RAND Corporation and Our Policy Makers." *Atlantic Monthly* 212 (September): pp. 61–68.

FRYE, WILLIAM R.
  1963 "Characteristics of Recent Arms-control Proposals and Agreements," in D. G. Brennan, ed., *Arms Control, Disarmament, and National Security.* New York: Braziller.

GALBRAITH, J. K.
  1956 *American Capitalism.* Boston: Houghton Mifflin.

———
  1962 "Poverty Among Nations." *Atlantic Monthly* 210 (October): pp. 47–53.

1967 *The New Industrial State.* New York: Signet.

1969 *How to Control the Military.* New York: Doubleday & Co.

GANS, HERBERT J.
1964 "Some Proposals for Government Policy in an Automating Society." *The Correspondent* 30 (Jan./Feb.): pp. 74–82.

GREEN, PHILIP
1963 "Alternative to Overkill: Dream and Reality." *Bulletin of the Atomic Scientists* (November): pp. 23–26.

HAYAKAWA, S. I.
1960 "Formula for Peace: Listening." *New York Times Magazine* (July 31): pp. 10–12.

HEILBRONER, ROBERT
1970 "How the Pentagon Rules Us." *New York Review of Books* 15 (July 23) p. 5.

HOROWITZ, DAVID
1962 *World Economic Disparities: The Haves and the Have-Nots.* Santa Barbara, Calif.: Center for the Study of Democratic Institutions.

HOROWITZ, I. L.
1963 *The War Game: Studies of the New Civilian Militarists.* New York: Ballantine.

HUMPHREY, HUBERT H.
1962 "The Economic Impact of Arms Control Agreements." *Congressional Record* 108 (October 5): pp. 2139–94.

ISARD, WALTER, AND E. W. SCHOOLER
1963 "An Economic Analysis of Local and Regional Impacts of Reduction of Military Expenditures." *Papers* I, Chicago Conference of the Peace Research Society International.

JANOWITZ, MORRIS
1957 "Military Elites and the Study of War." *The Journal of Conflict Resolution* 1 (March): pp. 9–18.

1960 *The Professional Soldier.* Glencoe, Ill.: The Free Press.

KELLER, SUZANNE
1963 *Beyond the Ruling Class.* New York: Random House.

KNEBEL, FLETCHER, AND C. BAILEY
1962 *Seven Days in May.* New York: Harper & Row.

KNOLL, ERWIN, AND JUDITH MCFADDEN, *eds.*
1969 *American Militarism 1970.* New York: The Viking Press.

KNORR, KLAUS
   1963   "Warfare and Peacefare States and the Acts of Transition."
          The Journal of Conflict Resolution 7 (December) : pp. 754–62.
LAPP, RALPH E.
   1962   *Kill and Overkill.* New York: Basic Books.

   _____

   1968   *The Weapons Culture.* New York: Norton.
LARSON, ARTHUR
   1961   "The Internation Rule of Law." A report to the Committee
          on Research for Peace, Program of Research No. 3, Institute
          for International Order.
LASSWELL, HAROLD
   1958   *Politics: Who Gets What, When & How.* New York: Meridian.
LIPSET, SEYMOUR M.
   1959   *Political Man.* Garden City, N.Y.: Doubleday & Co.
LITTLE, ROGER W.
   1968   "Basic Education and Youth Socialization in the Armed
          Forces." *American Journal of Orthopsychiatry* 38 (October) :
          pp. 869–76.
The Long Island Sunday Press
   1964   February 23.
LOWI, THEODORE J.
   1964   "American Business, Public Policy, Case-Studies, and Political
          Theory." *World Politics* 16 (July) : pp. 676–715.
LUMER, HYMAN
   1954   *War Economy and Crisis.* New York: International Publishers.
LYND, ROBERT S., AND HELEN MERRILL
   1959   *Middletown.* New York: Harcourt.
MCDONAGH, JAMES J., AND STEVEN M. ZIMMERMAN
   1964   "A Program for Civilian Diversifications of the Airplane In-
          dustry," in U.S. Senate Subcommittee on Employment and
          Manpower, *Convertibility of Space and Defense Resources to
          Civilian Needs.* Washington, D.C.: U.S. Government Printing
          Office.
MCNAMARA, ROBERT S.
   1963   "Remarks of the Secretary of Defense before the Economic
          Club of New York." Washington, D.C.: Department of Defense
          Office of Public Affairs.
MANNHEIM, KARL
   1956   *Freedom, Power and Democratic Planning.* London: Routledge
          and Kegan Paul.

MEISEL, JAMES H.
    1962   *The Fall of the Republic*. Ann Arbor, Mich.: University of Michigan Press.

_____

    1958   *The Myth of the Ruling Class*. Ann Arbor, Mich.: University of Michigan Press.

MELMAN, SEYMOUR, *ed.*
    1962   *The Peace Race*. New York: Braziller.

_____

    1963   *A Strategy for American Security*. New York: Lee Offset, Inc.

_____

    1970   *Pentagon Capitalism*. New York: McGraw-Hill.

MERBAUM, R.
    1963   "RAND: Technocrats and Power." *New University Thought* 3 (December–January): pp. 45–57.

MICHAEL, DONALD
    1962   *Cybernation: The Silent Conquest*. Santa Barbara, Calif.: Center for the Study of Democratic Institutions.

MILBRATH, L. W.
    1963   *The Washington Lobbyists*. Chicago: Rand McNally.

MILLS, C. WRIGHT
    1958   *The Causes of World War III*. New York: Simon & Schuster.

_____

    1959   *The Power Elite*. New York: Oxford University Press.

MINNIS, JACK
    1964   "The Care and Feeding of Power Structures." *New University Thought* 5 (Summer): pp. 73–79.

MOLLENHOFF, CLARK R.
    1967   *The Pentagon: Politics, Profits, and Plunder*. New York: Putnam.

NOSSITER, BERNARD
    1964   *The Mythmakers: An Essay on Power and Wealth*. Boston: Houghton Mifflin.

OSGOOD, CHARLES E.
    1962   *An Alternative to War or Surrender*. Urbana, Ill.: University of Illinois Press.

PARSONS, TALCOTT
    1951   *The Social System*. Glencoe, Ill.: The Free Press.

_____

    1959   *Structure and Process in Modern Societies*. Glencoe, Ill.: The Free Press.

PAUL, J., AND J. LAULICHT
1963   "Leaders' and Voters' Attitudes on Defense and Disarmament,"
in *In Your Opinion* 1. Clarkson, Ontario: Canadian Peace
Research Institute.

PECK, M. J., AND F. M. SCHERER
1962   *The Weapons Acquisition Process*. Cambridge, Mass.: Harvard
University Press.

PERLO, VICTOR
1963   *Militarism and Industry*. New York: International Publishers.

PIEL, GERARD
1961   *Consumers of Abundance*. Santa Barbara, Calif.: Center for
the Study of Democratic Institutions.

PILISUK, MARC
1963   "Dominance of the Military." *Science* 139 (January 18): pp.
247–48.

──────
1965   "The Poor and the War on Poverty." *The Correspondent* 34
(Summer): pp. 107–110.

──────
1968   "A Reply to Roger Little: Basic Education and Youth Socialization Anywhere Else." *American Journal of Orthopsychiatry*
38 (October): pp. 877–881.

"The Power of the Pentagon"
1969   *The Progressive* 33 (June): p. 6.

RAPOPORT, ANATOL
1960   *Fights, Games, and Debates*. Ann Arbor, Mich.: University of
Michigan Press.

──────
1964   *Strategy and Conscience*. New York: Harper & Row.

RAYMOND, JACK
1964   *Power at the Pentagon*. New York: Harper & Row.

REAGAN, MICHAEL
1963   *The Managed Economy*. New York: Oxford University Press.

REINER, THOMAS
1964   "Spatial Criteria to Offset Military Cutbacks." Paper presented
at the University of Chicago Peace Research Conference,
November 18.

"Report on the World Today"
1964   *Atlantic Monthly* 214 (September): pp. 4–8.

ROGOW, ARNOLD A.
1963   *James Forrestal*. New York: Macmillan.

SCHERER, FREDERICK
 1964 *The Weapons Acquisition Process: Economic Incentives.* Cambridge, Mass.: Harvard University Business School.

SHILS, EDWARD
 1961 "Professor Mills on the Calling of Sociology." *World Politics* 13 (July): pp. 600–621.

SINGER, J. DAVID
 1962 *Deterrence, Arms Control and Disarmament.* Columbus, Ohio: Ohio State University Press.

———
 1964 "A Study of Foreign Policy Attitudes." *Journal of Conflict Resolution* 8 (December): pp. 424–85.

———, ed.
 1963 "Weapons Management in World Politics." *Journal of Conflict Resolution* 7 (September): pp. 185–90 and *Journal of Arms Control* 1 (October): pp. 279–84.

STACHEY, JOHN
 1963 *On the Prevention of War.* New York: St. Martin's Press.

STRAUSS, LEWIS L.
 1962 *Men and Decisions.* Garden City, N.Y.: Doubleday & Co.

SUTTON, JEFFERSON
 1963 *The Missile Lords.* New York: Dell.

SWOMLEY, J. M., JR.
 1959 "The Growing Power of the Military." *The Progressive* 23 (January): pp. 10–17.

———
 1964 *The Military Establishment.* Boston: Beacon Press.

U.S. ARMS CONTROL AND DISARMAMENT AGENCY
 1962 *Economic Impacts of Disarmament.* Economic Series 1. Washington, D.C.: U.S. Government Printing Office.

———
 1964 *Toward World Peace: A Summary of U.S. Disarmament Efforts Past and Present.* Publication 10. Washington, D.C.: U.S. Government Printing Office.

U.S. CONGRESS
 1964 *Military Posture and Authorizing Appropriations for Aircraft, Missiles, and Naval Vessels.* Hearings No. 36, 88th Congress, 2nd session. Washington, D.C.: U.S. Government Printing Office.

———
 1964a *Pyramiding of Profits and Costs in the Missile Procurement*

Program. Report No. 970, 88th Congress, 2nd session. Washington, D.C.: U.S. Government Printing Office.

U.S. CONGRESS, COMMITTEE ON BANKING AND CURRENCY
1963 *Bank Holding Companies: Scope of Operations and Stock Ownership.* Washington, D.C.: U.S. Government Printing Office.

U.S. CONGRESS, COMMITTEE ON FOREIGN AFFAIRS
1964 *Foreign Assistance Act of 1964* (Parts 6 and 7) Hearings, 88th Congress, 2nd session. Washington, D.C.: U.S. Government Printing Office.

U.S. CONGRESS, COMMITTEE ON GOVERNMENT OPERATIONS
1962 *Pyramiding of Profits and Costs in the Missile Procurement Program* (Parts 1, 2, and 3). Hearings, 87th Congress, 2nd session. Washington, D.C.: U.S. Government Printing Office.

———
1963 *Government Information Plans and Policies* (Parts 1–4). Hearings, 88th Congress, 1st session. Washington, D.C.: U.S. Government Printing Office.

———
1964 *Satellite Communications* (Part 1). Hearings, 88th Congress, 2nd session. Washington, D.C.: U.S. Government Printing Office.

U.S. CONGRESS, COMMITTEE ON LABOR AND PUBLIC WELFARE
1964 *Toward Full Employment: Proposals for a Comprehensive Employment and Manpower Policy in the U.S.* Washington, D.C.: U.S. Government Printing Office.

U.S. CONGRESS, JOINT ECONOMIC COMMITTEE
1963 *Impact of Military Supply and Service Activities on the Economy.* 88th Congress, 2nd session. Washington, D.C.: U.S. Govment Printing Office.

U.S. CONGRESS, SENATE COMMITTEE ON ARMED SERVICES
1961 *Military Procurement Authorization Fiscal Year 1962.* 87th Congress, 1st session. Washington, D.C.: U.S. Government Printing Office.

U.S. CONGRESS, SUBCOMMITTEE ON EMPLOYMENT AND MANPOWER
1964 *Convertibility of Space and Defense Resources to Civilian Needs.* 88th Congress, 2nd Session, vol. 2. Washington, D.C.: U.S. Government Printing Office.

WARNER, WILLIAM LLOYD, AND J. D. ABEGGLEN
1955 *Big Business Leaders in America.* New York: Harper & Row.

WARNER, WILLIAM LLOYD, P. P. VAN RIPER, N. H. MARTIN,
AND O. F. COLLINS
1963   *The American Federal Executive.* New Haven, Conn.: Yale
       University Press.

WATSON-WATT, SIR ROBERT
1962   *Man's Means to his End.* London: Heinemann.

WEIDENBAUM, MURRAY L.
1968   "Arms and the American Economy: A Domestic Emergence
       Hypothesis." *American Economic Review* 58 (May): pp.
       625–29.

WESTIN, ALAN
1963   "Anti-communism and the Corporations." *Commentary* 36
       (December): pp. 479–87.

WISE, DAVID, AND THOMAS ROSS
1964   *The Invisible Government.* New York: Random House.

WRIGHT, QUINCY, WILLIAM EVANS, AND MORTON DEUTSCH, *eds.*
1962   *Preventing World War III: Some Proposals.* New York: Simon
       & Schuster.

Chapter 7

THE DOMINICAN CRISIS

In April 1965 American marines were sent to Santo Domingo where, after several days of street fighting, they suppressed a revolt by supporters of former president Juan Bosch. This sudden action left a group of rightist generals in command of the country. The background of this incident lends insight into the goals and tactics of American foreign policy.

The Trujillo Era

The Trujillo dictatorship in the Dominican Republic was infamous, even among military dictatorships, for its corruption and brutality.[1] During the latter days of Trujillo's rule, the tyrant was so despised that he could not longer trust even his own police or his regular army. He concentrated his arsenal of tanks and infantry troops under the command of his own son at the San Isidro Air Base. Colonel Elias Wessin y Wessin commanded the tank corps.

Trujillo was the Dominican strong man for 31 years. Like his Cuban counterpart, Batista, he had been a beneficiary of President Roosevelt's Good Neighbor Policy toward Latin America. In the 1950s Trujillo strengthened his grip on the economy of the Dominican Republic by dispossessing small

---

[1] An excellent biography of Trujillo is Robert Crassweller's *Trujillo: The Life and Times of a Caribbean Dictator* (New York: Macmillan Co., 1966).

landowners and concentrating the economy around the production of sugar and cane by-products for export, particularly to the United Kingdom. In return, Trujillo imported military equipment from England (Goff and Locker 1969).

During the late fifties, after the successful Cuban revolution, the American import quota for Cuban sugar was cut drastically. Trujillo used his most influential American contacts to arrange for a rise in the import quota for Dominican sugar. His contacts included a number of politicians and newsmen, whose sympathy he bought with a combination of bribery and blackmail (Martin 1966). In Congress, Representative Harold D. Cooley, chairman of the House Committee on Agriculture, spoke on Trujillo's behalf. Cooley's family and three other congressmen and their families were treated to expense-paid vacations in the Dominican Republic (*Hispanic American Report*, September 1962). Senator George Smathers advocated Trujillo's cause faithfully enough that the dictator called him "a very good friend of our country." Senator Strom Thurmond called the Dominican Republic under Trujillo "a true and loyal friend" of the United States (*Congressional Record*, August 31, 1960). Trujillo gained special favor among southern members of Congress, and several of them journeyed to Santo Domingo at the dictator's request (Crassweller 1966).

In 1960 an act of Congress rewarded the Dominican sugar lobby by transferring the largest share of the suspended Cuban sugar quota to the Dominican Republic. The victory provided for a dramatic upsurge in Dominican sugar productivity and profit. But it was short-lived, for the Organization of American States then voted for economic sanctions against the Dominican Republic. Since the Eisenhower administration was at the time very sensitive to charges of "communism 90 miles from the American coast," it was particularly concerned with cementing its relations with the Organization of American States. Such relations might be used to create sanctions against Cuba and to prevent other Latin nations from following the Cuban example. Although Congress managed to end its session without implementation of the OAS sanctions against the Dominican Republic, the administration announced a special import tax on the reallocated sugar. This sharply cut profits, and in March 1961, the new Congress approved a total embargo on Dominican sugar.

Two months later Trujillo was assassinated in a coup led by Colonel Antonio Imbert Barrera, chief of the Dominican national police. Imbert is believed to have been working closely with members of the United States CIA (Gall 1963, cited in Goff and Locker 1969). The president of South Puerto Rico Sugar Company, whose wholly-owned subsidiary is the largest employer in the Dominican Republic, then testified before Congress that a permanent United States quota at premium prices was necessary to the economic and political stability of the Dominican Republic. Without such assistance, the country might succumb to "Communist–Castroite" groups (United States Senate Finance Committee, 417). Congress agreed and Representative Cooley added an amendment obliging the United States government to repay the $22 million in tax penalties levied on Dominican sugar before Trujillo's death. Cooley's amendment was thrown out before the bill was passed, but President Kennedy was sufficiently moved by the pleas of the Dominican sugar interests to create a special fund to pay back the $22 million (Martin 1966).

The continuing conversion to a single-product economy, even with extreme profits from sugar sales, was having an adverse effect on the masses of impoverished Dominicans. Small landowners were dispossessed; food had to be imported at prices too high for general consumption, and thousands fled to the cities in the vain hope of finding employment.

The resources of the Dominican Republic, even after Trujillo's death, were dominated by a small class of wealthy aristocrats and by foreign-owned corporations. Such elite domination is the pattern in most nations in Latin America, Asia, and Africa. The durability of governments in these nations depends on their control over externally financed police and military services and is little affected by the condition of landless peasants (or miners or factory workers), who live as serfs, as an expendable commodity either in congested cities or in rural shanties in their own country.

Seventy percent of all Dominicans live in rural areas and work the fields when such work is available. Seventy-six percent of the farmers own only 14 percent of the cultivated land; the remainder is divided among large estates and sugar cane plantations (*Hispanic American Report*, February 1963).

The 1962 Elections

Following the assassination of Trujillo, and under the eyes of the Organization of American States, two political parties contested for power. The Union Civica Nacional, a conservative party which included members of the former aristocracy, assumed that it would win an easy victory on the strength of its anti-Trujillo rhetoric. The Partido Revolucionario Dominicano, led by Juan Bosch, ran on the policy of a peaceful social revolution based on major agrarian reform and financed by nationalization of the Trujillo holdings (which comprised more than one-third of the nation's land) (*Hispanic American Report*, February 1963). Bosch advocated distribution of the Trujillo land to peasants, formation of cooperatives for the sharing of agricultural equipment, an increase in agricultural wages, and the construction of eating halls to feed the hungry in the larger towns. Agriculture was to be diversified to produce more of what was needed for domestic consumption, and unemployment was to be attacked through public works and the development of new industry around untapped mineral resources.

There were three separate communist parties active in the Dominican Republic before the 1962 election. The Partido Socialista Popular was a communist group with a long history in Dominican politics. It actively collaborated with the conservative UCN by providing it with badly needed organizational cadres. The Fourteenth-of-June Movement was a Castroite group which also collaborated with the UCN and managed to give it important ties to Dominican youth. Its leader, Manual Tavarez Justo, accompanied representatives of the UCN to Washington, D.C. when the UCN was planning the interim government immediately after the assassination of Trujillo. Only the third communist group, the Movimiento Popular Dominicano, had any association with the party of Juan Bosch. The MPD, in fact, infiltrated and dominated the youth section of Bosch's party. In response, Bosch disbanded that section completely. Not until later in the 1962 election campaign did the conservative UCN sever its ties with communist groups. The extent of these ties was demonstrated by the fact that the end of the alliance resulted in the resignation of 18 of 24 UCN leaders (Draper 1965). At this time the communists urged a boycott of what they considered to be an electoral farce. Shortly before the elections Láutico García, a Jesuit priest, accused Bosch of being a communist. A television debate was arranged, and García could produce no evidence to support the charge (Bosch 1965). Bosch and his party won a landslide victory.

The Failure of Reform

The history of Bosch's independence from communist groups is important for understanding what happened after the election. When he took office in February 1963, Bosch was denounced by some as a Yankee tool, by others as a communist. The police, the army, and the press remained right-wing bastions, exactly as they had been under Trujillo. The strength Bosch brought to the presidency was an active concern with conditions in the Dominican Republic, which he had studied extensively during his years of exile. He was the darling of the Kennedy liberals, who saw in him an opportunity for a non-communist alternative to social development. Newell F. Williams, head of the Alliance for Progress in the Dominican Republic, regarded Bosch with great favor, and Bosch showed ability to work with United States Ambassador John B. Martin (Draper 1965).

Part of Bosch's strength, and perhaps his weakness, lay in his refusal to govern by any force other than moral force. For most of his 31 years' rule Trujillo had labeled his opponents "communists" and then had them destroyed or exiled, including Bosch himself. Bosch adamantly refused to purge anyone from the country. Above all, he wished to avoid civil strife.

He took steps to strengthen non-communist labor unions, with considerable financial aid from American foundations. (Unknown to Bosch, some of his sources of assistance at the time were conduits for funds from the CIA.) On numerous occasions Bosch answered his anti-communist critics by saying that he refused to make martyrs of communists. His thesis was that communists become guerrillas and terrorists if they are suppressed (Draper 1965).

It is important here to examine the communist thesis of revolution. Its stance is not that peaceful social reform is undesirable, but rather that it is impossible. A Batista or a Trujillo helps to confirm the communist thesis that there can be no real reform without revolution. The United States State Department intelligence report on *World Strength of the Communist Party Organizations* listed communist strength in the Dominican Republic as negligible in 1962. The 1964 report indicated only small and isolated sectors of communist support (United States State Department 1962 and 1964). Yet even in these circumstances there was a strong campaign of defamation against Bosch, extending from the conservative newspapers in the Dominican Republic to conservative newspapers in the United States.

A noted UCN leader, Dr. Viriatio A. Fiallo, issued the specific charge that communists had been appointed to key positions in the Bosch government. Bosch challenged Fiallo to produce the names of these people. A list of the names of visitors to Cuba's 26th of July celebration in 1963 was brought into the controversy. The actual list showed many people who had formerly occupied positions in the UCN, but none in Bosch's own party (Draper 1965).

One person who became a target of the UCN's bitter abuse and criticism was Sacha Volman. Volman headed the Inter-American Center for Social Studies (CIDES) which received its funds and direction from the American-based Institute of International Labor Research (IILR) (Shereff 1967). The Institute's director was Norman Thomas. In order to circumvent communist entrenchment on the economic planning board, Bosch had turned over most of the state planning activities to CIDES, a private organization. Volman himself was a socialist with a long-term record of anti-communist activities. Ironically, the Institute of International Labor Research was in turn funded by the Kaplan Foundation, in this case shown later to be a funnel for funds provided by the CIA (*New York Times*, September 3, 4, and 10, 1964).

Juan Bosch himself was an inspirational leader of unusual caliber, an intellectual and a scholar of peasant origins. His role as president was that of the nation's conscience. During his time in office, the American press frequently criticized Bosch as a weak administrator. Certainly he had a weak and difficult bureaucracy to lead, but he was elected for four years and overthrown after seven months amid charges in the American press that he had not overcome the plight of the Dominican Republic—which had developed over 31 years. During his seven months in office, Bosch survived four attempted coups. Despite the Kennedy administration's talk of building a "showcase of democracy" for Latin America (Schlessinger 1965, quoted in Goff and Locker 1969), AID Director Williams and Ambassador Martin both have commented on all the trouble Bosch had in getting American aid (Goff and Locker 1969). In spite of these obstacles, Bosch effected substantial reforms. During the seven months of his leadership, Trujillo's 57 personal enterprises were brought under an independent state agency which reinvested all profits in the economy. A progressive tax law was enacted. Wages rose and unemployment declined. There were, however, two very striking problems left to the Bosch administration after the rule of the interim UCN government.

The first was a hastily enacted postliminy law which re-awarded land to property owners who had been dispossessed by Trujillo. This law filled the courts with a backlog of jurisdictional cases, in which it had to be decided what land had legally belonged to the Trujillo family. The law blocked the road to any major agrarian reform.

The second and even more damaging remnant of the brief interim UCN government was a modification of the nation's police and military forces. *The Hispanic-American Report* of October 1962, four months before the election that brought Bosch to office, indicated that Council of State members Colonel Antonio Imbert Barrera, and Luis Amiama Tió, whose duties included supervision of the army and the police, were "fast making themselves the new dictators of the republic, using the threat of Communism as their pretext" (*Hispanic American Report* 716, October 1962). There was a sudden rise in the police force from 4,000 to 12,000 men, trained in riot control by two Los Angeles policemen (Evans 1963, and *Hispanic American Report*, February 1963). The effect of this buildup was to bequeath to Bosch a military and police operation responsive not to him but to the officers who remained from a previous era. In addition, the military and police in the Dominican Republic had become highly dependent for equipment, training, and supplies on assistance from the United States Department of Defense.

Bosch knew that a much-needed purge within the leadership of the police and military organizations could trigger a military coup and plunge the country into civil war. Since he was determined to rule peacefully, Boach's only alternative was to leave the old Trujillo armed forces intact.

President Bosch's uncompromising opposition to corruption seems to have been a critical factor in the success of the coup which overthrew him. In fact, one week before the coup brought down his government, Bosch was flying with the Dominican Air Force chief, General Pablo Atila Luna, to Mexico. On that flight, the general proposed a six million dollar purchase of British war planes. There was some scandal at the time over the fact that high-ranking military officers were taking a kickback of 10 to 15 percent from military purchases. Bosch learned that the military wanted 20 percent of the British deal. His reaction was incredulity that the general could think a country in which people died of hunger had money to throw away on war planes (Bosch 1965).

Bosch's independent foreign policy also added to the precariousness of his position, robbing him of potential allies. He tried, and failed, to steer to the right of Castro without running aground on American domination. Despite long-standing differences between Bosch and Castro, Bosch refused either to approve or condemn the Cuban revolutionary government (Draper 1965) at a time when the United States was seeking censure of Cuba by other Latin nations.

The purpose of this report is not essentially to indicate why Juan Bosch was overthrown in 1963, but rather why American marines prevented his return in 1965. Still, some of the details of the 1963 coup are helpful to an understanding of the events which followed.

After the coup Brigadier General Antonio Imbert Barrera, who had been one of its leaders, disclosed that in his role as head of internal security, he had given Bosch on September 19th a three-page document in which it was claimed that Dominican communists were planning to stage an uprising the following January. Supposedly, his information had come from an informer's account of a secret meeting of communist leaders. The military had used Imbert's report to demand that Bosch provide them with orders to "repress the communists and 'crack their heads.' " When Bosch refused, the military apparently decided to get rid of him. That his was the first constitutional government Dominicans had seen for three decades gave the conspirators no pause. The measure of General Imbert's concern for the constitution was shown in his statement: "Sure, we violated the Constitution by ousting Bosch, but I believe that it was absolutely necessary to place the Constitution in recess in a desk drawer" (Dubois 1963, quoted in Draper 1965, p. 9).

An important question arises: How could a popular Latin American government regarded as a "showcase of democracy" by the United States, as was the Dominican Republic under Juan Bosch, be suddenly overthrown by a military coup? One clue comes from the position of one of the Dominican trade union confederations, CONATRAL (financed by the AFL–CIO, USAID, and possibly the CIA), which ran advertisements in the Dominican press urging people to put their faith in the armed forces to defend them against communism (Bodenheimer 1967). A second clue is the fact that Bosch had made enemies of powerful oil interests by canceling an oil refinery contract which Esso, Texaco, and Shell had negotiated with the Trujillo government. Duane D. Luther of Texaco, a former member of the OSS (the major American intelligence operation during World War II), had contributed $2,500 to Bosch's opponent, Fiallo, and was reported to have planned the anti-Bosch coup. Luther refused to accept a phone call from columnist Drew Pearson seeking to confirm the report (Pearson 1965, cited in Goff and Locker 1969). A third clue was given by Bosch himself, who asserted that the Dominican government could be overthrown in an hour because even a captain from the American military mission had more authority over the Dominican military command than the people, the constitution, and the president (Bosch 1965). This view was supported by observations of an American journalist, Sam Halper, who stated that the Dominican military decided to oust Bosch "as soon as they got a wink from the U.S. Pentagon" (Halper 1965, p. 4, quoted in Draper 1965, p. 9). Whether such reports are true is not easy to determine, but it is very clear that the Dominican armed forces were at the time dependent on the United States military establishment.

Despite the army's dependence, the United States was apparently unwilling to exercise any restraining influence against the overthrow of the democratic government. The official attitude among people in the Kennedy administration was disillusionment and surprise, but it seems clear that the facts of the revolt were presented to at least some important Kennedy people as a fait accompli. The Kennedy administration, to its credit, withheld recognition from the military junta.

After the assassination of President Kennedy, however, his successor, Lyndon Johnson, recognized the new regime. In his May 2, 1965 speech celebrating the failure of the pro-Bosch revolt, Johnson even referred to the 1963 coup (with a spray of linguistic perfume) as a "revolution" (Draper 1965). Whoever wrote those words into President Johnson's speech showed either a great misunderstanding of revolution in Latin America or a great desire to deceive. (We shall soon look at the persons who were in a position to advise the president.) The word "revolution" has a particular meaning for destitute Latin Americans long abused by corrupt officials who wield military and economic power to stay in office and prevent the people from rising out of their bitter poverty. A revolution is by definition popular and aimed at eliminating an exploitative regime. The return of the military junta in 1963 was just the opposite—a military undertaking removing from office a popular, democratically elected government which was leading a movement toward peaceful revolutionary change.

When the president's speech-writers referred to the coup as a revolution, they unwittingly validated the Cuban premise that the United States will not permit a social revolution in Latin America. As the Cuban newspaper *Hoy* noted, Bosch had failed to establish diplomatic relations with Cuba, to purge his right-wing military, to make a commercial pact with the USSR, and to nationalize American businesses (*Hoy* 1963, cited in Draper 1965). The lesson was clear. A model representative government steering an independent course to peaceful change would not be left alone either by its own military strong men or by the United States, which armed them. As *Hoy* put it, "the middle way does not exist."

Rebellion and American Intervention

The head of the junta in 1965 was a former automobile dealer, Donald Reid Cabral. Reid, however much he favored the military, was opposed to corruption. Immediately before the 1965 revolt, Reid fired two army colonels for graft and disloyalty (Bethel 1965, cited in Draper 1965). His intention to eliminate a contracts racket operated by top military men was his downfall. The desire to topple Reid was added to a widespread resentment against the military among supporters of the former Bosch regime. Reid was forced to resign as head of the ruling junta. Then a group of young officers headed by Colonel Francisco A. Caamaño Deñó, hoping to return Bosch to Santo Domingo as the head of state, installed as provisional president the former president of the Chamber of Deputies under Bosch, Dr. Jose Rafael Molina Ureña (Draper 1968).

The pro-Bosch rebellion under the direction of Molina Ureña proceeded with great speed. General Wessin y Wessin had sent a small force to guard the Duarte bridge between Santo Domingo and the San Isidro air base to the east; but most of his troops were still at San Isidro, and no shots had yet been fired. Many of the generals were undecided whether the rebellion should be aided or crushed. About a dozen miles west of the capital, General Montas Guerrero held his army regiment in a state of arrest. Naval and air units waited also for an appropriate sign and withheld action (Draper 1968).

The revolt was immediately popular in the streets of Santo Domingo, and the rebels were able to take control of Santo Domingo within two days, almost without resistance and with little violence. By April 25 they were in control. The chronology of the events that followed is illuminating.

April 25. A member of the United States State Department expressed fears that the return of Bosch as head of the Dominican Republic would pose a threat of communism within six months (Szulc 1965). The State Department vetoed a suggestion by embassy officials that it should initiate contact with Bosch in Puerto Rico (Draper 1965). The American embassy in Santo Domingo informed Washington that embassy military attachés had given "loyalist" leaders a go-ahead to do everything possible to prevent what was described as the danger of a communist takeover (Geyelin 1965, quoted in Draper 1968). The embassy naval attachés worked specifically and successfully at the task of persuading Captain Rivero Caminera, the Dominican naval commander, either to cast his lot with the loyalists or, at the least, to remain neutral (Szulc 1965).

April 25–26. Dominican air force planes began strafing the capital city. Both naval and air force fire centered around the presidential palace, which was controlled by Molina Ureña and his aides (Draper 1968).

April 26. Wessin y Wessin sent tanks from the San Isidro Air Base toward the capital (Draper 1965). (Within two days the Wessin forces were virtually routed by Bosch supporters.)

April 27, P.M. Some pro-Bosch leaders faltered and asked United States Ambassador W. Tapley Bennett, Jr. to arrange a cease-fire. He refused, saying, according to his own account, that he had not been authorized to intervene.

In San Juan, Bosch learned from the Dominican Republic's Papal Nuncio, Msgr. Emanuele Clarizio, that Wessin y Wessin's forces were almost defeated and the pro-Bosch forces were winning. Bosch said that in spite of his imminent victory, further death and destruction were unwarranted. He approved negotiations to call off the fighting (Draper 1965).

April 28, A.M. American officials yet unapprised of the change in the war were expressing relief over the failure of the insurrection (Draper 1965). Meanwhile, the newly formed three-man military junta, under air force Colonel Pedro Bartolome Benoit, was beginning to smell defeat (Draper 1968).

April 28, P.M. Ambassador Bennett informed the administration of a complete loss of control of the situation by the Dominican police and military, which could no longer guarantee the safety of Americans there. He went on to say that Wessin y Wessin and Imbert had requested American assistance in restoring law and order.

As Bosch relates, the Papal Nuncio brought the offer of negotiations from Bosch to Wessin y Wessin. Wessin y Wessin, now assured of American support, refused to negotiate (Draper 1965).

April 28, evening. American marines landed in Santo Domingo. They first evacuated American civilians and then assisted the remnants of Wessin y Wessin's forces in subduing the revolt.

During the time of crisis Juan Bosch sought passage to return to Santo Domingo from San Juan, Puerto Rico. On May 1 he spoke to one of President Johnson's most trusted advisors, Abe Fortas, and in the following days to other United States representatives, who made it clear they did not want him to go back (Goff and Locker 1969). Meanwhile, the State Department made a point of keeping in touch with Joaquin Balaguer, former president under Trujillo, who had been driven into exile by the conservative UCN interim government in 1962 (Draper 1968). The liaison was I. Irving Davidson (Goff and Locker 1969). Over a year later, when elections were held in June 1966, the United States backed the conservative Balaguer, who repaid his American benefactors after taking office by clinging tightly to American coattails. Balaguer promulgated a new constitution to American liking, accepted large loans and grants which brought with them hundreds of American advisors and administrators, and placed training programs for the police and military in the hands of AID, the Defense Department, and the CIA (Goff and Locker 1969).

Recently, in preparation for the May 1970 elections, Balaguer removed any remaining doubts about his disdain for a government responsive to the Dominican people. On April 7, 1970 he closed the national university and two major union headquarters and occupied them with army and police units. There were a number of political arrests. When all the opposition parties threatened to boycott the elections, Balaguer finally yielded power to an interim government during the election campaign. But Hector Garcia Godoy, Balaguer's replacement, died shortly afterward of a reported heart attack.

American Policy and Its Apologists

One thread in the tangle of American policy is the official statements of Johnson and the State Department, attempting to explain the events. These statements are significant for two reasons. First, they help illustrate the mode of thought of those who make the major day-to-day decisions about the execution of diplo-military policy. Secondly, however much the State Department statements are interpretive rather than reportorial, these statements are reported by the press as news. To a large extent this is the nature of news in mass industrial society; that is, news is the statements agencies make regarding their own activities and the rationales needed to justify them.

There is more than one official American version of what happened in Santo Domingo. The first statements indicated that the prime concern of American policy was to evacuate those who might be injured during the revolt (Draper 1968). In keeping with promises both rebel and anti-rebel groups made to the American embassy, 1,000 people were safely evacuated from the Hotel Embajador on April 27. They were transported by road from the hotel to Jaina, seven miles west of Santo Domingo. Although the United States claimed that a group of armed rebels that came to the hotel "engaged in indiscriminate firing . . . endangering the lives of many people" (Mann 1965, pp. 733–34), the evacuation was carried out without even an injury (Draper 1968). Yet the message that the police authorities "could no longer be responsible" and the fear that there were "no constituted authorities of any kind in the city" were the reasons provided for sending 500 marines, who were stationed around the Hotel Embajador for the express purpose of assisting further evacuation by helicopter on April 28. On the evening of April 28, several hundred more people were evacuated, again without casualties (Mann 1965).

The landing of even this group of marines was a sharp violation of the mandates of international law and of United States commitments to the charter of the United Nations, which precludes the unilateral intervention with force by one nation state in the affairs of another. The action also violated a similar commitment to the Organization of American States. The excuse provided by Under Secretary for Economic Affairs Thomas Mann for bypassing the OAS was that innocent civilians might be hurt by the delay.

Mann's article in the *Department of State Bulletin* (November 8, 1965) states that the administration had not assumed from the beginning that the revolution was communist-dominated, nor that it should be opposed by military force. He expresses the view that the United States had hoped to withdraw its troops as soon as evacuations were completed. The hope was that non-communist elements on the rebel side "would either reach a cease-fire agreement with the bulk of the armed forces opposing them or bring the armed civilians and paramilitary on the rebel side under effective control" (Mann 1965). Under Secretary Mann then explains how American hopes were dashed. The military forces under General Montás that entered the city from the west on April 29 completely failed to stop the revolt. What of Wessin y Wessin's forces? Here Mann writes:

> By the evening of April 29 it became clear that the armed forces at San Isidro would be nothing but observers. General Wessin, for reasons best known to him, elected not to support General Montás' column which . . . after some initial success, disintegrated. As it turned out, Wessin never did move his forces into the city. (Mann 1965, pp. 734–5)

Yet Mann, in his earlier release to Max Frankel of the *New York Times* (May 9, 1965), had noted that Wessin's military forces had suffered a "virtual collapse . . . by the afternoon of April 28." Perhaps Wessin "elected not to support General Montás" because he had no troops to do it with. The *New York Herald Tribune* had reported on May 2 that the military junta was highly unpopular and regarded by most Dominicans as corrupt. The *Tribune* article suggested that the anti-rebel soldiers showed a certain lack of enthusiasm for battle: "The demoralized dwindling group of perhaps 2,000 loyalist troops under strongman Brigadier General Elias Wessin y Wessin have virtually given up." The UPI reported that Wessin's forces had lost tanks, and the AP noted the unverified report that two-thirds of the military defected after the civil war started (Draper 1965).

Mann expresses United States concern with a known communist movement which was, according to his description, the only group of rebels roaming through Santo Domingo on April 29 with any degree of cohesion. The United States, according to Mann, had been concerned with the communist leaders, who were said to have committed the crime, before the revolt, of distributing arms to civilians. Mann says a decision was made on the eve of April 29 to reinforce a small number of troops holding the perimeter near the beach and to land troops at San Isidro airport a few miles east of the capital city. He explains that this second wave of American troops was to function as a "line of communication, a corridor . . . between the troops in the San Isidro area and the troops in the International Safety Zone. This corridor had the effect of interposing troops between the two contending armed factions" (Mann 1965, p. 735).

Through the flimflam of State Department jargon, it seems clear that the United States evacuated civilians at the first signs of failure of the junta forces, and then sent its marines to revive the disintegrated loyalist forces and squash the rebels, some of whom were believed to be communists. Exactly why American marines have more right to be present in the Dominican Republic than Dominican communists is never questioned.

Mann's judgment is that a government with even an alliance with communists would be intolerable to the United States.

> The need to distinguish between a reform movement allied to the Communists, and a movement dedicated to reform in freedom should be emphasized over again. Indeed, it is precisely the failure to make this distinction—the tendency of some to lump all "reformers" together and to evaluate them solely on the basis of their rhetoric—that causes a great deal of confusion. (Mann 1965, p. 736)

After the pro-Bosch rebellion had been crushed, the State Department produced as part of its justification for intervention a list of 58 supposed communists who allegedly had taken part in the rebellion. Revised and expanded lists were issued after a few days. But the lists lost all credulity as reporter after reporter found that some of those listed had been out of the country at the time of the crisis, others had been in prison, others had had no involvement in the revolt, and still others could not by any stretch of the imagination be called communists.[2] When confronted with these revelations, the State Department turned defensive. Mann suggested that "the strength of the Communist component of the rebel side must be measured not only by its men and arms and its superior discipline, but by the weakness, the divisions, and the lack of leadership within the rebel movement" (Mann 1965, p. 736).

It seems to be an odd set of international rules by which the United States is playing. Apparently the United States reserves for itself the right to determine if a new government shall be prevented from coming into being on the basis of the estimated strength of a minority group of communists within that new government—as judged by the United States. The question remains: What is left to be judged by the people of the country whose government is at stake? It is interesting that in his protestations of a lack of

---

[2] For a complete discussion of the numbers game engaged in by the State Department, see Draper 1968, pp. 133–50, 159–70.

leadership among the rebels, Mann gives no mention to the name of Juan Bosch. Mann closes his defense of the American action in Santo Domingo with a very strong condemnation of popular fronts. "Popular fronts do not have as their principal objective the noble purpose of democratic reform. Their principal objective is political power" (Mann 1965, p. 736). He then proceeds to defend the Latin American military juntas as follows: "The Latin American military contain in their ranks many able and dedicated men who do not deserve to be smeared with the brush that ought to be reserved for the few" (Mann 1965, p. 737). He then defends the oligarchical church organization and organized labor, a sizeable faction of which was virtually created and dominated by the AFL–CIO, and which stood behind government policies contrary to the most basic demands of workers (Bodenheimer 1967).

Most interestingly, Mann sees fit to include as part of his apology for the American actions in the Dominican crisis a comparison of the values of American society and the 1776 revolution with Russian society and the 1917 revolution. The assumption is clear that the underdeveloped countries of the world cannot select their own form of revolution, but they must choose between one of two models already available; and the United States will do anything within its power to influence the choice.

The article in which Thomas Mann marshals his defense of the American action in the Dominican Republic is important both as a statement of rationalization for the American activity and as a personal account of the considerations of one of the political figures responsible for producing an explanation at the time. Under Secretary Mann assumes that the United States must intervene, in violation of international law and agreement, to prevent either communist or popular front uprisings against reactionary regimes. This need not inevitably be the case; why this assumption is a part of American policy, in Latin America particularly, must be seen from other quarters. We are obliged to ask not merely to know the terms in which the policy is defended, but rather to know the interests represented by the policy.

Thomas Mann and Business Ideology

For whom does Thomas Mann actually speak? A clue to this is provided by *Business Week*'s February 1, 1964 background story and interview of Mann written at the time he replaced both Edwin M. Martin, as Assistant Secretary for Latin Affairs, and simultaneously Teodoro Moscoso, as coordinator of the Alliance for Progress. According to *Business Week*, Mann is known as "a conservative friend of business" (*Business Week*, February 1, 1964, p. 65). Mann's views on land reform and military juntas, two most pressing Latin American problems, are consistent with his friendship with the corporate community. He emphasizes steps to raise farm output rather than land redistribution and reform. While the Kennedy administration tried to some extent to promote democracy by suspending diplomatic ties and economic assistance to military regimes, Mann "doubts the effectiveness of such attempts by the U.S. to try to impose democracy on other countries" (*Business Week*, February 1, 1964, p. 67). He views the problem of underdevelopment not as a need for social revolution to alleviate extensive poverty and eliminate corrupt leadership, but rather as a problem of how to secure American investment capital. Historically, when Latin American nationalism has conflicted with American business interests, American companies have called for stiffer measures to protect their interests. In *Business Week*'s interview Mann said he supports their position and emphasized "that the U.S. has an obligation to protect all legitimate U.S. investment interests" (*Business Week*, February 1, 1964, p. 68). *Business Week* makes clear the significance of Mann's appointment. ". . . Latin America is close to home, and the U.S. has a big stake there. Excluding Middle Eastern oil, Latin America accounts for more than 80% of the total U.S. investment in developing countries" (*Business Week*, February 1, 1964, p. 65).

One of the most fundamental insights of the Alliance for Progress was that American assistance had to be channeled to democratic, reform-oriented regimes lest the money go merely to preserve corrupt juntas and wealthy landowners. Mann's views on reform and the military juntas can be traced back to his remarks regarding the overthrow of the Arbenz government in Guatemala in 1954. Arbenz had been elected in one of the few free elections within a constitutional framework in Latin America. He was dedicated to land reform and favored nationalization of specific industries which were fleecing Guatemalan resources without raising the severely depressed living standard of the country. He was overthrown in a plot organized and assisted by the United States Central Intelligence Agency.[3]

Space does not permit a full discussion of American business interests in Guatemala; we merely note that they are extensive—and, as we know, Thomas Mann was a "friend of business." Mann made public his views of the Guatemalan coup in a speech at commencement exercises at the University of Notre Dame in 1964. In it Mann pretended that the coup was indigenous, rather than engineered by the CIA. After paying homage to the ideal of constitutional government, Mann went on to hint that certain unconstitutional regimes might be preferable to some constitutional ones. "Unilateral intervention" to force an unconstitutional government out of power in another country, said Mann, is not always the wisest course.

> . . . Not long ago, a majority of the Guatemalan people voted in free elections for Arbenz, a candidate for president. Later the Guatemalan people discovered that Arbenz was a Marxist–Leninist. Colonel Castillo led a suc-

---

[3] David Wise and Thomas Ross give a full account of the CIA's part in the coup in *The Invisible Government* (New York: Random House, 1964), pp. 165–83.

cessful revolt and was widely acclaimed by his people as he marched into Guatemala City. Had we been unconditionally committed to the support of all constitutional governments under all circumstances, we would have been obliged to do everything within our power to bring about the overthrow of Castillo and to restore a Marxist–Leninist power against the will of the Guatemalan people. (Mann 1964)

Apart from Mann's assumption that the will of the Guatemalan people is better determined by the United States State Department than by Guatemalan elections, the illustration shows very clearly the State Department's unwillingness to recognize the regressive role of military juntas or the need for basic economic reforms in Latin American development. The illustration also highlights the role of the Department of State as an apologist for policies already enacted by military or intelligence sources.

Originally a major insight recognized by the Alliance for Progress was that economic development, particularly the task of uplifting Latin Americans from circumstances of mass poverty, could not be directed from abroad but depended on progressive Latin leadership. Given the suspicion generated by American's long record of exploitation in Latin America, there seemed no choice but to depend on progressive planning under Latin leadership, even if the United States still had to supply the purse. To implement this quest for Latin leadership, the Inter-American Committee for the Alliance for Progress was created in November 1963 as a steering group with members from the United States and Latin American countries. The Latin American nations approved a noted Argentine economist, Raul Prebisch, for the committee chairmanship. But concurrent with the increase of Mann's responsibility over economic assistance to Latin America, the nomination of Prebisch was blocked in Washington, "presumably", said *Business Week*, "because of his controversial economic views that stress government planning" (*Business Week*, February 1, 1964, p. 66).

There is great fear of government planning among American business interests in Latin America, since planning could restrict the holding of land, the overly generous tax arrangements, and the exploitation of agricultural workers, miners, or dock workers. The great fear is always that the governments may attempt a program, highly popularized by the Castro regime, of nationalizing American firms, with payment in bonds of an amount equal to the firms' declared value in their own tax returns. The procedure strikes heavily at American industries which have been able to reap great profits from their foreign investments.

Two points are to be emphasized with regard to Thomas Mann. The first is that he seems to resign himself more easily to undemocratic rightist regimes than to any kind of leftist regime, whether democratic or not. The freedom Mann defends in Latin America is not the freedom to be self-governing but the freedom of American investors to make secure investments there. The second point is that the economic development he sees involves only a hope of greater total productivity, with the expectation that benefits will somehow trickle down to the people.

Sugar Power

The question yet to be raised is: Who are the investors so threatened by the social reforms and independent foreign policy of Juan Bosch? And why is their power to influence decisions great enough to cause American marines to be sent to the Dominican Republic? A list of people who hold influential positions both in business and in government should prove illuminating. We turn our attention to the East Coast sugar complex and related organizations.

The former representative to the Organization of American States (1964–66), Ellsworth Bunker, was a director of the National Sugar Refining Company from 1927 to 1966 and at various times also president and chairman of the board (*Who's Who in America*, 1968–69). National Sugar depends on rates of sugar export from the Dominican Republic for the determination of world sugar prices. Bunker is also a trustee of the Atlantic Mutual Insurance Company and is in this capacity related to the interests of another trustee of Atlantic (Dun and Bradstreet 1969), an influential financier with an interest in Dominican affairs: J. Peter Grace, president and a director of W. R. Grace and Co., which operates a shipping line from the Dominican Republic. Until 1965, J. Frank Honold was also an Atlantic trustee and at the same time vice-president in the Trust Department of Chase Manhattan Bank, which has two branches in the Dominican Republic (Dun and Bradstreet 1965, and Moody's *Bank*, 1965). J. Peter Grace is also associated with the conservative publication *Human Events* and is a director, along with AFL–CIO president George Meany, in the CIA-supported American Institute of Free Labor Development, which exerts influence on the policies of labor movements in Latin American countries (Jacobs 1967).

Another labor institute that influenced Dominican trade unions was the Institute of International Labor Research, one of whose directors was Sacha Volman. The IILR was funded by the liberal Kaplan Foundation, which in turn received funds from the Central Intelligence Agency. J. M. Kaplan first supported Bosch but later withdrew his support. The Kaplan family finances were based in Oldtyme Molasses, Southwestern Sugar, and American Sucrose (Shereff 1967). J. M. Kaplan is an influential contributor to the Democratic party (Goff and Locker 1969).

Ambassador-at-Large W. Averell Harriman (sent to Latin America by Johnson to explain the Dominican intervention) is listed as a "limited partner" in Brown Bros., Harriman & Co. (Moody's *Bank*, 1968), which owns substantial stock in the National Sugar Refining Company (Goff and Locker 1969).

Abe Fortas, formerly a Supreme Court justice and a close friend of President Johnson, was a director of the SuCrest Corporation (formerly the American Molasses Company) from 1946 to 1966 (Moody's *Industrial*, 1946–1966). SuCrest in its 1963 annual report mentions its purchase of blackstrap molasses from the Dominican Republic. The same issue expresses concern over the loss of Cuban sugar and the necessity for further imports to compensáte for the loss. Former ambassador to Brazil Adolf A. Berle, Jr., who has been involved in policy making toward Latin America in various capacities, has been a director of SuCrest since 1946 and was chairman of the board until 1964 (*Who's Who in America*, 1968–69). Berle's book *The Twentieth Century Capitalist Revolution* refers approvingly to the direct dealings of American corporations with foreign governments, with specific references to "American sugar companies doing business in the Dominican Republic" (Berle 1954, p. 131).

Joseph S. Farland, ambassador to the Dominican Republic from 1957 to 1960, has been a director since 1964 of the South Puerto Rico Sugar Co. (*Who's Who in America*, 1966–67), whose subsidiary, Central Romana, is the largest employer in the Dominican Republic, with up to 20,000 workers, depending on the season. Central Romana owns 275,000 acres of choice Dominican land (Moody's *Industrial*, 1965).

Senator George A. Smathers, a consistent defender of former dictator Trujillo and an opponent of Juan Bosch, is a founding member of the law firm of Smathers, Thompson, Maxwell, and Dyer, which is the legal counsel for Atlantic Mutual. Smathers is also a partner in Gulf and Western Industries, a huge conglomerate which acquired South Puerto Rico Sugar in 1967 (Gulf and Western Industries *Annual Report*, 1969).

The legal counsel for National Sugar is the firm of Cravath, Swaine and Moore. Its managing executive partner is Roswell Gilpatric, former deputy secretary of defense (1961–64), a position whose holder would possibly be consulted if marines were to be sent to a country. Wall Street attorney Max Rabb, whose law firm Stroock, Stroock, and Lavan is the legal counsel for SuCrest, was secretary to President Eisenhower's cabinet from 1953 to 1958. Rabb was also a member of the National Committee for Johnson and Humphrey (Goff and Locker 1969).

The man who kept the State Department in contact with Balaguer, I. Irving Davidson, has been a lobbyist for the Equadorian sugar industry. He was also involved in an illegal Haitian meat packing deal with Clint Murchison, Dallas businessman, who controlled Greatamerica Corporation jointly with another Dallas man. Abe Fortas was a board member and general counsel of Greatamerica Corporation (Goff and Locker 1969).

Ellsworth Bunker was honored for his success in the political world by an appointment as honorary director of the New School of Social Research. His son is president of the second largest beet sugar refining company in the United States (Goff and Locker 1969), and his brother has been a director of Lehman Brothers, a large New York investment house.

The limited wealth of the Dominican Republic is bound to American corporate interests which have a great stake in assuring that no major reforms are activated to redistribute that wealth to impoverished Dominicans. The corporate men involved were obviously well placed to protect their concerns. Except for the roles of Davidson and Fortas, the informal operations of these men remain a secret. But the multiple connections between Dominican industry and United States policy circles make a far more convincing explanation for the marines than the after-the-fact State Department messages of Thomas Mann.

Illusions and Realities

American military intervention is no novelty to Dominicans. In 1898 the United States supported a secret military expedition. Former ambassador John Martin, describing events in the years between 1904 and 1916, writes:

> ...the United States moved from the Roosevelt Corollary to full scale marine occupations of the Dominican Republic. First we collected customs, then we forbade insurrection in order to maintain stability, then we held elections with warships in the harbor and sailors or marines at the polls, then we demanded full control over internal revenues and expenditures as well as over customs, then we demanded the disbanding of the Army and establishment of a Guardia Nacional (Constabulary); then we sent the marines. (Martin 1966, p. 28, quoted in Goff and Locker 1969, p. 250)

Our industrial involvement is also long-term. It began with the New York banking house of Kuhn, Loeb and Co., which took over the extensive Dominican foreign debts and floated a $20 million bond issue in 1904 (Goff and Locker 1969). From 1928 on, a host of industrial and political figures maintained close contact with the interests of Dominican dictator Rafael Trujillo. The occupation of 1965 was not an accident of American foreign policy. It merely reiterated a policy crafted by interlocked corporate, military, and political interests for their own purposes. These purposes do not include the independence or the economic security of the Dominican people, who still live in extreme poverty.

There are three major elements in the expressed long-term goals of United States foreign policy in Latin America. These are (a) to promote the development of democratic institutions, (b) to assist less developed nations in economic development, and (c) to protect the security of the United States and of American interests. American involvement has not promoted democracy in the case of the Dominican Republic. It surely has not promoted democracy in Greece (see chapter 8). Popular democracy is an important symbol that helps make interventionist policy palatable both to the American public and to the target population, which suffers most from interference in support of the status quo. The symbol has little reference to such United States actions as sending marines into the Dominican Republic in 1965. Rather, the symbol is State Department packaging designed specifically to legitimize less benign objectives. To the State Department, promoting "democracy" means defeating socialist or communist movements, no matter how democratically these movements may be functioning.

The goal of assisting in economic development was also not fulfilled in the Dominican Republic. American corporations there continue to do well, with sugar export remaining a bulwark of the economy. The benefits of this prosperity have not yet trickled down to Dominican field workers. Clearly, what is meant by economic assistance in development is the creation of a stable environment for American investors. This undoubtedly creates some jobs, but it prevents any reorganization of the economy that might bridge the tremendous gap between the poor and the elite.

Whether the United States has achieved its third professed objective, the protection of its military security, is also open to question with regard to actual actions such as the Dominican intervention. American security was served only if one assumes that pro-American regimes dependent militarily on the United States are a greater asset to United States security than popular regimes with independent foreign and domestic policy. In South Korea and again in Vietnam the United States has paid heavily for its support of unpopular pro-American regimes. It is not clear, then, that even the objective of military security is served by such policies as the Dominican intervention.

But the value of showing how the overt objectives of American policy are undermined by the actual operating procedures is limited. Day-to-day operations are not the product of explicit long-term national goals. They are more an outgrowth of unpublicized administrative dealings of corporation officials and of agents of the Central Intelligence Agency. Only when such business and military intelligence activities cannot sustain themselves is an official action, for example sending in the marines, called for. Here, the close ties between the State and Defense Departments on the one hand, and major corporate interests on the other assure us that the local agents know how to formulate their requests correctly so that they can be granted within the framework of the avowed ideals and limits of United States policy. There is evidence that during the 1965 crisis Ambassador Bennett told Colonel Benoit, the junta leader, precisely what pretext to give for his request to the American government to send marines (Draper 1968).

The official agents of government policy, officials in the executive branch of the government, are called on to execute major policy, not to formulate it. Later, they are called on once again to explain it, and their press releases and public remarks make the news and shape the reporting of the events themselves. The avowed long-term goals of American foreign policy are precisely this type of after-statement, a rationalization for the protection of those very same corporate and intelligence interests which customarily handle the day-to-day policy making without fanfare and without the need for public policy support.

Frequently, policy making occurs in just this covert manner. An ambassador to the Organization of American States who is also chairman of the board of a corporation dependent on strong control over the Dominican economy is likely to identify American interests with American *business* interests, and to try to prevent radical social change in Santo Domingo. Each of the activities of his corporation plays a major part in the economic status of the Dominican Republic and is a significant detail in the operation of United States "policy" in Latin America. Likewise, each intelligence agency decision, whether to infiltrate a Dominican labor union or to finance its political advertisements, is policy on the operating level.

It is useless merely to point out the inconsistency between expressed objectives and the actions which have occurred. The actions are not accidents resulting from happenstance misinformation in the hands of well-meaning officials. The very process by which intelligence is gathered by agencies with a stake in controlling a foreign government assures a flow of information which can be used to justify either military intervention in support of questionable governments or refusal to intervene on behalf of popular reform leaders. The very process of selection of key personnel assures an overrepresentation from corporations, investment houses, and the major law firms which serve them. The board of directors of SuCrest does not have to answer to either the American or the Dominican voter, and the local CIA offices are barely accountable to anyone. As far as the major long-term guidelines for foreign policy are concerned, official public administrators, from the president on down, appear to play a supportive role to the more primary paramilitary and business bureaucracies that create policy as they go about their daily operations.

If this analysis represents the actual state of policy formation, then it is clear that objection to specific public or official policies is not adequate to change them. Democracy in the Dominican Republic is inconsistent not merely with specific American policies but with the existence of an American agency which takes an active role in local Dominican policies. Similarly, land reform and economic programs to alleviate poverty are inconsistent with the existence of large concentrated corporations with special privileges to exploit the physical and human resources of the Dominican Republic.

References

BERLE, ADOLF A., JR.
  1954 *The Twentieth Century Capitalist Revolution.* New York: Harcourt, Brace.

BETHEL, PAUL
  1965 Article in Hearst newspaper chain (May 4).

BODENHEIMER, SUSAN
  1967 "The AFL-CIO in Latin America: The Dominican Republic: A Case Study." *Viet-Report* 3 (September/October): p. 15.

BOSCH, JUAN
  1965 *The Unfinished Experiment.* New York: Praeger.

CRASSWELLER, ROBERT
  1966 *Trujillo: The Life and Times of a Caribbean Dictator.* New York: Macmillan.

DRAPER, THEODORE
  1965 "The Roots of the Dominican Crisis." *The New Leader* 48 (May 24): pp. 3–18. Reprinted by the League for Industrial Democracy.

  ――――
  1968 *The Dominican Revolt.* New York: Commentary.

DUBOIS, JULES
  1963 Article in *Chicago Tribune* (September 27).

DUN AND BRADSTREET
  1965 *Million Dollar Directory.* Also 1969 edition.

EVANS, ROWLAND, JR.
  1963 "First Steps in Dominican Democracy." *The Reporter* 28 (January 3): pp. 21–23.

GALL, NORMAN
  1963 "How Trujillo Died." *New Republic* (April 13): pp. 19–30.

GEYELIN, PHILIP
  1965 Article in *Wall Street Journal* (June 25).

GOFF, FRED, AND MICHAEL LOCKER
  1969 "The Violence of Domination: U.S. Power and the Dominican

Republic," in Irving Horowitz, Josue deCastro, and John Gerassi, eds., *Latin American Radicalism*. New York: Random House.

HALPER, SAM
    1965   "The Dominican Upheaval." *The New Leader* 48 (May 10): pp. 3–4.

HISPANIC AMERICAN REPORT
        September 1962; October 1962; February 1963.

HOY
    1963   September 27.

JACOBS, PAUL
    1967   "How the CIA Makes Liars out of Union Leaders." *Ramparts* 5 (April): pp. 25–28.

MARTIN, JOHN B.
    1966   *Overtaken by Events*. New York: Doubleday & Co.

MANN, THOMAS
    1964   "The Democratic Ideal in our Policy Toward Latin America." *Department of State Bulletin* 50 (June 29): pp. 995–1000. (Commencement address at University of Notre Dame, June 7, 1964.)

_____

    1965   "The Dominican Crisis: Correcting Some Misconceptions." *Department of State Bulletin* 53 (November 8): pp. 730–37.

MOODY'S
    1946–1966
        Industrial Manual.

_____

    1965   *Bank and Finance Manual*. Also 1968 edition.

PEARSON, DREW
    1965   "The Washington Merry-Go-Round." *Washington Post* (May 21).

SCHLESINGER, ARTHUR M., JR.
    1965   *A Thousand Days*. Boston: Houghton Mifflin.

SHEREFF, RUTH
    1967   "How the CIA Makes Friends and Influences Countries." *Viet-Report* 3 (January/February): p. 15.

SZULC, TAD
    1965   *Dominican Diary*. New York: Delacorte Press.

U.S. SENATE FINANCE COMMITTEE
    1962   *Hearings on Sugar Act Amendments*. 87th Congress, 2nd session. Washington, D.C.: U.S. Government Printing Office.

U.S. STATE DEPARTMENT, BUREAU OF INTELLIGENCE AND RESEARCH
  1962   *World Strength of Communist Party Organizations.* Also 1964
      edition.
Who's Who in America
  1968–69
WISE, DAVID, AND THOMAS ROSS
  1964   *The Invisible Government.* New York: Random House.

Chapter 8

AMERICAN
RESPONSIBILITY
IN THE GREEK COUP

Early Friday morning, April 21, 1967, on the eve of the parliamentary election campaign, a group of Greek army colonels took over the government of Greece, arrested thousands of political leaders, and suspended the constitution. For at least three years the Greek people had been awaiting an election that might return to power a progressive government which would tackle the chronic economic and social problems of Greece and institute badly needed reforms. But the rightists entrenched in the powerful Greek army were unready to allow the government to escape their control—and they calculated on United States support.

At three o'clock on the afternoon of April 20, the army officers of the Supreme Military Council held a meeting under the chairmanship of Lt. General Grigoris Spantidakis.[1] They met ostensibly to discuss questions of promotions and retirement. Actually, it was a secret meeting to consider using Prometheus II, a plan developed by the North Atlantic Treaty Organization to put down communist insurgency, as part of the coup d'etat they were planning. Reports indicate that the generals were opposed to telling Prime Minister Panayotis Kanellopoulos about the planned coup, and the group split on whether to warn King Constantine.

---

[1] The following account is taken largely from Robert McDonald, "Greece: April 21, 1967," *The Massachusetts Review* 9 (Winter 1968), pp. 59–78, one of the most detailed chronological accounts of the coup available. Specific page references are given periodically.

The issue of whether to tell the king became a matter of no importance, for the coup was preempted by the colonels, who got wind of the generals' meeting that afternoon and quickly convened their own "war council." Probably the information leak came through Lt. General George Zoitakis, commander of the northern Third Army Corps. Those who attended the meeting were reportedly the "inner circle" of the 60 or so junior military officers who would later constitute the new regime's revolutionary council.

That same Thursday evening, Prime Minister Kanellopoulos was holding a cabinet meeting to plan his strategy for the coming elections. Afterward he continued the discussions at his own apartment, covering, among other things, the possible use of the military to control the crowds at the first campaign rally of his Center Union Party opponents, Andreas Papandreou and his father, George.

While the colonels were plotting, Andreas Papandreou, a widely popular symbol of progressive forces in Greece, spoke before the executive committee of the Democratic Unions of Athens. In his talk he warned that the military and the judiciary were participating in a giant "plot against the nation." He urged that the army should belong to the nation, rather than vice versa, and said, "the king does not require praetorians. His shield is the constitution, and the army is the shield of the nation (McDonald 1968, p. 60). But Papandreou's struggle to secure government control over the rightist strongholds of the army and the Greek intelligence agency had gotten him into trouble before, and was about to do so again.

Apparently none of the leading figures in Papandreou's Center Union Party was forewarned of the coup. Only one got word at 9 PM Thursday evening, and he promptly set sail for Turkey and then sought asylum in France.

The NATO plan left little to chance, and the coup proceeded with extreme efficiency. By three o'clock on the morning of April 21, the Tank Corps, commanded by General Pattakos, who had joined the coup the night before, had occupied all strategic points in Athens and cut off all internal and external communications (McDonald 1968). About 2:15 AM the military began its first wave of arrests, exactly as specified in the NATO plan. Anyone who might be likely to lead organized resistance was arrested (McDermott, Mallet, and Maspero 1967). Among those arrested were cabinet members, leaders of the several opposition parties, advisors to the king, newspaper editors, and thousands whose names were associated with communist or former resistance groups. Prime Minister Kanellopoulos was arrested only after a combination of ruse and threat got him to leave his home in the middle of the night. Andreas Papandreou, a former cabinet member and a Center Union Party candidate in the scheduled elections, tried to hide on the roof terrace of his house, but gave himself up when a soldier threatened one of his children in an attempt to locate him. Other leading political figures who were arrested included Minister of Public Order Rallis, the ERE (conservative party) Defense Minister Papaligouras, the Center Union leader of the House, a Liberal Democratic Center deputy, the leader of the left-wing EDA, and Manolis Glezos, a former leader of the Greek resistance fighters in World War II who was considered a key link between the EDA and the communist KKE (McDonald 1968).

The NATO plan for stopping communist subversion was extensive, though somewhat dated. It used three lists prepared by the Greek secret service classifying subversives by degree of potential danger. But the "gamma list" (active militants) had been, like most police lists, assembled over a long period of time, and the first wave of police repression hit the old above all. The former patriots of the resistance against Nazi occupation—people who had been subjected to persecution through most of the period following the Greek civil war (1947–49)—were arrested first. Some of them had actually done nothing of record for over 17 years. Eventually the arrests covered every potential opponent, whether young or old (McDermott, Mallet, and Maspero 1967). In the first wave, Papadopoulos said, 6,000 were arrested. The number grew, until by the end of May the total was said to be approaching 20,000 (Stanislas 1967, cited in McDermott, Mallet, and Maspero 1967).

The king learned of the coup in the early morning hours as arrests were begun, but he was unable to set off effective resistance. Colonel Michael Arnaoutis, personal secretary and confidant to King Constantine, managed to reach the king by phone, but was arrested shortly afterward. Demetrios Bitsios, a diplomat and royal political advisor, was arrested. The minister of public order, George Rallis, learned of the coup before he was actually arrested and called the king, who reportedly told Rallis to instruct the Third Army Corps in the north, troops with a special reputation for loyalty to the crown, to start for Athens. Rallis called but could get no cooperation when he tried to convey the royal command. Evidently General Zoitakis, who had joined the colonels' coup, had left instructions to thwart any attempt by the king to mobilize the Third Army in opposition to the coup. Meanwhile the king reached the residence of Defense Chief Lt. General Spantidakis by phone, but Spantidakis too was shortly arrested. The king apparently did get through to the navy at Skaramanga Base, and ordered the ships to remain at port but to prepare to put to sea. When Rallis called the king to report his failure to move the Third Army, the King was already meeting with a junta triumvirate of Colonel Papadopoulos, Colonel Makarezos, and General Pattakos. Rallis's call was interrupted by his own arrest. By this time the combination of arrests and severed communications had virtually destroyed any chance of resistance (McDonald 1968).

During the night newspapers were closed down, and news of the coup never reached the newsstands in the morning. Editors were arrested in their homes, including Leonidas Kyrkos, editor of *Avghi*, the press of the non-communist left-wing party, EDA.

The colonels' original plan is said to have called for an all-military cabinet, with Lt. General Spantidakis as premier. Spantidakis is believed to have been persuaded during the course of his arrest and the ride from his home to the Defense Ministry building to throw his lot in with the colonels and accept the premiership. When the junta triumvirate met with the king in the palace, shortly after 3 AM, they presented him with a fait accompli and asked him to sign a royal proclamation of the coup. The king, however, following Rallis's advice not to take action without the approval of his advisors, refused to sign the proclamation and attempted to dismiss the colonels. It is reported that the king held a private meeting with General Spantidakis, during which the general told the king that he had joined the junta for the purpose of keeping watch on its activities for the king. Evidently this was not completely satisfactory to the king, who still refused to sign the proclamation. By 6 AM the National Broadcasting Institute (EIR), which had been taken over in one of the earliest pre-dawn movements of the coup, began broadcasting reports of a royal proclamation endorsing the coup and declaring a state of emergency, restricting all civil liberties, and announcing a strict curfew on the streets. At this point the junta was taking a chance, because the king had not actually signed the proclamation. At daybreak soldiers and military police were everywhere in the streets, preventing crowds from gathering.

While militarily the coup was a fait accompli, the king still had something in his power which the junta very much needed, that is, the sanction that would be necessary in order for the new government to hope to gain international diplomatic recognition. On the morning of April 21, King Constantine commenced to bargain with the junta. Some of the junta members wanted to send the king off on the next plane; others knew that his presence was necessary. What Constantine was striving for was a possibility of continuing to rule with the junta in existence, with the hope of exercising some moderating influence but with the minimum goal of saving his crown and preventing bloodshed (McDonald 1968).

The king eventually endorsed the government and salvaged his figure-head position. But it was the colonels who ruled, and they began tightening their grip on the nation.

The American Response

United States policy in reaction to the coup was muddled and indecisive, but its ultimate effect was to lend support to the new regime and to gloss lightly over its brutality and wholesale suppression of civil rights.

The coup was made possible by a military body integrated into NATO and funded by the United States. Several of its leaders were members of the Greek Intelligence Agency (KYP), which had been set up and financed largely by the United States Central Intelligence Agency. The plan for the coup was known to American officials and to the Greek king. If there was a surprise, it lay only in the personnel who executed the plan. There had been strong hints that neither the king, nor the Greek army, nor the CIA, nor the American military would tolerate the return of a progressive Center Union government under Andreas Papandreou, and that a coup was very likely in the offing. But the colonels stole the coup from the generals, and caught the king off guard.

American Ambassador Talbot, who had worked closely with the king, was at first horrified by the coup, and cabled Washington describing it as the "rape of Greek democracy" and asking an immediate strong condemnation of the coup (Drew 1968, p. 59). An immediate firm denunciation by the United States would have weakened the junta seriously. The king's forces were potentially far more powerful than those of the colonels, but he was cornered and could not mobilize them. In fact, the Greek army, navy, and air force in the north outnumbered the southern division involved in the coup by ten to one, and they stood ready to launch a counter-coup if the Americans gave them any hint of support.

But the State Department played a waiting game, doing nothing for a week. The Assistant Secretary of State for Near Eastern and South Asian Affairs was new to his post and unfamiliar with affairs in Greece. His deputy, Stuart Rockwell, was inclined from the start toward an accommodation with the colonels. Daniel Brewster, Director of Greek Affairs, had served the United States in Greece at critical periods—from 1947 to 1952 when the United States intervened in the Greek civil war, and from 1961 to 1965 when the United States was deciding that Andreas Papandreou was not an acceptable leader for Greece.

A mild note was finally prepared regretting the coup, but secretary of State Dean Rusk refused to issue it because it might hamper future relations with the new government. On April 28, the United States released a statement that was the model of conciliation. In the note Rusk expressed gratification "that Greece will continue its strong support of NATO," encouragement at King Constantine's call "for an early return to parliamentary government," and hope "that the new Greek government will make every effort to re-establish democratic institutions." To avoid offending the colonels, the note did not even mention the fact that military aid would be partially suspended. Rusk did say he trusted that political prisoners would be set free in a few days, as Papadopoulos had promised, but little was done to enforce American wishes. The United States continued shipping small arms to Greece, and political prisoners remained in jail (Drew 1968).

Walt Rostow and John Roche, moderate intellectuals in positions close to the president who might have swung some weight, could not even be persuaded to present the case for American intervention to save the life of Andreas Papandreou, who had developed strong ties with American scholars during twenty years of studying and teaching in the United States. Only after John Kenneth Galbraith, then outside the good graces of the Johnson administration, begged for such action did the president respond (Rousseas 1967).

United States policy was purportedly to support the king, and since the king was trying to live with the junta, the Americans did likewise. In December 1967, however, the king tried to overthrow the colonels with the aid of Greek troops loyal to the monarchy. The United States gave him no overt support, although it is reported that State Department officials privately wished him success. But the counter-coup was badly timed and badly organized, and the king was quickly forced into exile. As a result the United States temporarily suspended diplomatic relations with Greece, but resumed them not long afterward (Drew 1968).

American support of the junta continued in spite of the heavy-handed cultural restrictions and political restraints imposed by the new regime. In 1968 the junta proposed a farcical new constitution with provisions for a "free" press—bound by numerous regulations—yet a State Department official said approvingly, "The purpose of our policy has been to influence these people to move in the direction of constitutional government, and it has had that effect" (Drew 1968, p. 66).

The Rule of Fascism

Under the colonels Greece has exhibited many manifestations of fascism. The draft constitution, issued by the junta in March 1968, declared that "the press is free" but in the same breath said that it "exercises a social mission, that entails obligations." So that no one would mistake what social obligations the junta had in mind, the constitution specified that confiscation of the press is permitted "when it insults the Christian religion, insults the person of the King, the King's parents, the Queen, the Crown Prince, their children and wives, insults the honor and reputation of individuals holding public office or having held public office..." (Drew 1968, p. 66). As of the summer of 1967, the supposedly "free" press was required to submit its copy for official review each night before publication and to print government handouts as news. Censors told the newspapers where to print articles, how much space to give them, and how large the headlines should be (Anastaplo 1968).

The junta not only clamped down on the Greek press, but cramped every phase of Greek life and culture. Its zeal for moral purity showed striking parallels to the Nazi drive in the 1930s. Beards and miniskirts were banned, musical compositions of suspected communists could not be played (Drew 1968), and Greek classical drama was censored (Rousseas 1967). Greek artists who no longer manifested the "Greek spirit" had their citizenships revoked (Heineman 1968). Following the coup, church attendance was made compulsory for students, who were instructed to turn in their history books for new ones which contained a full section on the Greek kings (Rousseas 1967).

Political repression was perhaps even more pervasive than cultural repression. Along with the summary arrests of thousands of citizens, there was extensive use of military tribunals, and outlawing of parties distasteful to the junta. With the suspension of the constitution and the hunting of political opponents, the death penalty for political offenders was reintroduced. The brilliant Athenian lawyer Nikiforos Mandilaras was an early victim. His defense had made a shambles of the Greek army high command charges in the "Aspida" case in which Andreas Papandreou and 28 army officers were accused of high treason. After he had been arrested in the first wave of arrests, Mandilaras's body was found washed ashore on the island of Rhodes (Rousseas 1967).

In the more than three years since the coup, reports have trickled out of Greece that many political prisoners have been tortured. The descriptions of beatings, electric shock, and more exotic horrors rival stories of medieval Europe, or of the French in Algeria. The colonels have refused to allow investigators to enter Greece and verify the charges, but the Commission on Human Rights of the Council of Europe has found conclusive evidence of torture by interviewing witnesses who had escaped Greece.[2] The purpose of this chapter is not to describe the methods human beings have devised to inflict extensive brutality on each other. But if the study of international conflict is ever to result in anything more than an abstract understanding

---

[2] Details of the allegations of torture may be found in C. S. Wren, "Greece: Government by Torture," Look 33 (May 27, 1969), pp. 19–21; James Becket, "Greece: The Rack and the Bomb," Nation 290 (July 7, 1969), pp. 6–7; John Corry, "Greece: The Death of Liberty," Harper's Magazine 239 (October 1969), pp. 72–81; "Torture: Activities of the Greek Junta," Newsweek 74 (December 15, 1969), p. 52; and James Becket, Barbarism in Greece, Walker and Company, 1970. A follow-up article in Look, October 7, 1969, describes the refusal of Papadopoulos to allow investigations of charges of torture. In mid-December 1969, Greek representatives walked out the Council of Europe just before the council was to take up the question of expelling it for denial of basic democratic rights to the Greek people. The council had hemmed and hawed, but when the Human Rights Commission Report came out, it finally was compelled to take action.

of the course of history, then it is necessary to permit ourselves the empathic experience of those remote victims of our own foreign policies. Sickening documentation of the most extreme forms of physical abuse imaginable have leaked out of Greece. These are not, of course, unique to Greece. Current reports from Brazil and from the Santa Rita Rehabilitation Center in California suggest similar atrocities at the hands of government authorities in many areas. But the documentation compiled by James Becket in *Barbarism in Greece* must be an ingredient of any serious attempt to understand the new face of fascism.

The ideology that underlies the new regime is one of moral absolutism and rabid anti-communism. Colonel Papadopoulos, leader of the coup and once the contact man between the American CIA and its Greek counterpart (Drew 1968), is a virulent hater of communism. In an interview four months after the coup, Captain D. M. Alexandrou, a young naval officer who firmly supported Papadopoulos, expressed well the regime's Manichaean depiction of the world in terms of angels and demons. Alexandrou sees himself as a staunch ally of the United States in a crusade against the ambitions of communist Russia. He warns that the United States and Greece must never be fooled by the Russians, who do not and could not want coexistence. "They are barbarians. They have no civilization for they are slaves and peasants. They threaten what we in Greece stand for." In the face of the Soviet threat, the criticisms of the monarchy and the military by former Center Union premier George Papandreou are not merely criticisms but outright subversion. Alexandrou sees every repressive measure as a "necessary" part of the stand for "democracy, morality, and virtue" (Heineman 1968, pp. 79–82). The assuredness of "true believers" like Captain Alexandrou leaves little opening for meaningful discussion. Yet such men now rule Greece.

Greece in the Aftermath of World War II

Aside from isolated modern urban areas, Greece is a semi-feudal state with a small aristocracy of extreme wealth, a military establishment loyal to the aristocracy and externally funded, and a general population living in poverty. The Greek political situation bears strong resemblance to that of the Vietnamese and, perhaps, to others.

Betrayed by pro-fascist generals, Greece was quickly overwhelmed by the Nazis in 1941. A few months later Greek resistance fighters organized the highly effective EAM, or National Liberation Front. They were known as Antartes—partisans (Thermos 1968)—and the 40,000 to 60,000 guerrillas (Gitlin 1967) in their military arm had liberated almost all of Greece by the spring of 1944. The remaining small portion of Epirus fell to a much smaller conservative resistance group (Thermos 1968). The EAM was the only truly popular force in the nation at the time of liberation. It numbered about two million members out of a total population of over seven million (McNeill 1947). That a broad range of organizations supported the EAM was partly the result of its guerrilla policies, which included no entering of peasants' houses, village elections with broad slates (even including traditional royalists on occasion), voting privileges for women, village schools, highly localized and reportedly fair people's courts, and complete respect for the custom of individual land holdings (although this must certainly have run counter to the wishes of certain communist and socialist parties affiliated with the EAM).[3]

During World War II the Greek monarch and a largely royalist army of about 20,000 men fled into exile in the Middle East. Through the royal family the British had exercised political and economic domination of Greece during the prewar years, and Britain's prime policy objective during the war was to regain its influential position in Greek affairs. When in February 1944 there was a power struggle among the exiles between republican elements on the one hand and a combination of royalists, fascist sympathizers, and anti-republicans on the other, the British intervened, shipping 12,000 of the republicans to concentration camps in northeast Africa, and saving the day for the royalists (Thermos 1968).

In March 1944, at a conference in Lebanon sponsored by the British, the royalists and republicans formed a coalition Government of National Unity with conservative George Papandreou as prime minister. The EAM, although it controlled most of the land and was superior in its armed forces and extremely popular, agreed the following August to submit to the authority of the compromise government for the sake of national unity (Thermos 1968).

The new government then signed an agreement with the British which, among other things, outlawed opposition to the pro-fascist Security Battalions, Greek units which had fought on the side of the Germans and Italians. An earlier agreement had declared that all resistance and volunteer armed forces would be dissolved, and that a national army would be raised by conscription. But in actual fact the hated Security Battalions were never dismantled, and they continued their attacks on the EAM. In November and December of 1944, Premier George Papandreou announced again that all volunteer forces would be dismantled, with the exception of the Sacred

---

[3] Gitlin, pp. 145–46. Gitlin's sources are Stefanos Sarafis, *Greek Resistance Army: The Story of ELAS* (translated and abridged by Marion Pascoe), (London, 1941), p. 33; Frank Smothers, William H. McNeill, and Elizabeth D. McNeill, *Report on the Greeks* (New York, 1948), pp. 24–25; and L. S. Stavrianos, *Greece: American Dilemma and Opportunity* (Chicago: H. Regnery Co., 1952), pp. 80ff.

Battalion and the Mountain Brigade, two recently organized units that were largely fascist or royalist. These two units would form the core of the new national army (Thermos 1968).

Britain took a deep interest in the parry and counter-parry of Greek politics, and Stalin sanctioned that interest in an agreement with Churchill concluded in October 1944, placing Greece within the British sphere of influence. Meanwhile, British General Scobie and George Papandreou were negotiating with the EAM. The British held firm for a return of the monarchy, the arming of the pro-royalist Mountain Brigade, and the disarming of the EAM (McNeill 1947). Their demands provided no basis for compromise. However, many Greeks still regarded the British as allies and did not anticipate the lengths to which the British would go to get their way.

British troops had begun arriving in Greece in October. On December 3, 1944, the British opened fire in Athens on a leftist demonstration against the Papandreou government amid cries of "Long live Churchill! Long live Roosevelt! Down with Papandreou! No King!" (Rousseas 1967, p. 78, and Gitlin 1967, p. 152).[4] Within 24 hours the British inflicted 13,700 casualties. On December 6, General Scobie ordered British aircraft to strafe one of the poorer neighborhoods in Athens, which was most heavily dominated by EAM supporters (Gitlin 1967).

Even during the fighting in December the EAM's position was conciliatory. When Papandreou proposed establishing a government under Sofoulis, the EAM accepted, but the offer was withdrawn before it could be put into effect. When Churchill visited Athens in late December, the EAM asked for an appointment with him, but Churchill refused. By the end of December, the EAM was still in control of most of Greece and most of Athens. But the British, assured of Soviet permission for hegemony over Greece, sent two more divisions in American transports. On January 4 and 5 the organized EAM military slipped out of Athens, leaving a populace of armed snipers (Gitlin 1967).

Then began the horror and brutality of civil strife. When the British arrested thousands of suspected snipers and transported them to North Africa, the EAM retaliated by marching 14,000 rightist sympathisers out of Athens under guard, reportedly causing 4,000 deaths from the rigors of the forced march (Forster 1958, cited in Gitlin 1967). Charges of terror and brutality on both sides became increasingly a self-fulfilling prophesy.

One last effort to constrain further internal strife occurred when the EAM, the imposed Greek government, and the British signed the Varkiza Agreement on February 12, 1945. It provided for an end to hostilities;

---

[4] The story that a *Chicago Sun* reporter heard these slogans shouted is taken from National Liberation Front (EAM) *White Book, May 1944–March 1945* (New York: Greek American Council, 1945).

disarming of all popular or volunteer armies (except the controversial Sacred Battalion, which would be incorporated in the national army) ; a purge of the security battalions, the public services, and the police; repeal of martial law; amnesty for all political offenses committed between December 3 and February 12; release of all hostages; free expression for all political opinions including those of the EAM and the Communist Party (although neither was to be represented in the new Plastiras government) ; an early (1945) plebiscite on the question of constitutional republic versus monarchy; and free elections to form a new Constituent Assembly (Thermos 1968; Rousseas 1967; Stavrianos 1952, cited in Gitlin 1967).

The EAM, though still in control of three-fourths of Greece (Gitlin 1967) and still the most popular resistance group emerging from the war, actually overfulfilled its promise to disarm, turning in more weapons than the agreement required. Then, during the next 13 months until the election, a reign of terror was unleashed against the EAM. The entire left-wing press was suppressed, hostages were taken, and former political and military resistance leaders were arrested and murdered. With a rightist military in control, the purge extended to government officials, civil services, the universities, and the church. EAM records showed 84,931 arrests, 31,632 cases of torture, and 1,289 persons killed in the purge (Thermos 1968).

The Soviet Union, maintaining its hands-off policy, suggested that the Communist Party take part in the British-sponsored elections (Gitlin 1967). The elections, however, were openly a farce involving forgery, terror, and "every possible form of corrupt practice" (American Council for a Democratic Greece 1949, quoted in Thermos 1968, p. 121). Even cabinet members were aghast. The foreign minister resigned, charging that free elections were impossible unless "a wide amnesty is granted" and "terrorism by state organs ceases." The vice-premier, Kafandares, resigned, calling the forthcoming elections a "comedy" (Gitlin 1967, p. 161).

The five parties of the EAM bloc were joined by four other political parties in boycotting the election. With a very small turnout, the royalists won and the monarchy was restored. The left was effectively ruled out of any participation in the government, whose first program was apparently to exterminate its opposition (Thermos 1968). Yet even in April, after the elections, the communists did not endorse armed struggle in opposing the government (Zografos 1964, cited in Gitlin 1967). But bands of armed guerrillas were already forming in the Greek mountains. The government branded this group, which had once been the Antartes (patriots), as Symmorites (outlaws), to be pursued with official anti-left fanaticism (Thermos 1968). Guerrilla strength increased rapidly. In August the communist party, still without any form of assistance from the USSR, sent General Markos Vafiades to coordinate the guerrilla activities (Gitlin 1967). As a series of inept governments faced with civil war failed to make any of the economic or social reforms imperative to alleviate the poverty and chaos of a war-ravaged country, the opposition grew in size and strength.

American Intervention and the Truman Doctrine

In 1947, with the civil war turning toward the rebels, British Foreign Minister Ernest Bevin told United States officials that without American assistance, Great Britain could not maintain its position of influence in Greece (Macridis 1968). The American response, which did more than anything else to launch the cold war, was the Truman Doctrine.

> Assistance is imperative if Greece is to survive as a free nation.... At the present moment in world history nearly every nation must choose between alternative ways of life.... One way of life is based upon the will of the majority, and is distinguished by free institutions, representative government, free elections, guarantees of individual liberty, freedom of speech and religion, and freedom from political oppression. The second way of life is based upon the will of a minority forcibly imposed upon the majority. It relies upon terror and oppression, a controlled press and radio, fixed elections, and the suppression of personal freedom. (*New York Times*, March 13, 1947)

Surely American officials recognized the quality of the government they were supporting. Secretary of State Acheson admitted that the armed challenge, while led by communists, was supported by many non-communists who were dissatisfied with the Greek government (U.S. Department of State 1947). A State Department speech writer, Joseph Jones, who helped draft the Truman Doctrine speech, also showed recognition of the quality of government his country was defending. The choice, he said, was not "between black and white but between black and a rather dirty grey. With the United States aid and pressure" this dirty grey government might "become a respectable white" (Jones 1955, p. 186 quoted in Gitlin 1967, p. 179).

Our protection of Greece took the form of $400 million in military aid and $300 million in economic assistance between March 1947 and June 1949 (Gitlin 1967). Americans organized and trained the Greek army and placed the Greek military under NATO (essentially American) command (Macridis 1968). A United States public health team did wipe out malaria in Greece. It did not, however, produce a popular government. Inflation was rampant, and the rich Greek oligarchy refused to pay taxes. Premier Sofoulis was powerless to make any reforms that would reduce the grip of the extreme right on the economy. The many small political parties that continued to exist represented a narrow part of the spectrum of Greek political opinion. The effect of the American policy was to neutralize and weaken the moderate forces, thus posing for Greece the alternatives of insurgency from the left or suppression from the right (Gitlin 1967).

President Truman was not acting because of anti-communist pressure from the American public. In the month of his speech setting forth the Truman Doctrine, polls showed 48.3 percent of the public opposed to sending military supplies to help the Greek government put down armed attacks by Greek communists, with 14.5 percent undecided (Gitlin 1967). Public opinion followed the American military intervention, but did not cause it.

With the United States providing direct military intervention and the Soviet Union maintaining a strict neutrality, the rebels were soon crushed. Not a single communist government had recognized General Markov's revolutionary (Free Democratic) government. American artillery, dive bombers, and napalm, and General Van Fleet's campaign for "the systematic removal of whole sections of the population" caused rebel resistance to end in October 1949 (Barnet 1968, p. 122). After the hostilities ended, a highly visible American presence remained, through the embassy, the military, and the CIA. The American ambassador hunted with the king and the embassy staff worked closely with politicians and businessmen from the extreme right. The CIA created, trained, and controlled the Greek Intelligence Agency. The United States "approved prime ministers, interfered in elections and passed upon military promotions" (Drew 1967, p. 56).

For American military strategists, our policy toward Greece has been essentially a success. For them Greece is a component in the doctrine of the Joint Chiefs of Staff. Greece lies on the perimeter of the United States–dominated Western world. The doctrine holds that only a strong NATO presence protects Greece from an attack by Bulgaria or from an insurrection directed and aided by Moscow. Since the United States is heavily committed to serving the same role elsewhere, any deficiencies in Greek defense will have to be met by an already overextended United States military. Hence the doctrine holds that support of an anti-left Greek military must be the cornerstone of American policy not only toward Greece but toward NATO in its entirety (Drew 1967).

Whether the Bulgars have ever intended to attack Greece is not frequently discussed in American policy circles. There is even substantial doubt whether Greek troops and weapons concentrated in the northern plains of Greece are poised against Bulgaria or against Greece's NATO partner Turkey, also supplied with arms by the United States (Clark 1967). Senator Joseph Clark, returning from a fact-finding mission in December 1966, wrote: "The justification for military aid to Greece is simply no longer there. The fact that we have given military aid to Greece for so many years should not blind the Congress to the desirability of terminating further military aid to Greece and to Turkey. . . ." (Drew 1968, p. 60). Still, the military strategists have created their own reality. Since Bulgaria has not attacked Greece, they reason that their assumptions must be correct and their strategy successful.

Walt Rostow, an influential advisor to Presidents Kennedy and Johnson, considers communist insurgency to be a disease of the transition to modernization. His thesis is that if one can only rob communist insurgents of their opportunity to foment trouble during the limited time of under-development, then Westernization will take hold (Gitlin 1967). But post–civil war events in Greece belie this theory. More than nine years after the guerrillas had been vanquished, an Athens newspaper reported, "In the nearly 15 years since the Second World War, we have been unable, despite Truman doctrines, Marshall plans, American aid, and so on, to make Greece capable of maintaining and feeding her own population" (Zografos 1964, pp. 48–49, quoted in Gitlin 1967, p. 178). Jean Meynaud (1965) docu-ments a long (and still existing) period of economic stagnation and political chaos. The countryside is overpopulated, urban workers are underpaid, and the rich oligarchy who work closely with the American mission refuse to pay taxes or to permit reforms (Gitlin 1967). The price of military success has been, and perhaps always is, a destitute population.

The Center Union Party and the Movement for Greek Autonomy

With the throne, the Greek military, the highly protected business oligarchy, the United States embassy, and NATO all having con-gruent interests (all pursued in the name of democracy or at least of anti-communism), any move for effective social reform seemed hopeless. In the early 1960s, however, the conservative Karamanlis government was under attack both from the royal family, for its independence, and from George Papandreou's Center Union Party, for its failure to act on pressing economic and social problems (Drew 1968).

The Center Union Party won a plurality in 1963 and an absolute majority in 1964. The elder Papandreou, a crafty pro-royalist and vehe-mently anti-communist statesman (once selected by the British for this quality) played the delicate game of balancing the right against the left. On one hand he approved a sizable pension to Queen Mother Frederika and forbade public criticism of her. He made numerous conservative cabinet appointments, including the appointment of beer baron Petros Faroufalias, a palace favorite, as minister of defense. On the other hand, he broke the control of the rural police over the countryside, diminished the power of the dossier-keeping security forces, proclaimed an amnesty for political prisoners, and renegotiated contracts with large foreign monopolies on terms more favorable to Greece (Rousseas 1967).

The critical elements that led to his downfall, however, were three: his failure to weaken the organization of the right-wing military establish-ment; his pro-Greece position in the Greek–Turkish dispute over Cyprus; and the appointment of his son, Andreas, as minister of coordination.

Andreas Papandreou, exiled from Greece as a student in the 1930s for opposing the Greek military dictatorship, lived in the United States for 20 years. He became an American citizen and a distinguished Harvard-trained economist. He was an active supporter of Senator Hubert Humphrey in Minnesota and of Adlai Stevenson. When he returned to Greek political life, Andreas proved to have great talent and appeal. He drew up the first comprehensive economic plan for Greece and pushed for extensive reforms along the models of the social democratic programs of Western Europe. He forced through a plan giving the Greek cabinet, rather than the United States Central Intelligence Agency, direct control over the Greek Intelligence Agency. He struggled to reduce palace control over the military and to increase the autonomy of Greece under NATO. Although first subject to charges that his return to Greece after almost 21 years' absence was either opportunistic or the work of the CIA, Andreas stirred the nationalism of the people and rapidly became the most popular political figure in Greece (Drew 1968).

When in 1965 the issue of control over Cyprus exploded, the United States tried to exert influence on Greece to resolve its differences with Turkey, also a NATO member, on terms which would have meant political suicide for the Center Union government. When even a personal effort by President Lyndon Johnson failed to change the Center Union policy, the United States embassy staff decided to get rid of Andreas Papandreou (Rousseas 1967). Its opportunity came when the Center Union party backed Archbishop Makarios in his struggle for control of the Cypriot army. Makarios sought military assistance from Czechoslovakia and the Soviet Union, hoping to exert leverage on the Americans and the NATO powers by appealing to the communists. Meanwhile, the association of the Center Union government with Makarios, and of Makarios with the communists, spelled only one thing to the Greek royalists. In a scheme in which the American CIA was later reported to have been involved, a Greek general on Cyprus drew up charges that Andreas was plotting to overthrow the government by force. He said Andreas had secretly formed a conspiratorial club (called "Aspida") of dissident army officers, who planned to take over the army, depose the king, and impose a Nasser-type dictatorship. These obviously trumped-up charges were elaborated in a report containing nothing but hearsay, and devoid of evidence. When King Constantine appointed Garoufalias, the minister of defense, to look into the case, George Papandreou warned that the king was using Garoufalias to smear the Center Union government. He tried to dismiss Garoufalias, who refused to resign without a writ from the king. Instead, George Papandreou himself was obliged to resign; a puppet government replaced him (Rousseas 1967).

Since the United States had informed the king that only technically constitutional moves would be supported (Drew 1968), it was essential that a date be set, however reluctantly, for elections to replace the interim government. The attitude of the monarchy toward democracy is best summed up in Queen Frederika's statement in 1960. She would, she said, "be the first to fight for democracy if she thought it had anything to offer the people other than modern bathrooms" (Rousseas 1967, pp. 32–33, footnote). To the king, the 1964 vote of 53 percent for the Center Union party and additional 12 percent for the left-wing party meant that 65 percent of his subjects were suspect. When Andreas Papandreou brought the Greek Intelligence Agency under cabinet control and was making overtures to replace the most extremely rightist army officers, the monarchy felt deeply threatened. The Greek army had traditionally been the personal shield of the monarchy; 16 years of American control, through NATO and through $100 million of military and economic aid per year, had done nothing to force the king to think otherwise (Rousseas 1967). The king managed to delay elections for two years, until they were finally forestalled by the coup.

From the dissolution of the Center Union government in July 1965 until the actual military coup, a series of sometimes open, sometimes clandestine political maneuvers took place. They were aimed at insuring that the Center Union party would not win an absolute majority, and at minimizing the influence of the reform-minded Andreas Papandreou. A key figure was Christos Lambrakis, publisher of two leading Greek newspapers. While supporting the elder Papandreou, the Lambrakis papers virtually blacked out Andreas and pressured for repressive police measures against the left (Rousseas 1967).

The Center Union in its 1964 victory had won a substantial amount of support from voters who had previously supported the left-wing EDA. The monarchy hoped to alienate these voters and to force the older Papandreou to form a coalition with the conservative government and resolve all differences with the king. The king also wanted a free hand in appointing ministers to the new government. If he could regain this measure of control, not only the king but also American industrialists and the American NATO command would be satisfied (Rousseas 1967).

The aging Papandreou, in his desire to regain the premiership, agreed to all the monarchy's demands without consulting his party. Had he rejected them, elections could have been postponed, under the constitution, for more than a full year. In accepting the conditions George Papandreou also agreed to support a new caretaker government under the governor of the National Bank of Greece for a five-month period. Andreas was then urged both by American officials and by Greek industrialists to accept the terms. He refused, and refused further to engage in any secret deals with the king (Rousseas 1967). But the elder Papandreou demanded that his party back the caretaker government.

During the struggle for power that followed, it became immediately clear that Andreas's popularity had been underestimated. Andreas was, in fact, in a position to oust his own father from the party leadership. Although father and son were not now on speaking terms, Andreas could not bring himself to do this. After negotiations through intermediaries, Andreas accepted his father's agreement on the interim government, but with one important concession. Andreas Papandreou, and not the conservative wing of the Center Union party, was to have prime say in determining the party's candidates for election to parliament (Rousseas 1967).

In a sense, the plan to destroy the influence of Andreas and the long overdue reform politics of Greece had backfired. Now, with the king, the conservative party, and the Center Union party all firmly committed to elections within five months, the de facto leadership of the party had changed. With Andreas emerging again as a popular hero it seemed possible that the Center Union would again win an absolute majority (Rousseas 1967). But just before the official opening of the election campaign, the neo-fascist coup took place. The immediate effects of the coup in Greece have already been described. But Greece is highly dependent on the United States. We must examine the extent of United States involvement in Greece before and after the coup.

American Responsibility

In 1950 the American CIA established a counterpart Greek intelligence agency, the KYP. Since then both organizations have been hard at work to influence Greek politics. Under American tutelage the KYP has undergone extensive growth and moved its agents into the armed forces and into many branches of the Greek government (Vachliotis and Diakogiannis 1967).

From 1964, the prime target of the KYP was Andreas Papandreou, perhaps because Andreas sought to make the KYP responsible to the Greek cabinet. The KYP investigated Andreas, screening his mail, infiltrating his household staff of servants, and plotting to oust him (Vachliotis and Diakogiannis 1967).

In the months before the July 1965 crisis in which Prime Minister George Papandreou was forced to resign, a Greek businessman learned from an American CIA source that the palace and the minister of defense were plotting to overthrow the Center Union government. He passed the word on to the prime minister, who uncovered other evidence of CIA involvement. Shortly before the crisis the elder Papandreou also learned that a suspected CIA agent had made visits to two Center Union parliamentary deputies. After the crisis, these deputies both joined a renegade Center Union faction that wanted to sacrifice George Papandreou and form a government without him—an outcome that might well have suited the CIA (Rousseas 1967).

But the KYP was not satisfied with unseating the Center Union and Andreas's father, and continued to plan the demise of Andreas himself.

When Andreas was finally arrested on the night of the coup, a document of charges against him was in the hands of the KYP. It was signed by his friend and Center Union colleague, Vachliotis, and it charged Andreas with plans to organize a coup d'etat among dissatisfied young officers, to remove the king, and to take Greece out of NATO. The document affirmed that Andreas held pro-communist sympathies and was guilty of treasonous activities. The testimony of another colleague, Diakogiannis, asserted that Andreas intended to use violent means to replace certain key military and police leaders. The document, however, was a frame-up. Both men have since stated that they produced this perjured testimony only under direct personal threat (Vachliotis and Diakogiannis 1967).

The importance of the American-backed and American-financed Greek Intelligence Agency in the colonels' coup cannot be overestimated. The new officials in charge of "interior security" and "espionage and counter-espionage" and the staff director of the prime minister are all KYP men (Vachliotis and Diakogiannis 1967). The junta dictator himself, Colonel Papadopoulos, was a key figure in the KYP; Andreas has charged in public that Papadopoulos is the first CIA agent to make it as head of government (Rousseas 1969). The sad fact is that Papadopoulos is not the first one—South Vietnam's Diem preceded him, and several other Asian, Latin America, and African heads of state, if not directly subsidized by the CIA, at least owe their positions to the workings of that agency.

In the 20 years of the KYP's existence, it has leaned heavily on the CIA for training and financial support. Whether the colonels' coup was directly a product of CIA policy or whether it was engineered by the Greek protégés of the CIA seems to make little difference. The results in Greece are wholly consistent with the aims and activities of the CIA in the rest of the world—in Guatemala, Vietnam, and all other nations in desperate need of social progress.

American Industry and Diplomacy in Greece

The United States Department of Commerce listing (October 1967) of *American Firms, Subsidiaries and Affiliates in Greece* reports over one hundred large commercial firms operating in Greece in which Americans have the major capital investment. American holdings are particularly prevalent in chemical and pharmaceutical industries and in tobacco. The list includes the following powers of American industry:

Allied Chemical, American Broadcasting Company, American Life Insurance, Associated Press, Bendix, Bristol Myers, Colgate Palmolive, Continental Can, Control Data, Dow Chemical, Eastman Kodak, First National City Bank of New York, Ford, Hertz, Hilton, IBM, International Harvester, International Telephone and Telegraph, John Hancock Mutual Life Insurance, Kaiser Engineers, Litton Industries, Mobil Oil, National Cash Register, Pan American World Airways, Proctor and Gamble, Rexall Drugs, Singer Sewing Machine, Squibb, Standard Oil, Trans World Airlines, Union Carbide, all the major United States tobacco campanies, and the investment house of Merrill Lynch, Pierce, Fenner and Smith International (U.S. Department of Commerce, Washington, 1967).

The giant of American-owned Greek manufacturing is the Esso–Pappas industrial complex, which is engaged in oil refining and the production of ammonia, petrochemicals, and steel. During the years of Papandreou's regime the government insisted on renegotiation with Esso–Pappas on terms more favorable to the Greek economy. In so doing, they created a powerful American enemy. It is important to note that Greek laws have favored big industry by providing exemptions in taxes and in import duties on investments outside of the Athens–Piraeus area, and on investments in various kinds of equipment and fuels. Investments—regardless of type or location— which are approved under provisions of the foreign investment laws also rate certain privileges, and are free from import duties (U.S. Department of Commerce, April 1967).

During the months before the coup, when suspected CIA agent Richard Barhum quit the State Department (his earlier cover) and went to find private employment in Greece, it was at an Esso–Pappas office in Athens that he found work (Rousseas 1969). Pappas himself has close connections with the Nixon administration through Vice President Spiro Agnew, a fellow Greek whose family comes from the same village as Pappas. The two have been friends at least since Agnew became governor of Maryland, and Pappas has boasted of exerting influence on Nixon's choice of vicepresident. Today Agnew is in a position to repay Pappas for his favors (Pearson 1968).

The great economic crime of Andreas Papandreou was looking toward the day of Greek economic independence. Investments for short-term profits, as in tourism, were rejected in favor of those which might provide longterm expansion, increased planning, and more direct trade relations with Common Market countries. Foreign investors were particularly annoyed by such policies (Macridis 1968). A United States Department of Commerce report published the same month as the coup refers to the Papandreou policy as "bureaucratic red tape and delay in acting on investment applications" and gives assurance that "high government officials have . . . called attention to certain of these problems, and the situation has shown signs of improvement" (U.S. Department of Commerce, April 1967, p. 4).

Since the coup, the junta has done all in its power to lure American investment. It has created the impression, and for a time the reality, of stability by politically sterilizing Greece. The fantastic number of arrests at the beginning was followed by stern warnings to family heads in workingclass districts not to discuss politics. New targets of suspicion, such as mayors and municipal officials, were intimidated. The entire facade of acceptance took place behind a total news blackout (McDermott, Mallet, and Maspero 1967). Most top political leaders are now in jail or in exile, but recent sporadic bombings calculated to shake the regime attest to continuing resistance among the Greek people.

Perhaps the most striking case of American industrial intervention in Greece is the example of Litton Industries. Litton's bid for a large contract to undertake regional development and to encourage tourism had been defeated in Greek parliament a few months before the coup by progressive forces led by Andreas Papandreou (Macridis 1968). But the contract was approved by the military junta within three weeks after the coup. Under the terms of the contract, Litton Industries agreed to produce $840 million in capital for Greece over a 12-year period. In return the military junta agreed to repay Litton all of its costs, plus 11 percent profit, plus a commission of about 2 percent of all capital directed to Greece through Litton's efforts. It has been noted by Robert M. Allan, Jr., president of Litton's International Development Corporation, that the "return on investment here, of course, is very large because we don't have any basic investment. Our real investment is our good name which, of course, is the most valuable thing we own" (Horowitz and Ehrlich 1968).

The value of the Litton name comes from Litton's position as one of the great American industrial conglomerates (along with Gulf and Western Industries and Ling–Temco–Vought). It is a holding company for more than 80 large corporations operating in 18 distinct industrial categories. Its strength lies in its ability to play the stock market and to use contacts to influence the direction of prime contracts from government sources. Since the junta was, and still is, highly dependent on official United States reaction, connections are very important. It was Litton President Tex Thornton who pulled strings in 1967 (during a Washington visit ostensibly to attend a meeting of the President's Advisory Commission on Civil Disorders, of which he was a member) to open for junta representatives the doors of the vice president, the secretary of the treasury, the chairman of the House Armed Services Committee, and the speaker of the House of Representatives. Litton provided public relations support to the junta through the person of its chief public information officer, Barney Oldfield. Oldfield is a former air force colonel with important Pentagon and Republican party connections. It was not surprising, therefore, that Secretary of Defense Clark Clifford asked for, and got, a major extension of American military assistance to Greece not long after the coup. An equally important boost for the junta came through the activities of still another secretary of defense, Robert McNamara, the former president of Ford Motor Company (which operates a branch in Athens) and a personal friend of Litton President Tex Thornton. In one of the first actions of the World Bank following McNamara's appointment as its president, a $12.5 million loan was made to the junta. This effectively broke the freeze on loans to Greece from European Common Market countries following the coup (Horowitz and Ehrlich 1968).

Within the United States, Litton's Robert Allan made speeches emphasizing the new "stability of environment" for investment in Greece, attacking actress Melina Mercouri and Andreas Papandreou, and defending the soldiers, who he said were responsible for the survival of Greece. In an interview, Allan belittled reports of massive torture and imprisonment and offered a list of other "free world" dictatorships in which he would like to try the "Greek approach" (Horowitz and Ehrlich 1968).

The junta has used full-page advertisements in the *New York Times* to emphasize the stability and safety of the new Greece for investment. While its expenditures on advertising have not yet produced rich dividends in American capital, the junta might well view such advertising as a partial repayment of its debt to the *New York Times*. On October 5, 1966, C. L. Sulzberger, an owner–editor of the *New York Times*, warned of a dangerous leader of the left, Andreas Papandreou, and foreshadowed a royal coup: "If Constantine feared the country faced disaster I suspect he might even temporarily suspend some of the Constitution...." (Rousseas 1967, pp. 118–9).

Sulzberger described the young king of Greece as "an up-to-date sensible young man ... more liberal than his enemies concede and tougher than they suspected...." (Rousseas 1967, p. 119). In an October 7 article, Sulzberger labeled the majority Center Union party "The Bourgeois Barbarians" (Rousseas 1967, p. 121). Andreas was described in a later column as "political hatchet man," "ruthless," "vain and ambitious," whose "talent for fulmination is not equated by his reputation for veracity" (Rousseas 1967, p. 126). Referring to the Aspida case, Sulzberger added that Andreas was under "very serious charges of conspiracy."

Mr. Sulzberger is not, as he later tried to claim, merely an American journalist reporting on a visit to some foreign country. He has personal connections with the king (his Greek wife is related to intimate friends of the royal family) (Rousseas 1967), and as the figure selected to transmit personal messages from the Soviet premier to the president of the United States, he has been close to the channels of influence in American policy (Rousseas 1967).

The Greek press, knowing of Sulzberger's relationship to the king, interpreted his columns as a threat by King Constantine to overthrow a Center Union government, if it should be elected. Andreas, incensed, wrote a letter to the *New York Times* asking Sulzberger whether Americans should condone a situation in which the president of the United States, out of fear of a Republican victory at the polls, decided to suspend the election and the American Constitution. The letter went on to assert that "the Greek people are determined to . . . fight any attempt to impose a dictatorship. A Constitution is a precious document in a democracy, guaranteeing as it does the civil liberties of the people and their protection from the potential tyranny of the state. In Greece's case it also guarantees the rights of the King" (Rousseas 1967, p. 127).

On April 15, a week before the coup which no one expected, *New York Times* correspondent Richard Eder reported from Athens that efforts by the conservative party's two-week-old service government to solve Greece's "political crisis" had collapsed and that the parliament had been dissolved. Eder continued that despite attempts to moderate the situation by King Constantine and the United States, the door was open for a political confrontation which would represent "serious danger to Greece's democratic institutions" (Rousseas 1967, p. 128). The same story later explained what the political confrontation and the moderating efforts were. The impending confrontation was the scheduled election. The king and Prime Minister Kanellopoulos planned to keep the conservative government in office by passing a new proportional representation law assuring representation for each of a number of small, diverse right-wing parties. The Kanellopoulos government then announced its intentions to remain in office during the campaign and the elections—a policy which violated the Greek tradition that a non-political caretaker regime should take over during election campaigns (Rousseas 1967). At this point Eder's story edged into the area of fomenting policy rather than just reporting the news, with his account that "after Mr. Talbot saw Mr. Papandreou yesterday, word began to leak out that the seventy-nine year-old leader had warned that if the King allowed the National Radical Union (the conservative party) to run the elections, the Center Union campaign would become an attack not only on its political rivals but on the King as well." The article clearly stated what the king might do on advice from his army leaders, court advisors, and extremists of the conservative party—namely, suspend the constitution and establish a dictatorship. On the very next day Eder softened this insinuation with an article on how the balmy air had affected the logic of the Greek voter so that anything which might happen in the next few days would appear to some aspect of the Greek population to be a logical conclusion.

Stephen Rousseas, a Greek political observer, concludes that:

". . . the editorial policy of the *Times* regarding this subject consistently overruled the facts. The *Times* very clearly was, for reasons which are only partially evident, actively engaged in foreign-policy making. . . . In the case of Greece, the *Times* has its share of the liability that is entailed in the present dictatorship." (Rousseas 1967, p. 133)

During the following weeks, the *New York Times* in general and Sulzberger in particular strove to create the image of a monarch who at first resisted and finally succumbed to the pressure of the colonels with great personal conflict (Rousseas 1967). To the *Times*, the king was the hero; but would the coup have been different had the king carried it out himself? Would the mass arrests, the suspension of civil liberties, the censorship of the press, a blocking of elections, and the suspension of the constitution have been better under the monarchy? Yet news reports since that time have sought to assume that since the dangerous leftists have been silenced and the fear of elections has now passed, all that remains is to restore the powers of the king under a new constitution and a conservative government acceptable to the junta.

It is clear that long-term support for the junta derives from American military, as well as economic, interests in Greece. In keeping with American military objectives the Greek army remains strong, thus requiring little need for American ground forces. Greece provides a much-needed port for rest and recreation for the Sixth Fleet in the Mediterranean. Even though the junta dismissed 500 NATO-trained officers and purged American support troops (Drew 1968), it was still better in the eyes of the American military to maintain such a government than to risk a government that might pursue an independent policy.

For 20 years the CIA has intervened clandestinely in Greek affairs to preserve American economic and military interests, oblivious to the fact that its means include opposing progressive governments and supporting governments whose every act is contrary to professed American ideals. And as in the case of the Dominican Republic, the State Department and news media have rationalized the most dubious of American policies even when such policies evolve from the activities of the CIA. Though the 1967 coup may not have been the work of the CIA, there is little doubt that if the colonels had not acted, the CIA would have had a hand, one way or another, in thwarting Andreas Papandreou and the forces of social reform in Greece.

Greece is the only European nation that failed to purge the Nazis after World War II. Its monarchy, with American support, has represented feudal traditions of superstition and ignorance and has favored the special interests of an aristocratic oligarchy in a country in vast need of social reform, of democracy, and of hope. Poverty remains a major problem of contemporary Greece and results in an annual exodus of 12,000 young men from Greece to Common Market countries in the hope of finding decent jobs (Macridis 1968).

Ever since 1947, the United States has claimed that its purpose in Greece and elsewhere is to protect the "free world," to save it from being engulfed by communism. John McDermott comments:

> It is said that the Truman Doctrine "saved Greece from Communism." But what accomplishment is that? The Greek people have not suffered less than

their Bulgarian and Yugoslav neighbors. In the Communist world of eastern Europe there has been a significant social and economic development and, for over a decade, the slow growth—however erratic—of personal freedom and governmental accountability, while Soviet influence has radically declined. By contrast, Greece is as backward as ever, her prisons as full, her police as free and, more than ever she remains an American satellite." (McDermott, Mallet, and Maspero 1967, p. 8).

Stability in Greece comes at great expense. In a police state it is difficult to separate fact from rumors circulated by the government regarding the organization and movements of opposition forces. It seems clear, however, that continued oppression will lead to continued revolt and to further strife. Continued American military assistance to the junta is apparently going to be needed to protect the Greek government, not against Bulgaria, not against communism (although that may yet come true), but against the Greek people themselves.

The tragedy of Greece is the tragedy of the United States. The depth of United States responsibility was reaffirmed in two recent *New York Times* dispatches:

> Despite U.S. restrictions on arms shipments to the Greek junta, the Defense Department is reported to have secretly supplied this year nearly twice the military aid to Greece authorized by Congress. . . . (as reported in the *San Francisco Chronicle*, April 16, 1970)

The forked tongue of the administration then replied through the State Department that:

> . . . deliveries of military equipment to Greece have been "generally consistent with our military assistance program policy of suspended shipment of major end items. . . . The fact that the U.S. delivers materials no longer useful to it to some of our allies is not secret." (as reported in the *San Francisco Chronicle*, April 17, 1970)

If the American Constitution still stands for anything, then Greece is not an ally but an oppressed colony. The arms we have sent are part of that oppression. Those weapons are as likely as not to be captured by a liberation movement, turned against the junta and against the American military which supports it. That is precisely what happened in Vietnam.

References

AMERICAN COUNCIL FOR A DEMOCRATIC GREECE
    1949   *Facts on Greece*. New York: American Council for a Democratic Greece.

ANASTAPLO, GEORGE
  1968   "Retreat from Politics." *The Massachusetts Review* 9 (Winter):
         pp. 83–113.

BARNET, RICHARD J.
  1968   *Intervention and Revolution.* New York: World Publishing
         Company.

CLARK, SENATOR JOSEPH S.
  1967   "War or Peace in the Middle East." Report to the Committee
         on Foreign Relations of the U.S. Senate, 90th Congress, 1st
         session.

DREW, ELIZABETH B.
  1968   "Democracy on Ice." *Atlantic Monthly* 222 (July): pp. 56–67.

FORSTER, EDWARD S.
  1958   *A Short History of Modern Greece, 1821–1946.* London:
         Methuen and Co.

GITLIN, TODD
  1967   "Counter-Insurgency: Myth and Reality in Greece," in David
         Horowitz, ed., *Containment and Revolution*, pp. 140–81. Bos-
         ton: Beacon Press.

HEINEMAN, B. W., JR.
  1968   "Grecian Summer—1967." *The Massachusetts Review* 9 (Win-
         ter): pp. 79–82.

HOROWITZ, DAVID, AND REESE EHRLICH
  1968   "Litton Industries: Proving Poverty Pays." *Ramparts* 6 (De-
         cember 14): p. 40.

JONES, JOSEPH M.
  1955   *The Fifteen Weeks.* New York: Viking Press.

MCDERMOTT, JOHN, SERGE MALLET, AND FRANCOIS MASPERO
  1967   "The Greek Coup." *Viet-Report* 3 (September/October): pp.
         8–12.

MCDONALD, ROBERT
  1968   "Greece: April 21, 1967." *The Massachusetts Review* 9 (Win-
         ter): pp. 59–78.

MACRIDIS, ROY C.
  1968   "Greek Political Freedom and United States Foreign Policy."
         The Massachusetts Review 9 (Winter): pp. 147–54.

MCNEILL, W. H.
  1947   *The Greek Dilemma: War and Aftermath.* Philadelphia:
         J. B. Lippincott Co.

Meynaud, Jean
  1965 *Les Forces politique en Grèce*. Lausanne, Switzerland: Études de Science Politique.

Pearson, Drew
  1968 "Spiro Agnew and U.S.–Greek Policy." San Francisco *Chronicle* (November 1).

Rousseas, Stephen
  1967 *The Death of a Democracy*. New York: Grove Press.

  ———

  1969. Personal letter to the author (October 1).

Stanislas, Eve
  1967 *Le Nouvel Observateur* (May 24), cited in McDermott 1967, p. 12, footnote 4.

Stavrianos, L. S.
  1942 *Greece: American Dilemma and Opportunity*. Chicago: H. Regnery Co.

Thermos, Elias
  1968 "From Antartes to Symmorites: Road to Greek Fratricide." *The Massachusetts Review* 9 (Winter): pp. 114–22.

U.S. Department of Commerce
  1967 *American Firms, Subsidiaries and Affiliates—Greece*. Washington, D.C.: U.S. Government Printing Office.

  ———

  1967a *Establishing a Business in Greece*. In series Overseas Business Reports, OBR 67–16, April. Washington, D.C.: U.S. Government Printing Office.

U.S. Department of State
  1967 *Aid to Greece and Turkey: A Collection of State Papers*. (Bulletin Supplement) Washington, D.C.: U.S. Government Printing Office.

Vachliotis, Andreas, and Kyriakos Diakogiannis
  1967 "The Framing of Andreas Papandreou." *Ramparts* 6 (October): pp. 42–46.

Zografos, Zizis
  1964 "Some Lessons of the Civil War in Greece." *World Marxist Review* 7 (November): pp. 43–50.

Chapter 9

CONCLUSION AND PROJECTIONS FOR NEW POLICY DIRECTIONS

In this country at this time an educated, politically moderate military and industrial elite have created the policy making machinery and brought into being the events described in this book. The arrogance of the clique is obvious from its claim that the system that has elevated them to success must be made universal. Such a group assumes that that government is best which provides both the forms of free choice and the assurance that through the exercise of power such choice will always be used to ratify the group's own position of privilege. This premise differs only in detail from the absolutist doctrines of Germany and the USSR in the 1930s. It is instructive to pursue the comparison of the United States today with earlier totalitarian military systems.

If one looks at the training of a United States marine, the attempts by military intelligence to maintain its own surveillance of war protestors, the instances of overly brutal police responses to protest demonstrations, and the new conspiracy laws, the parallels between the United States and earlier totalitarian states seem clear. But so, too, are the differences. In this country, the forms of free participation in government, which are historically associated with the rise of entrepreneurship, are carefully preserved. And why not? Every American is free to contribute the $20 billion necessary to finance a candidate through the electoral process (see Ashmore 1969). But there are relatively few real actors in this game. These few are alike in their great stake in the international status quo. But for the majority of our population, who have for too long seen their own actions to be inconsequential in the making of foreign policy, there is only a sense of deep passivity. What exists is what is shown on the television screen, and what is must be—including overkill, germ warfare, profit pyramiding in the missile industry, and even a massacre of civilians by American soldiers. It is this passive separation from policy, particularly from foreign policy, that reduces the American populace to a pawn in the hands of effective opinion molders and makes the forms of democratic process more shadow than reality. The use of technical experts (like the type described among the military planners in chapter 6) accentuates the division between ruling elite and ignorant populace. Here again there is some similarity to the mental set of Germans in the 1930s. There were, according to one study, but a handful of butchers who planned and perpetrated the crimes of Nazi Germany. But the quiet sanction of the "good people" who did not know or want to know gave license to the others (Hughes 1964).

The current pattern of United States foreign policy includes the assistance which makes possible the torture and execution of political prisoners in Greece, Brazil, Bolivia, and Vietnam. It includes the extermination of large civilian populations through bombing and crop destruction. But the pattern is not best described by alluding to these specific crimes against humanity. The pattern is more one of economic exploitation (see chapter 2) which dooms most of the world to a mere subsistence economy, and one of ever widening applications of science to the control and manipulation of people.

This is where we enter in the early seventies. The chapters of this book have stressed the period of transition from the nuclear arms race to its combination with counter-insurgency and limited war. This combination has persisted through the sixties into the present. It is reasonable to project that in the next decade the technological race will continue and the means for control of revolution will expand. Such achievements are a testimony to the capabilities of human ingenuity for destruction.

The irony of the arms race is that nuclear powers find themselves less secure now than before they diverted the incredible sum of $1,300,000,000,000 away from human needs and into defense (Raser 1969). Yet A. T. & T. was able to pressure through Congress the open-ended ABM expenditure even in the face of overwhelming scientific testimony that such hardware would not succeed in defending against actual nuclear attack (see Wald 1969). Even if it would succeed, the ABM defense could be permeated by still more novel technology. Chemical and bacteriological warfare research was described in chapter 1. The toxic arsenal is cheap, easy to make, and easy to use. There could be no greater inducement for small nations to enter into this kind of weapons research than the fact that the United

States already stocks tularemia, Q fever, botulism, and nerve and nauseous gases. The major powers, however, have the still more sinister option of wrecking the geophysical environment. The possibility exists of precipitating an earthquake in California by setting off explosions in the China Sea. It is, in principle, possible to create a tidal wave by tipping loose material off the continental shelf, or to create a new Ice Age by redistributing the antarctic ice cap. The day lies ahead when we will be able to destroy the layer of protective ozone over selected areas of the earth, thereby permitting entire regions of the earth's surface to be burned by the sun's intense ultraviolet rays. It may even be possible to augment natural low-frequency electrical oscillations in parts of the ionosphere and thereby induce permanently damaging electrical activity in the brains of people in a particular region (Raser 1969).

Unfortunately, in the age of human visits to the moon, these new technologies of warfare are not science fiction. They can and will be actualized, not by any one individual's malevolent decision, but because the managerial and technical agencies for their development are already in operation. The army of defense intellectuals is already in harness to extol the virtues of "defensive-environment modification," while the contractors are ready to bid for it and the State Department is prepared to justify it as an extension of military deterrence to ensure peace.

Then, as now, people who criticize such new destruction and call for an end to all arms races will be called cowardly, naive, and unwilling to face the unbelievably hard task of what to do if our enemies develop still more vicious weapons. To this charge it must be replied that the easy task now is to augment man's already great ability to exterminate himself. The hard task is to arrange for the sharing of his abundance for the preservation of his environment and of human life.

It is clear now that no nation is technically able to defend itself against attack. We are not even able to defend ourselves from the radiation, the epidemics, and the gross environmental effects of the weapons testing originating in our own country. Recently a United States colonel indicated that he could no longer be responsible for the danger presented by a stockpile of nerve gas rockets if the government failed to give immediate orders to transport the deadly cannisters by rail to a place where they could be dumped into international waters of the Atlantic Ocean. Neither the legal challenge raised by the governor of Florida nor the ethical challenge raised by the secretary general of the United Nations could prevent the dumping. It is a fine example of the hard thinking of the military when we must act quickly to speed the already increasing industrial contamination of the ocean in order to save ourselves from the immediate consequences of our destructive ingenuity.

In a larger sense one may ask whether our destructive and manipulative capabilities are in fact designed to defend us at all. A measure of dehumanization—detachment from and disregard for life—is the necessary ingredient that permits the military–industrial machine to roll on. Once one group can be targetted and considered expendable—Chinese, Jews, Viet Cong, commies, Yippies, Black Panthers, or police—then the psychic disease has germinated, and it knows no bounds. When a congressional group was sent to investigate and whitewash the situation in Vietnam in 1970 (five years after the American troops had begun fighting), some of the group overstepped the bounds and discovered that the Saigon government was using tiger cages to restrain its human political prisoners. Days later Senator Mondale revealed that such tiger cages were also used in Texas to contain migrant farm workers. Even as the sightings of toxic sprays in Indochina were being denied by military spokesmen, the use of some of these chemicals was already in practice in the United States. Mace, part of the chemical arsenal developed for overseas use, is now in common use by local police despite medical testimony suggesting that it results in visual impairment.

The methods used to restore an uneasy truce in the ghettos and on the campuses were first developed for overseas use. Helicopter surveillance by police, the use of M–16 rapid-fire rifles, the aerial spraying of a peacefully assembled crowd of students with CN and CS tear gas, the Army's data bank on dissenters, the raiding of homes, and the shooting of protesters are not a projection of some future tyranny. They are part of the contemporary American record.

The similarities between pacification of our own people and pacification of an unwilling Vietnamese population are not accidental. Some of the same industries—like Litton, which contracts both for national defense and for the Greek military junta—also take on the training of ghetto youths in job corps centers. Many of the youths are then shunted into the army. More directly, the same army of social scientists, think-tank analysts, and weapons planners who were called to develop counter-insurgency for Vietnam are now moving into the area of "urban planning," "law enforcement," and "urb-coin" (domestic counter-insurgency).

RAND Corporation's New York City office employs 40 social scientists working in teams in various departments of the city government. The police department team has the largest budget (Leman 1968). The Institute for Defense Analyses, which has handled studies of small arms and aircraft for counter-insurgency, was commissioned to create a "task force" on science and technology in crime control. IDA's own chemical warfare expert, Joseph Coates, was an advisor to the task force (Klare 1968). The task force report applauded the increasing use of scientists and social scientists to devise new techniques for domestic counter-insurgency, and it proposed setting up comprehensive intelligence-gathering forces on the state and local levels.

Facilities for training domestic police in intelligence, crowd control, incapacitating agents, small arms, mobile weapons, surveillance and detection, prisoner control, and such special operations as tactical or sharpshooting anti-sniper units have been in existence in the United States for several years as a result of policies described in chapter 1. There the transition from deterrence to more far-reaching control was described. The expert knowledge acquired by the Army Operations Center, by the Public Safety Division of the Agency for International Development, and by its associated International Police Academy is now being applied domestically. In 1968 the army's Military Police School at Fort Gordon, Georgia, began teaching a course in civil disobedience for police at all levels. The course includes a simulated practice confrontation in which an anti-war demonstration is dispersed and a black militant speaker charging police brutality is arrested (Klare 1968). The methods by which such operations may actually take over and destroy the institutions they were created to protect is described in chapter 7. In the case of the Greek coup an actual military coup replaced the constitutional government rather than risk a curtailment of military powers by the electorate.

The possibility of a recurrence of the Greek drama in the United States seems less distant than we might hope when we consider that Congress has passed amendments to the McCarran Act which grant extra-constitutional powers to the Subversive Activities Control Board. Even more to the point, *Look*'s Senior Editor, William Hedgepeth, investigated six government detention centers and observed:

> Military planners in Washington acknowledge that detention of dissenters on at least a limited basis could conceivably take place should prolonged, simultaneous and seemingly coordinated urban riots reach ... nationally disruptive proportions so as to require ... martial law. ... [This] would mean full military control of the designated area, suspension of bail and mass arrests on the basis of suspicion alone. (*Look*, May 28, 1968, quoted in Leman 1968, p. 19)

In Vietnam, as in Greece and the Dominican Republic, counterinsurgency has involved an ideological component aimed at winning the support of the people for the government in power, and for the police who protect that government against insurgents. This counterrevolutionary response to problems in the colonized third world was described in chapter 2. Service projects, intelligence on agitators, and pro-police propaganda were combined in Vietnamese pacification. The model, while hardly a success in Vietnam, shows up again in police storefronts in ghetto areas which combine the work of spying, liaison with the Negro news media, public relations in the schools, police recruitment, and referral to social services.

Some of the internal workings of official agencies and quasi-official organizations charged with the formation of international policy were described in chapter 5. Organizations like the CIA and the FBI have operations which are secret and virtually independent of other government organizations, particularly of Congress. Where they have created the events we have described, as in Iran and Cuba, they created conditions which determined the direction public policy had to follow. Other large federal organizations, like the Department of State, are capable of only the ordinary bureaucratic response of rationalization, no matter how great the tragedy of the occurrence. Organizations like the Council on Foreign Relations or the Council of Economic Advisors work to provide the assurance that special corporate interests will be protected in any major new direction of policy; and the interlocked military, corporate, and government complex (see chapter 6) manages a loosely structured empire in which its own protection and expansion matters most. Technology and centralized power dwarf the public and cast it into the role of passive assenter to remote events. Public opinion management and the public role in foreign policy were described in chapter 3, where we saw that even the drive of a strong leader can have only a small effect on the major policy directions in a country constrained by large and powerful interests. These interests currently require a high degree of militarism in many forms. Whether or not these forms will turn even further toward domestic control, their international effect is likely to be the suppression of peaceful revolutionary change that makes violent change inevitable. What a hungry world needs is less of the ideological salesmanship of the wealthy powers and more of the wealth. What basic human dignity requires is much less willingness to subvert cultural autonomy for the sake of political and economic control.

If military efforts do continue their domestic turn, it seems quite reasonable to assume that the strategists will provide the essential rationale for the suspension of civil liberties and whatever secretive or repressive measures ensue. The movement in foreign policy has been toward the elimination of the public from public policy. Not long ago two of the better-known civilian defense associates prepared a Pentagon paper on "Constraint of Public Attitudes." The pair, Clark C. Abt (Abt Associates) and Ithiel de Sola Pool (Simulmatics), wrote:

> Limited strategic war strategy [must be] designed to assure its being carried out regardless of the eventuality of extreme public opposition. The retaliatory forces and their commanders, including the President, might be located in completely isolated and heavily defended areas. They might be given advance instructions and training to cut themselves off completely from

external influences and go ahead at all costs with the retaliatory strategy. (Burgess, *Limited Strategic War*, quoted in Brightman 1968, p. 4)

The ideology of winning the game, even the wrong game, at all costs, comes through here as it did in chapter 6. Whatever the moves, the strategists will continue to defend them on the grounds that they are vital to the nation's security.

The domestic protest against which counter-insurgency is taking new aim results almost directly from our foreign military policy. Military preparedness assures the insufficiency of funds to provide adequate food, housing, education, and health care to millions of Americans. Resistance to the war itself and to the draft has led to the prosecution of thousands of young people who are now either in jail or in self-imposed exile. Paradoxically, the suppression of dissent has created some hope, small though it may be, of a day when ways of resolving international conflict may reflect the real and informed needs of the public. Opposition to the draft, to the "pre-staged" 1968 Democratic convention in Chicago, and to the university-affiliated CBW facilities has been met with a degree of suppression that exposes the weakness of the system. The pronouncements of planners, strategists, and bureaucratic officials show clearly that they have only one category for those who do not concur with the expansion and protection of the American empire. The category is "expendable." In one instance, prisoners received vicious punishment at the hands of guards at Santa Rita prison near Oakland, California, following their mass arrest for a crime (assembly) for which charges were not even pressed. The case is unusual only in the frankness of official explanation. The governor of California and the sheriff of Alameda County explained such brutalization by noting that many of the prison guards were Vietnam veterans who looked upon protestors as no better than Viet Cong. The extent and the dangers of dehumanization inherent in that excuse cannot be exaggerated.

For an increasing number of Americans, especially for young Americans, it is becoming clear that the experts are just not good enough, and that the powerful interests behind them have the wrong aims and the wrong means. They do not need to see the full deployment of domestic counter-insurgency to know that the American system has robbed them of the experiences necessary to conduct a humane foreign policy. They are reasserting their right to hear the anguish of people being "saved" by American intervention. They are feeling the freedom of refusing to bow to illegitimate authority which asks them to give their careers, even their lives, to a bizarre dream of omnipotent control. Call them reformers, resisters, revolutionaries, or just human beings—it is the ability of these people to say "enough" in the face of such concentrated power that gives hope to those who desire that international conflict may someday become a matter in which a free public exercises an international policy befitting the dignity of man.

References

ASHMORE, HARRY S.
  1969 "Electoral Reform." *The Center Magazine* 2 (January): pp. 2–11.

BRIGHTMAN, CAROL
  1968 "The Science of Control." *Viet-Report* 3 (January): p. 1.

HUGHES, EVERETT C.
  1964 "Good People and Dirty Work" *Social Problems* 10 (Summer): pp. 3–11.

KLARE, MICHAEL
  1968 "The Intelligent Agitator's Guide to Domestic Counterinsurgency." *Viet-Report* 3 (Summer): p. 43.

LEMAN, BEVERLY
  1968 "Social Control of the American Ghetto." *Viet-Report* 3 (Summer): pp. 43–47. Reprinted in R. Perrucci and M. Pilisuk, *Triple Revolution Emerging*. Boston: Little, Brown & Co., 1971.

RASER, JOHN
  1969 "ABM and the MAD Strategy." *Ramparts* 8 (November): pp. 36–37.

WALD, GEORGE
  1969 "Therefore Choose Life." Speech delivered at ABM Choice Conference, Washington, D.C., May 2.

DATE DUE

DATE DUE			
JY 23 '79			
AP 9 '81			
OC 18 '81			
GAYLORD			PRINTED IN U.S.A